Healing the Children of WAR

A handbook for
ministry to children
who have suffered
deep traumas

Edited by
Phyllis Kilbourn

HEALING THE CHILDREN OF WAR
A handbook for ministry to children who have suffered deep traumas

Phyllis Kilbourn, editor

ISBN 0-912552-87-5

Published by MARC, a division of World Vision, 800 West Chestnut Avenue, Monrovia, California 91016-3198, U.S.A.

Printed in the United States of America. Editors: John A. Kenyon and Edna G. Valdez. Interior page layout: Edna G. Valdez. Cover design: Richard Sears. Cover photo: Terri Owens.

First printing: 1995
Second printing: 1997

Contents

Part 4 - Theological Implications for Intervention Planning

Part 5 - Concluding Reflections

Contributing Authors

Marlys Blomquist. Ph.D., educational psychology. Psychologist in the Robbinsdale area schools and in a private child psychology clinic (North Psychology) in Minneapolis, Minnesota, U.S.A. Doctoral dissertation in field of moral development (Peru and U.S.). Field experience in Chile and Peru.

Cynthia Blomquist. A clinical psychology doctoral student at Fuller Theological Seminary Graduate School of Psychology, Pasadena, U.S.A. Also working towards a theology M.A. with an emphasis in cross-cultural studies. Field work and thesis research with MEDAIR in Liberia.

Perry Downs. Ph.D. from New York University. Professor of Christian education and director of the doctor of education program at Trinity International University, Deerfield, Illinois, U.S.A. Author of *Teaching for Spiritual Growth* (Zondervan, 1994). As licensed foster parents, Dr. Downs and his wife have cared for 28 children in difficult circumstances.

Sue H. Enoch. Minister of childhood education at Pelham Road Baptist Church in Greenville, South Carolina, U.S.A. Formerly served as elementary program supervisor, Kentucky School for the Blind, Louisville, Kentucky, U.S.A.

Delores Friesen. Associate professor of pastoral counseling and director of the Marriage and Family Counseling program at Mennonite Brethren Biblical Seminary, Fresno, California, U.S.A. Missionary in Nigeria and Ghana (1965-1978), including experience of the Biafran conflict. Facilitated healing and reconciliation workshops in Liberia (1991). Author of *Let Love Be Your Greatest* (Editions Trobisch), and *Living More With Less Study Guide* (Herald Press).

Clare Hanbury. Program officer of the Child-to-Child Trust (U.K.) for English-speaking Africa, Southeast Asia, the Far East, Eastern Europe and the U.K. As a qualified middle school teacher, she has taught in Kenya and Hong Kong. Her master's dissertation, "Education in Developing Countries," examined education programs in refugee camps. Ms. Hanbury travels extensively and is particularly interested in training and in programs that assist children in difficult circumstances.

Mickie Heard. M.A. in religious education, Trinity International University, Deerfield, Illinois, U.S.A. Master of philosophy, University of Aberdeen, Scotland. Member of American Association for Marriage and Family Therapy, with a private practice in child and family therapy. Part-time professor at Trinity College, Illinois, and minister of Christian education at the Village Presbyterian Church, Northbrook, U.S.A.

Phyllis Kilbourn. Ph.D. in education from Trinity International University. Missionary with WEC International since 1967, serving in Kenya and Liberia. Attended the course on "Care of Children in War and Disaster," University of London. Dissertation for doctor of education degree entitled "Responses to the Psychological Trauma of Children in War," with field research conducted in Liberia.

Margaret Lloyd. (Art sketches) Former kindergarten teacher who spent one year in the classroom and ten years on the Romper Room television program. Since 1981, she has been a teaching leader in Bible Study Fellowship International.

Carole A. McKelvey. Editor, journalist and co-author (with Ken Magid) of *High Risk: Children Without a Conscience* (Bantam, 1988). Co-author with JoEllen Stevens of *Special Needs in America: Foster Care and Adoption Issues* (Fulcrum Books, 1994). Former editor with the Rocky Mountain News, Denver, Colorado, U.S.A., she is currently a graduate student in psychology at Regis University in Denver and associate director and counselor of Accelerated Schools in Denver.

Ann Noonan. Nationally certified counselor and assistant director of Agape Counseling Associates, Rochester, New York, U.S.A. Works with adult survivors of childhood sexual abuse and with children; manages a counseling branch and supervises counselors. Lecturer, workshop leader and speaker.

Dale Henry Schumm. D.Min., pastoral counselor and personnel consultant for Mennonite Board of Missions, Elkhart, Indiana, U.S.A. Former pastor, teacher and educational administrator; missionary to India (1966-72). Other short-term assignments in Nepal, Afghanistan and Liberia. Worked with missionary team development in Asia, Latin America, Europe and the Middle East. Former consultant to the Christian Health Association in Liberia in developing the Healing and Reconciliation (H and R) program for traumatized war victims and H and R Workshop leader in 1991.

Edward T. Welch. Ph.D. in neuropsychology from the University of Utah, Salt Lake City, Utah, U.S.A.; M.Div. in biblical studies from Biblical Theological Seminary, Hatfield, Pennsylvania, U.S.A. Licensed psychologist, director of counseling at The Christian Counseling & Educational Foundation, Laverock, Pennsylvania, and faculty member at Westminster Theological Seminary, Philadelphia, Pennsylvania. Author of *Banquet in the Grave* (forthcoming from Baker Book House) and numerous articles.

Josephine Wright. Child psychologist and clinical psychologist with wide experience in the field of trauma and abuse, both with children and adults, as a clinician and in service planning. M.A. in child psychology at Nottingham University (1984); M.Sc. in clinical psychology (1988); Ph.D. in child psychology (1992). Works with MEDAIR and has served with them short-term in Liberia during the civil war in that country. Recently completed a book entitled *How to Cope When Your World Falls Apart*.

Acknowledgements

I want to express my deep gratitude to each member of the writing team who, firmly believing that the kingdom of God belongs to children (Mark 10:13-16), have so generously given their time and expertise as a gift to children traumatized by the atrocities of war. Each writer has many responsibilities in addition to their professional work, making it evident that without their sacrifice of time this book would not have become a reality.

I am also indebted to several other people who have given advice or helpful suggestions, especially to those members of my "think tank" at Trinity International University; Jeanette Kpissay, secretary of the American board of the Christian Health Association of Liberia (CHAL), who has gone "above and beyond" in helping me locate resource people and material; and Perry Downs who, along with assisting with the writing task, was always ready to serve as my sounding board and mentor.

The art sketches drawn by Margaret Lloyd are a much appreciated contribution to this book.

A special blessing in this project was working with World Vision editors John Kenyon and Edna Valdez. They not only did a superb job of pulling together the various contributions into a meaningful whole, they also shared in the authors' burden and compassion for war-torn children.

And I must not forget to mention another vital team of workers, too many to mention by name, who worked alongside the writers and were a vital part of the writing effort—those who supported us with their prayers and encouragement. They, too, will have a share in this ministry to suffering children.

Our prayer is that this handbook will help you in your

i

task of facilitating the healing of children suffering from war-related trauma and so provide them with hope for a meaningful future.

Phyllis Kilbourn

Foreword

Children are war's most helpless victims. The shame of our era is that they also have become war's most numerous victims. When the twentieth century began, some 90 percent of war casualties were soldiers. Today, 90 percent are civilians.

Why?

Over the past 50 years, the nature of conflict has changed. Wars within nations, not between nations, now dominate the political landscape. But in civil wars, battlegrounds seldom have boundaries. When government forces square off with one or several adversaries, control of the population means everything. Consequently, no patch of ground escapes becoming a military objective and potentially drenched in blood.

By the millions, war's children are uprooted from their homes and exposed to fearful dangers. They suffer direct injuries, malnutrition, disease, exposure, exploitation, abuse and neglect. Often they are left with nowhere to go and no one to be with. Many see their parents murdered. Some are even made to pull the trigger themselves, a maneuver designed to forever break their spirits.

There is a sense in which all the children of the world belong to all the people of the world. Because we all are implicated, we all need to take action to stop the wanton destruction of young lives and restore childhood's hopes and dreams.

Healing the Children of War is intended to help equip us for the task, an anthology of wisdom from people of action. Many of the Christian professionals who contributed to this volume have themselves lived through civil wars as they worked directly with children who had suffered unspeakable horrors.

But it is not enough only to care for war's young victims. We must do everything possible to reduce the madness of armed conflict. We must be unwearying in working towards the banning of land mines, the reduction of the arms trade and the mitigation of tensions that lead to conflict, including economic and social injustice.

As you read through the following pages, may you be affirmed and reaffirmed in a calling to serve, to witness, to walk with children in the shadows, to nurture hope in the resurrection of their lives.

Graeme Irvine
International President
World Vision International

Introduction

Phyllis Kilbourn

A normal part of children's growth and development revolves around their day-by-day childhood woes, crises, and traumas. Although brutal and inhuman war-related traumas and crises are far from what we would consider "normal" everyday childhood experiences, they are fast becoming a reality for thousands of children who become embroiled in the violent wars fanning out across a large portion of the world.

Those working with children caught up in such violence witness their psychological traumas along with the ensuing feelings of guilt, fear, lack of trust, loss of self-esteem and distorted ideas about God's character and how God works in the world. These severe war-related traumas have proved to be most damaging to children's normal development.

It has also been proven, however, that intervention by committed, loving caregivers who recognize that the children's future growth and development depend on successfully intervening in their emergency situations can enable children to pass through these intense crises with a strengthened sense of self, a renewed trust in their coping skills, and a firmer faith in the love and care of their heavenly Father.

There are three vital steps that caregivers seeking to assist children traumatized by the experiences of war must take to be effective. The first step is to develop an awareness, understanding, and sensitivity to the kind of experiences the children have had, the trauma they have suffered as a result of those experiences, and how

1

they feel about what has happened to them. Understanding their experiences will help the caregiver to interpret the children's war-related stresses and psychological traumas.

The second step requires the provision of interventions that will alleviate the children's suffering and pain and restore them to full health—physically, emotionally, mentally, and spiritually. Only then can a foundation be laid for the desperately longed-for and needed restoration of hope for the children's future. Intervention planning must also be holistic, providing care at the individual, family, and community levels.

The third step concerns the care of the caregivers. Other individuals must provide support, personal care, and ministry for the caregivers to ensure their effectiveness in providing care to the children.

This handbook provides assistance to caregivers in accomplishing each of the above steps. Part One describes the impact of war on children and details the resulting psychological trauma from these war experiences. Part Two examines special intervention concerns arising from the children's war-related experiences.

Parts Three and Four address vital intervention issues and strategies—psychologically, educationally, and theologically—with a special focus on the family and community structures. Part Three also provides insights into providing caregivers with much needed support networks.

In the planning of interventions, caregivers must be aware of the targeted people's rich cultural resources and strive for cultural sensitivity and relevance in the planning and administration of interventions. Caregivers must also discuss the implications of intervention issues and planning with the community, making the intervention plans culture-specific and community-oriented. What works in one culture may not work in another.

Part Five reflects on an important desired result of intervention planning—restoring hope

The authors' desire is that this handbook, written for the lay-caregiver, will become an effective tool for equipping and preparing individuals who minister with children living in the terrifying grip of warfare. We also hope that it will open many doors for blessing the hurting children, bestowing blessings on them that communicate God's love and acceptance (Mark 10:13-14).

Goal = restore hope.

Part I

Children's Encounter
with War

1

The Impact of War on Children: A Kaleidoscope of Experiences, Emotions and Traumas

Phyllis Kilbourn

War has a host of devastating effects on children that can forever change the normal development of their childhood. One word best describes the underlying cause of their resulting trauma: loss.

War has become a global, not an isolated, experience for children. Just how global is graphically portrayed by UNICEF:

Out of the ashes of World War II, the United Nations was founded in 1945 in the hope it would guard a new world order based on peace. Since then, more than 150 wars and civil conflicts have been fought around the globe, almost all of them in poor, underdeveloped countries. At least 20 million people have been killed since then by battle, perhaps tens of millions more if one considers all those who have died from disease, hunger and poverty spawned by warfare.

> . . . perhaps *the* horrifying fact of our era [is] that the vast majority of these war dead and injured have been women and children.[1]

War always results in tremendous loss for children. Their war-related losses form a total experience, not just a series of isolated experiences, and involve all aspects of their lives: emotional, spiritual, physical, and developmental. War often damages or destroys the structures that in normal times provide the framework for their healthy development.

The following report from Mozambique paints an all too common scene of what life can be like for children caught up in the atrocities of war.

> It is estimated that almost half of the nation's children are victims of the civil war, in which they are a direct target of the Mozambique National Resistance Movement (Renamo). It is a war that attracts little attention these days, but its atrocities equal those of Cambodia's Pol Pot, according to Eima Barr, a field worker for UNICEF in Mozambique's embattled Zambezi province who describes children being routinely forced to kill their own parents and siblings, to watch as pregnant women's bellies are slit open and the babies carved out, to see men having their genitals sliced off before being ordered to eat them.
>
> Childhood here means the ever-present fear that the *banditos*, as the Renamo soldiers are widely known, will raid your village, shooting those who try to escape, gang-raping girls and women, burning down homes with people inside. In these raids, children as young as six are captured and taken to the military bases—which, for the boys, usually means being forcibly trained as soldiers and ordered to kill. . . . For the girls, it means being "wives" and domestic workers to the Renamo soldiers.[2]

It is from such experiences that children suffer incredible loss—loss of such childhood treasures as significant attachments, love, security, trust, self-respect, innocence, hope, moral development and perhaps even their faith.

In downtown Beirut, four displaced children stand in front of a destroyed building.

World Vision/David Browne

A girl sits outside a row of tents at a refugee camp near Dakovo, eastern Croatia.

Loss of family and home

Central to the children's losses in war is the loss of family and home. Especially for young children, home, together with the family, is the center of their world. At home children find love, security, trust, belonging, acceptance and care. So when the child has lost home, parents and siblings the loss is immense. Often such losses also include the loss of provision for the children's basic necessities, forcing them to live as a refugee or on the streets. Thus the children experience not only the loss of family, but also a loss of all that is familiar.

Separation from or loss of family members, especially parents, is the worst possible outcome of war for children. Children will tell you that they fear this more than something happening to themselves.

Loss of friends and other important attachment figures

Loss of friends represents a major loss to children—friends they have grown up with and shared the childhood joys of secrets and play. Sorrow from this loss is multiplied when a child witnesses a friend's death.

UNICEF/5425/Darko Gorenak

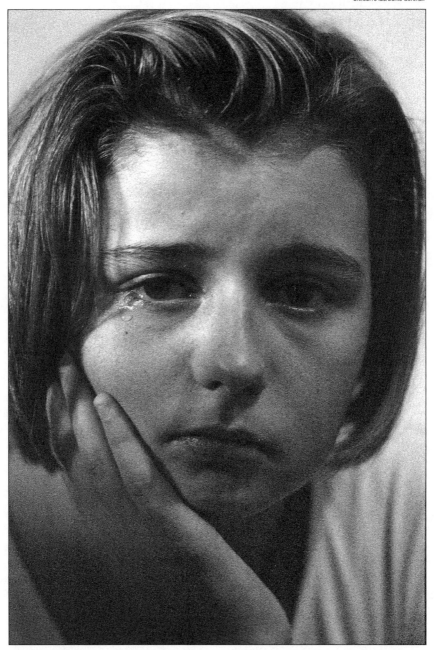

A girl refugee, living in temporary quarters in Zagreb, Croatia, remembers her war experience.

Loss of childhood

War leaves few choices for children. If they survive, they are often forced to grow up overnight, abandoning their childhood as they face adult responsibilities and the harsh realities of life.

The loss of childhood usually focuses around the death or absence of the child's parents or caregivers, which forces them into assuming adult roles. Lacking care from a loving attachment figure, unable to develop their personality through normal, stimulating play, these children lack important aspects of childhood, aspects that we usually take for granted.

The children have to "grow up quick" to care for orphaned siblings or to assume other adult responsibilities. In disaster or war-stricken communities it is not uncommon, due to the parents' death or disappearance, for a ten-year-old child to be a family's sole provider. Many children have to take on adult functions when living in stressful situations.

Seven-year-old Phala and her nine-year-old sister Leem of Cambodia.

A father accompanies his son as he learns to use crutches at the Red Cross hospital for war victims in Kabul, Afghanistan.

Loss of physical safety

Loss of the children's physical safety means they no longer have any protection against horrifying experiences involving their torture, arrest and detention, sexual and physical abuse, or being abducted into slavery, prostitution or recruitment into the armed forces. The children are left powerless and without a defender.

The experiences they endure when physical safety is lost often leads to severe physical injuries and debilitating physical and emotional handicaps. Also, children can lose their physical health due to illnesses contracted while living in severe and unsanitary living conditions with inadequate food; the illnesses, which generally go untreated, often leave the children with lifelong physical problems.

A fifteen-year-old boy wearing Rwanda Patriotic Front beret and military clothing stands holding a hand grenade and AK-47 automatic assault rifle.

Loss of moral development

Dr. Neil Boothby observed the effects of war on moral development at the Lhanguere Center where a group of 42 former Mozambican soldiers between six and sixteen years of age was receiving care. He noted the children's struggle to leave behind a world that sanctioned killing, and to re-enter a world that, once again, condemned it. He states,

> I have come to learn that his re-entry into a society is as much a moral struggle as a psychological one: a long, often anguished quest into one's own soul to discover the very moral sensibility that was obliterated through having committed what, in nearly every culture, is the gravest sin of all.[3]

The UN report, *Children and War: A Call for Protection*, describes the tragedy and senselessness of the abuse of using children as soldiers in war: *forcibly*

> In many parts of the world we see children, often smaller than the weapons they carry, being drilled in the art of war. Forced to lay aside the innocence of childhood, they are immersed in a sea of adult hatreds to learn to kill or be killed for causes they don't fully understand, in a world increasingly hostile to their experience.[4]

> *"I've killed more people than I can remember. We are given drugs in the daytime to make us brave to fight. In the evening we are given alcohol to make us forget what we did. But the memories keep coming back—I can't forget."* (A child soldier)

Loss of innocence and beliefs

War forces children into confrontation with death and horrible atrocities during their most impressionable age. They often have to give up their most treasured beliefs: in their parents' ability to always protect them and keep them safe; trust that adults will only do "good" things to others; and that their world is a safe and happy place to live.

Elizabeth Jareg states that, "When this happens, children cross forever a barrier dividing what is generally considered to be 'human behavior' to that usually condemned by society as being 'inhuman.'"[5] Children who have had such experiences will at some time or another have to confront themselves with this fact. They will deal with it psychologically in different ways, depending on many factors.

— loss of trust.
— total confusion.

Skulls and bones of some of the hundreds of people who died when shelling destroyed the warehouses where they were taking shelter, litter the port area of Freeport, Monrovia, Liberia.

Children warily watch an army patrol while playing in the streets of San Vicente, El Salvador.

Loss of schooling

For many children living under circumstances of threat and unrest, going to school every day is the only thing they have that gives them some feeling of security and stability. Young people also view school as their only opportunity to bring change into their lives and to provide them with a hope for their future. Thus the loss of school is a very heavy loss to bear. A sobering account from Afghanistan reflects the serious, long-term effects of such a loss on a nation, and on individuals:

> The numbers alone paint a horrifying picture. Two million children—the direct and indirect victims of a decade of war. . . . One million young people fatherless or orphaned.

> But numbers alone cannot convey the damage civil war and foreign occupation have done to the very fabric of Afghan society. The nation's educational system is in a shambles; three million children of school age receive no teaching. Hundreds of thousands cannot read or write. Most children have no concept of formal education and have had little exposure to rich Afghani cultures and traditions before the war. Truly, they are a lost generation, raised on terror, bitter ideological disputes and bloodshed.

> How will Afghanistan have a future, if this generation is not recovered? Even if peace were declared tomorrow, how could this army of youth rebuild the nation, if they cannot read or write? Most frighteningly, what kind of values will these children—knowing only insecurity and death—pass on to their offspring?[6]

— The next generation may well be one without a conscience, as we have become to understand conscience.

Loss of basic necessities

Hunger and extreme malnutrition are commonly found to be part of the children's distress in war. Losing home, clothing, and other personal belongings, they suffer cold from exposure. Long flights from the scene of danger can leave them exhausted, hungry, injured or ill, but with no resources to have their basic needs met.

Relief workers worry about the long-term physical and mental condition of malnourished children. They fear that in many countries the degree of starvation has been so great that many children who survive will suffer brain damage.

A girl rests beside a street in Phnom Penh, Cambodia, with her meager possessions.

Personal losses: identity, status, self-worth

Many times war causes families to flee from danger. Often these flights are sudden and families become separated, or the parents are killed. Children join themselves to other groups who are traveling. In these groups, very small children may be found of whom nobody can give any information as to their origins. Such events can result in a loss of identity and, subsequently, a loss of family history for the children; thus the children lose their true identity. This can cause psychological problems in adolescence, when the young person starts asking, "Who am I?" and "Where did I come from?" At other times, the family history of children can be lost if nobody takes the time to try and write it down while information is available.[7]

In some societies children who become orphaned lose status in the eyes of the community. Instead of valued persons, the community may see them as a threat to its survival, or an unwanted burden in times when it is a struggle simply to survive. Sometimes attitudes toward orphaned children may reflect this negative change in status, causing them to feel unloved and unwanted. This is reflected in the response of one small boy who, when questioned about his identity, stated, "I am nobody's nothing."

confusion

— It may be too late for many children who are already brain-damaged.
— Total blank memory of a previous life.
— Fear was not mentioned.
— Terror " " " .

Children share their breakfast at the Good Samaritan Orphanage set up for abandoned or orphaned children in Mount Barclay, Monrovia, Liberia.

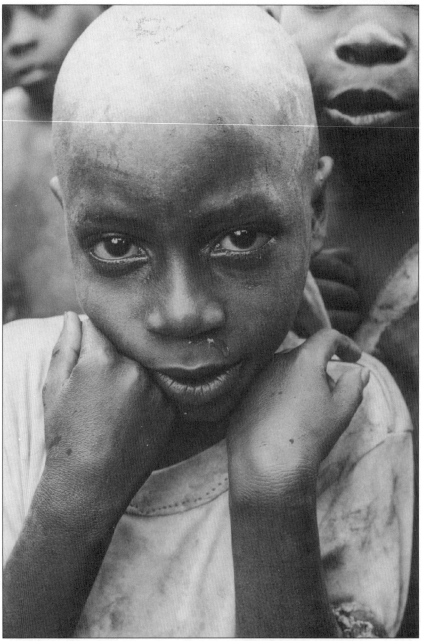

A child in Rutare, a grim "safe haven" outside of Rwanda's capital, Kigali.

Loss of security and trust

Developing a sense of trust in the world is important for children's identity formation. Yet many children in the world's troubled spots have never experienced a day of real peace. They live in the shadow of prolonged warfare, constantly surrounded by insecurity and violence. The unsolved conflict situations impose exorbitant demands on children who are forced to share responsibilities, fears, hatred and acts of revenge far too early in their lives.

War also revives the deep-rooted feelings of helplessness and inadequacy in the child's spirit. Facing continuous external threats, children find it difficult to trust other people and to look confidently to the future. $\succ$ *impossible?*

From their simple belief that the world is a "safe" place to live in, the world becomes a place of uncertainty, fear and anxiety. Children exposed to traumatic situations cannot be expected to establish a sense of security in their world. Ongoing war-related stresses will shatter their security altogether.

Laughter is the hallmark of a happy, carefree childhood. But war stifles the laughter of children as their losses and bereavements overwhelm them. The sum of their losses, and the resulting pain and loneliness of children in war are so vast that the reality of it becomes unimaginable to us. Confronting the children's distress through the printed page is emotionally painful, let alone having personal meetings with the children of war. In responding to the "why" of children being so victimized by the atrocities of war, Dr. Neil Boothby gives a very disturbing reply:

> Why are children, the future of any community, if not the world itself, being singled out in today's armed conflicts? As paradoxical as it may be, this is occurring precisely because children are so precious to many of us. To destroy what is of the highest value to someone is clearly among the most effective forms of terrorism imaginable; to kill and injure children is to rob a family of its future. What better way to undermine whatever popular support may exist for any given cause than to attack the very beings we love and value most in life?[8]

29

Children also represent what is precious and of the highest value to the church. That is why it becomes imperative for the church to reach out to these suffering members of the body of Christ—members we love and value—and accept the challenge and sacrifice required to demonstrate Christ's love and compassion toward them. In addition, the church must provide opportunities for them to experience healing, reconciliation, forgiveness and hope.

NOTES

1   Edgar Koh, ed., "More Can Be Done for the Children of War," *INTERCOM* No. 56 (UNICEF: April 1990), pp. 1-2.

2   Angela Neustatter, *The Independent*, London. Quoted in *World Press Review*, November 1992, p. 27.

3   Neil Boothby, "Living in the War Zone," *World Refugee Survey— 1989 in Review* (41).

4   From a one-page report, *Children and War: A Call for Protection* (UNICEF; no date given).

5   Elizabeth Jareg, "Children Under Stress: Especially Vulnerable Children," *Redda Barna Training Module No. 2* (March 1991), p. 10.

6   Edgar Koh, ed., "Afghanistan: What Does 'School' Mean?" *INTER-COM* No. 56 (UNICEF: April 1990), p. 14.

7   Jareg, p. 9.

8   Neil Boothby, "Children and War," *Cultural Survival Quarterly* (Vol. 10, No. 4, 1986), p. 29.

— Tools & pawns of War.

2
Recognizing and Understanding Troubled Children

Josephine Wright

Colleagues I work with in Africa and Europe frequently ask me, "How do I recognize when a child is in distress? How do I know when they need more than I can give them as a loving, listening person? Do children suffer from post-traumatic stress, and if so, how?"

In this chapter we shall explore together just how children show emotional as well as physical pain. Through this book, we will learn how to begin to help them through holding them, hearing them and, with God's hands, healing the hurts that disable their future.

What is a trauma?

There are several words commonly used to describe the experience that children go through when they are involved in a war, an earthquake, a famine or an accident. The most common are *disaster*, *crisis* and *trauma*. They all mean that children have had to cope with a situation that was out-of-the-ordinary, frightening, unexpected, and has demanded that they cope in a way that they have not had to before. The ways they have had to cope and the feelings, thoughts, and even physical abilities that they have are all new, or strange.

Children may be used to being physically able and active; now, suddenly, they cannot move without help. They may pride themselves on being calm, controlled or private children; suddenly they find themselves bursting into tears in public places, unable to sleep, being startled by sudden noises, experiencing nightmares or seeing pictures of the traumatic event in their heads in the daytime (we call these pictures "flashbacks").

These are all common symptoms of a condition called *post-traumatic stress* (PTS), that is, stress produced by the trauma, the effects of which we see *after* (or *post*) *the trauma*. We can expect the types of situations described in chapter one to cause PTS. Examples of these situations include:

- A serious threat to one's life or physical well-being;
- The sudden destruction of one's home or community;
- Seeing another person who is being, or has recently been, seriously injured or killed because of an accident, physical violence or rape; or
- The sudden loss of close friends or family.

All these examples are common occurrences in a wartime situation.

What is PTS?

Post-traumatic stress is the body's and mind's reaction to an *abnormal* event. Traumas are abnormal. We expect our lives to run along in a fairly predictable way. Traumas are unpredictable and represent danger and, therefore, they are threats to our usual existence. We feel insecure, vulnerable, unsure how to react, and afraid of further traumas happening.

Stress is a normal reaction to threats. When we are threatened by danger, our instinct is either to run away or to fight. Our bodies and minds prepare to fight or to run away by preparing for action. We breathe faster and our hearts beat faster to provide our muscles with more oxygenated blood.

Our body produces a substance in the blood called adrenaline, which tells the body to prepare to work harder and faster. Our muscles tense up, ready for action. We sweat, and find it difficult to eat or sleep.

During the stressful experience and afterwards, however, we are often unable to use this energy, and therefore, we have to keep it inside us. This produces stress reactions or PTS. Stress is not bad in itself. We need it to motivate us and to give us the energy to do our daily tasks. If we are unable to use our stress energy, however, it becomes stored up inside, making it hard to relax and causing us to be permanently and unnecessarily expecting danger to happen.

PTS is a normal reaction. If the signs of PTS do not go away after four to six weeks, however, a person will be diagnosed as suffering from *post-traumatic stress disorder* (PTSD).

What is PTSD?

Post-traumatic stress disorder (PTSD) is an illness that many people suffer from, especially those who have been through a war or similar disaster. The number of people who may be affected seems to vary in different studies and, although certain characteristics make it reasonably likely that a person will suffer from PTSD, it is difficult to predict who will suffer in this way.

Certain persons—either because of their basic personality types, previous experience of coping with trauma, or knowledge of and access to individuals who offer them appropriate support and ways of coping with crises—seem to cope better than others. Coping seems to require that a person can understand or make sense of what has happened to him or her, and can adapt to changed circumstances in a way that still permits the basic needs for meeting normal development. PTSD may develop when a person experiences an acute, single crisis event (Type 1 PTSD), or when a person experiences chronic traumatic stress (Type 2 PTSD).

Definition of PTSD

Doctors have a formal system for categorizing illnesses or diseases, known as DSM III-R (*The Diagnostic and Statistical Manual of Mental Disorders*, Third Edition, Revised, 1987). In this manual, persons suffer from PTSD if:

- God makes sense, thereby providing relief 33
from PTS, as the blame is placed on sin + Satan.

PTS

diagnosis

stipulations

1. They have experienced an event that is outside the range of usual human experience, and that event would be markedly distressing to almost anyone, and

2. They persistently re-experience the traumatic event in at least one of the following ways:

   a) Recurring and intrusive distressing recollections of the event that happen in situations that are unrelated to the trauma, and ones related to the trauma (for example, young children may repeatedly play out ideas that express the events or their feelings about the trauma).

   b) Recurring, distressing dreams of the event.

   c) Suddenly acting or feeling as if the traumatic event was recurring, including a sense of reliving the experience, and experiencing illusions, hallucinations (delusions), and flashbacks (feelings or mental pictures that are not related to what the person is doing at the time or are not connected with reality, and feel detached from reality). These may occur particularly if the person has just woken up or has been drinking alcoholic beverages.

   d) Becoming very distressed when exposed to events that symbolize or resemble an aspect of the traumatic event, including anniversaries of the trauma.

3. They persistently avoid anything that may remind them of the trauma and are less responsive (numb) than they were before the trauma. They do not react to events in the same way as they did before the trauma. At least three of the following indicate this:

   a) They try to avoid thoughts or feelings associated with the trauma.

   b) They avoid activities or situations that make them remember the trauma.

   c) They are unable to remember an important aspect of the trauma.

d) They are a lot less interested in significant activities (for example, young children may show a loss of recently acquired developmental skills, such as toilet training or language skills).

e) They feel detached or separate from others, and do not feel part of the family, school, or work situation.

f) They are unable to feel as deeply, or in the way that they usually can feel (for example, a father or mother may find it unusually difficult to show love for the partner and their children; a young child may be unable to enjoy playing or learning, and may withdraw from the parents' loving embraces).

g) They feel that their future has been cut short (for example, they find it difficult to make plans about their new school, or to see themselves having a job, or getting married and having a family, whereas they could do this before the trauma).

4. They show signs that they are more aroused (excited, tense, stressed) than they were before the trauma. At least two of the following indicate this:

a) They have difficulty falling or staying asleep.

b) They easily become angry, vexed, or irritable.

c) They find it difficult to concentrate or to remember recent events or pieces of information (such as lessons at school).

d) They are always on the alert, looking out for danger when it is not necessary for them to do so.

e) They are very jumpy and startle easily, in an exaggerated way.

f) They react physically by becoming tense and showing signs of stress (stiff muscles, sweating, faster breathing, faster pulse rate) when they experience events that are similar to the traumatic event.

For a person to be diagnosed as suffering from PTSD, he or she must display these symptoms for at least a month. Sometimes people do not show signs of PTSD immediately and may not show signs of distress until perhaps six months after the trauma. These persons are said to be suffering from delayed PTSD.

PTSD and children

In normal life situations, experts commonly acknowledge that children are a vulnerable subsector of the population, and yet the study of PTSD has only recently turned its attention to children. Many adults assume that children have a resilience in the face of disasters that they are never assumed to have in other situations. Some researchers believed that major disasters severely affected only a few children, and that most children recovered quickly from such events.

More recent studies, however, have studied children for a longer time, and the researchers have tried to get to know the children and to ask them how they themselves are feeling instead of just asking the children's teachers and parents to speak for them. Yule and Williams[1] did this in their study of child survivors of the Jupiter ship that sank. By studying the children in this way, Yule and Williams found that the disaster severely affected many children. They found that a large number of children showed signs of PTSD and high scores on the "impact of events" scale.[2] They also found that children's anxiety levels, which had been normal ten days after the ship sank, had significantly increased during another assessment five months after the ship sank. When Yule and Williams first assessed the children, they seemed depressed. Five months later, the children were even more depressed.

This and other recent studies have shown that children are very traumatized by disasters, and that they show signs of this distress even fifteen months after the incidents. They show similar PTSD symptoms to adults and their measured symptoms of distress were more severe than those of similarly traumatized adults. The actual symptoms that an individual child experiences will depend on several factors, which I will discuss later in this chapter.

Researchers have developed several assessment scales to measure a child's reactions, to see if their level of distress is abnormal (I am including a listing of some of these scales in the reference section at the end of this chapter).

The studies by Professor Yule and his colleagues have shown the importance of using specially designed scales when measuring children's reactions to disasters and of getting to know the children so one can question them directly, instead of getting the information secondhand. Secondhand answers can lead to severely underestimating the impact of a disaster on a group of children, and thinking that the children are unaffected when, in reality, they are very distressed. When faced with a large number of children, it is not easy to give each child a set of assessment scales to complete. Important information to note in administering the assessment scales to children follows the listing of these scales at the end of this chapter.

Vulnerable children

Children who are particularly vulnerable and may be in need of help include:

1. *Children who are showing signs of distress.* It is easy to misunderstand or to overlook signs of distress in children or to think of such children as naughty—e.g., not answering when spoken to, unwilling to go to school, not helping with everyday chores, being aggressive or disobedient, behaving like a baby and wetting the bed. Children may be distressed by:

    a) Not being looked after (or nurtured) and neglected by their parents. This lack of care may be emotional and physical.

    b) Living with abusive parents or caregivers.

    c) Family breakups due to their parents' own problems.

    d) Being separated from their parents and other emotionally important people.

    e) Not having enough food, water, shelter, or other material needs.

f) Not having the security and education offered by regular school activities.

g) Their parents are too distressed (anxious or depressed) to care for them physically or emotionally.

h) Being humiliated.

i) Being attacked sexually.

j) Witnessing others being attacked. — *school included.*

Some particular events that distressed children during the war in Liberia and that they had to cope with include:

- Their parent or someone close to them being killed or dying of malnutrition.
- Seeing people being killed or tortured.
- Having friends killed in the war.
- Killing someone themselves (especially if they had known that person before the war).
- Being a soldier or combatant.
- Becoming physically disabled because of the war.
- Having frightening experiences that they found difficult or impossible to talk about.

A child who has been in a war or other disaster usually will have had to cope with several of these distressing experiences. It is important, therefore, to assess fully what the child has experienced instead of just concentrating on one event. Again, listening (with your eyes and also your ears) to what the child finds most distressing is very important. Emotionally and physically, a child's main needs are to feel secure and to feel loved. These distressing experiences violate or deprive children of having their basic needs met, which include:

- Having enough to eat and drink.
- Feeling that they are loved, whatever they do or whatever they have done.
- Feeling special.

38

- ◆ Feeling that they are wanted.
- ◆ Feeling that someone understands them and will listen to them if they need to talk.

2. *Children who have experienced especially traumatic experiences include:*

   a) Unaccompanied children (children not in the care of their families or the main person who cares for them—their caregiver).

   b) Children who do not have the basics they need to survive, especially if they are close to death or are starving.

   c) Children who were forced to kill their parents.

   d) Children who were forced to join the fighting forces or armies, and took part in killing people or committing acts of violence.

   e) Children who were forced to witness the murder, violent death, or torture of their parents, other members of their family or their friends.

   f) Children who were tortured, raped, or beaten.

   g) Children who were captured, kidnaped, held hostage, or imprisoned.

   h) Children who were chased by the armed forces.

   i) Children who survived shelling, shooting, or a bomb at close distance.

   j) Children whose homes were attacked, shelled, or looted.

   k) Children whose parents have disappeared or were abducted.

   l) Children who have suffered the death of a parent, brother or sister, close family, or a friend.

3. *Children in difficult circumstances where their needs are not being met.*

Children understand things very much in the "here and now." They may not be aware of the level of danger that they are in

or how many of their needs are not being met. They are simply trying to survive. Children in difficult circumstances that often
deprive them of their basic needs include:

a) Children in detention camps and prisons.

b) Children living in orphanages and other residential
institutions that are often set up hurriedly in wartime.

c) Children alone on the streets.

d) Children living in homes where they are neglected or
abused.

When assessing a child's level of distress and the sources of
that distress, it is essential to assess the child within his family situation. Children often reflect the reactions of their parents,[3] so if parents are upset, the children are also upset. We must not assume that
because children have their parents with them that their parents are
giving the children proper care. Their parents may want to care for
them and may want you to feel that they are being good parents, so
they tell you that everything is okay, when in fact they are too distressed to care for their children or to listen to their distress. Children are very protective of their parents so they, too, may tell you
that everything is fine. We have to be very sensitive when we try to
discover what the true situation is so that we do not make the parents feel they are failures, that they are not coping and are not being
good parents to their children.

Recognizing that a child is in distress

So far we have discussed what post-traumatic stress disorder is and what experiences make a child particularly likely to
develop it. It is important to be aware that much of the research conducted with traumatized children has been done in the West, where
many incidents of children being traumatized take place "under
cover" or "in secret," such as childhood sexual abuse. The emotional
and practical aspects of the situation are very different from those
that prevail when a child is violently abused in a wartime situation.

For example, an uncle may rape a child in the child's home.
The violence, fear and danger operating at the time of that rape

may be very different from that operating when an armed gunman rapes a child on the street, with her raped and murdered mother lying next to her. We cannot say that one is worse than the other for the child, but in the second case more of the child's basic needs are not being met.

Children commonly show their distress in certain recognizable ways, depending on the following:

a) The child's personality

Both MacFarlane[4] in his study of the Australian bush fires and Yule in his study of the ferry disasters mentioned earlier noted how differently children reacted to similar experiences. Various reports on child soldiers illustrate the variety of ways that children cope with horrendous experiences. A child may be quiet, withdrawn, and may not appear to be in distress. We need to ask the child's caregiver what the child is usually like and whether the child is behaving in a way that is different from what they normally do. This is a good indication of whether he or she is in distress. We have to be patient, to allow the child to build up trust in us. We must listen to what the child does *not* say, as well as what she does say.

b) The child's understanding of the situation

Young children are very "concrete"—they understand things in the here and now. They do not easily understand what is happening to them and what the implications are for what has happened. They may not appear distressed that their mother is dead, because they think that she is just asleep. Although children may not intellectually understand the whole situation, however, they very quickly pick up feelings in their surroundings such as panic, pain and fear. Their lack of understanding may make the situation seem even more frightening, because they have no way of making sense of the events happening around them.

It is important to assess how a child perceives the situation, in terms of his own roles and actions, his family's response, his friends' responses, and people's general responses. Both children and adults desperately want to feel that their responses are normal

41

and "good enough," particularly in a crisis when it is hard for any-one to keep a clear idea of what is normal.

Children look to their friends, family, and others for reas-surance that they are coping well, and to give them a sense of hope for the future. The child's family is especially important in this respect. But if a child's parents and family are being murdered or tortured, or are running away, then the child, besides being trauma-tized by the actual events, has no one to provide this reassurance.

In these situations, children often feel guilty that they have failed to protect their parents from harm (although they know that they are unable to do so), overwhelming them with anger and a feeling of helplessness and guilt. Such children require special help, as do children who may have helped others commit—or may have themselves committed—immoral acts, even if they were initially motivated by genuine needs (such as those of a child soldier who killed many women, but who initially joined the army just to get some food).

c) Ways of coping

Children often withdraw and play in a very repetitive way at familiar games to try to restore a sense of order to their worlds. Thus you may see children playing in the street when all around are bombs and ruined buildings. It is not that they do not care or are not upset. They are trying to recreate a sense of security and normality for themselves. An older child may read a book that he has read many times, or may persistently talk about the same things (good memories of the past, or bad memories of the present trauma), or may start playing young children's games to achieve the same purpose.

Children who have been given a firm, caring home and acceptance and love, and have been helped to deal well with past distressing experiences, tend to cope better. The frequency, severity and consequences of these experiences affect how well a child copes.

When children are frightened, if they have been helped to know Jesus as their friend and Savior, they can turn to him, talk to him, sing to him, sit quietly with him, feel held by and safe with him when all around them a battle goes on.

The ability to retreat emotionally in this way from the fear of the situation to the safety and security of God's love protects children psychologically from being damaged by the danger around them. It is essential that we help children in danger to develop this protecting personal relationship with Jesus, and to help them to develop constructive rather than destructive ways of coping with their stress.

d) The culture

The culture that a child lives in determines how the child understands a trauma—how a child or adult shows distress and how they recognize distress. For example, many people in Liberia saw the recent war as a cleansing war to purify and punish God's people for not truly following him.

In Guatemala, Vietnam, Cambodia and elsewhere, there are great cultural differences in how people understand a trauma. We have to be careful not to assume that people in different cultures will all react in the same way. We need to spend time getting to know people and understanding their culture, their perceptions of the tragedy and its effects. When teaching workers about the effects of PTSD in Liberia, we had to explain how older children may wet the bed if they are distressed. Previously, these workers had seen these children as naughty, and had punished them in culturally specific ways.

e) The family's response and support

In most cultures the family remains the principal protector of, and provider for, children. Three important factors that may affect the child include:

1. How *intact* the family is—whether the family is separated or together, if a member is missing, or if the child is separated from his family. Freud and Burlingham say:

   The war acquires comparatively little significance for children so long as it only threatens their lives, disturbs

war

their material comfort, or cuts their food rations. It becomes enormously significant the moment it breaks up family life and uproots the first emotional attachments of the child within the family group (1943:67).[5]

I would challenge the idea that war is unimportant to a child if a child is simply in physical danger (especially if he or she is old enough to understand the danger), or not fed, given water or sheltered, but the emotional needs are most important. In Liberia, many children witnessed their parents' horrendous deaths, or were separated from their families as they ran from danger. Such children are particularly at risk.

forced
incest

2. How *nurturing* a parent is. In the war situation, parents may be unable to care for their children physically or emotionally or, as in Liberia, may be forced to abuse them physically or sexually, and thus break both family and cultural taboos. Such psychological damage to a child is enormous.

3. The amount of *support* available from other caregivers, and how reliable it is. Wars tend to break up the network of friends and family that support both the children and their parents, so the children lose the safe people with whom they might have shared their distress. They are deprived of social relationships that help to build their self-esteem, self-respect and ability to relate to others socially.

f) The child's age and development level

How children express their distress depends on their physical health and ability, their mental maturity (their thoughts and feelings), and their social maturity (how they play, talk, and relate to others). It is particularly important to notice if a child starts doing things again that they had grown out of.

A young infant in great distress may not eat, sleep, gain weight, or develop as he or she should. This is called a "failure to thrive." It can be fatal if the infant's distress is not relieved. A pessimistic outlook is one in which children dismiss the idea that any-

stress related

44

thing good will ever happen again, and feel that whatever they or anyone else does is bound to go wrong.

Psychosomatic complaints (physical pain or illness when there is nothing physically wrong, but that develops when they are hurting emotionally) are common in children. We usually ignore such complaints when we realize that children are not physically ill, but they can be very damaging and distressing. They are common in children, who often find it difficult to explain what they feel, or to sense that it is safe to say what they feel. They may believe that the people who are looking after them may get cross or upset. As one nine-year-old told me, "It is okay to have a pain in your tummy: it is not okay to be cross and cry."

Play and drawings are useful ways of helping a child express inner feelings (this approach is explained in chapter eleven), and children may need to use them repeatedly by children as a way to tell and make sense of their story. Chapter ten explores ways of helping children to express these thoughts, feelings, and physical needs more readily.

Everett Ressler[6] provides a good summary of the common signs of distress to watch for in children (see Figure 2.1 on page 46).

Summary

In this chapter we have explored together how a trauma may affect children and their families; how children show their distress or trauma; and what factors make it more or less likely that children are affected by a trauma. We have begun to see how this depends on the care the children receive—both at the time of the trauma and afterwards—and how the way in which children can understand and deal with the trauma influences the long-term effects on them.

We can do little to change some factors, such as the children's age and physical vulnerabilities. But we can do a great deal both during (sometimes) and certainly after the trauma to help a child express and understand her conflicting thoughts and feelings, allowing God to heal the memories and having basic needs for hope and security restored.

Figure 2.1: Common signs of distress in children

Thoughts and feeling states

- ashamed to be alive
- no wish to live
- inordinate guilt
- pessimistic outlook
- nightmares
- flashbacks
- uncharacteristic fearfulness
- depression
- sadness for an extended time
- generalized anxiety
- panic attacks
- irritability
- flat display of emotions
- fears of the commonplace
- fears of separation

Social interchange

- social isolation
- increased aggressive behavior
- defiance and rebelliousness
- excessive clinging

Individual behavior

- hyperactivity
- nervous tics
- over dependence
- easily startled
- easily moved to tears
- withdrawn
- sleeping difficulties
- regressive behavior
- thumb sucking and bed wetting
- repetitively describing or re-enacting a trauma
- uncharacteristic avoidance of talking about a trauma

Physiological functioning

- headaches
- psychosomatic complaints
- weight loss
- failure to thrive
- loss of energy
- no appetite

NOTES

1   W. Yule and R. Williams, "Post-traumatic stress reactions in children," *Journal of Traumatic Stress* (1990:3), pp. 279-95.

2   M. J. Horowitz, N. Wilner and W. Alvarez, "Impact of Event Scale: A measure of subjective stress," *Psychosomatic Medicine* (1979:41), pp. 209-218.

3   A. Freud and D. Burlingham, *War and Children* (New York: Medical War Books, 1943).

4   A. C. MacFarlane, "Family functioning and over-protection following a natural disaster: The longitudinal effects of post-traumatic morbidity," *Australian and New Zealand Journal of Psychology* (1987:21), pp. 210-218.

5   Freud and Burlingham, p. 67.

6   Everett M. Ressler, *Children in War: A Guide to the Provision of Services—A Study for UNICEF*, (New York: UNICEF, 1993), p. 174.

SCALES USED TO ASSESS PTSD IN CHILDREN

1   M. J. Horowitz, N. Wilner and W. Alvarez, "Impact of event scale: A measure of subjective stress," *Psychosomatic Medicine* (1979:41), pp. 209-218.

This is a version of a scale for adults that was adapted for children and can be used with children as young as eight years old.

2   P. Birleson, "The Validity of Depressive Disorder in Childhood, and the Development of a Self-rating Scale: A Research Report," *Journal of Child Psychiatry and Psychology* (1981:22), pp. 73-88.

You can use this scale to measure a child's depression.

3   C. R. Reynolds and B. O. Richmond, "What I think and feel: A revised measure of children's manifest anxiety," *Journal of Abnormal Child Psychology* (1978:6), pp. 271-80.

This scale provides a useful measure of children's levels of anxiety and what things make them anxious. They may also experience particular fears about certain parts of their distressing incidents. These can be measured and assessed using the scale in note 4 below.

4   L. C. Miller, C. L. Barrett, E. Hampe and H. Noble, "The Louisville Fear Survey for Children: Factor Structure of Children's Fears," *Journal of Counseling and Clinical Psychology* (1972:39), pp. 264-268.

When administering assessment scales, remember:

a)   It is important to act quickly. Children who are supported and given someone to talk to soon (within 48 hours of the incidents) generally recover better from their experiences and appear to be less distressed.

b)   The children may not be accustomed to filling out forms or expressing their feelings by answering specific questions, so they may say that they are okay, when in fact they are quite distressed.

c)   The forms and materials may not be easily available in a disaster situation. When paper and pencils are scarce, drawing in the sand or mud with your finger or a stick is a good substitute.

d) The forms are often in English, which—although it is the official language in many developing countries—is often not the language that the people express themselves in.

- To introduce the concept of God is to introduce the concept of sin + Satan. Sin + Satan are responsible for all evil - God is not. God could remove all evil but to do so He would have to remove all people. What people mean when they say why doesn't God do something, is that they want God to act decisively against all overt evil. If they really wanted God to eradicate evil they would be willing to forfeit their own existence.

Part 2

Intervention Concerns Stemming from War-related Trauma

3
Comfort for the Grieving Child

Cynthia Blomquist

Blessed are those who mourn,
for they will be comforted.
Matthew 5:4

Children around the world, living in places of warfare, carry hearts heavy with grief; they have no security, no homes, friends have disappeared and family members are dead. Children in war must struggle through the process of grieving these losses, even in the midst of continued pain and fear.

Some children must face the profound loss of a parent during their nation's war. For other children, death or distance separate them from their entire family. A child growing up in a war zone may find death commonplace, and not a secret. The loss of mother or father, however, is never commonplace. Caregivers need knowledge and strength to comfort the pain of a child overwhelmed with grief.

This chapter attempts to provide a basic framework of the child's grief experience, to empower the ministry worker with tools of caring. First, it is helpful to look at the experience of loss and death through the eyes of each age group. Differences in cognitive and emotional development lead to ways of understanding death that are very different from those of adults. With these age levels in mind, we can then make suggestions for helping these children move through the grieving process.

Finally, two factors are important to consider when working with children in war: first, the relationship between trauma symptoms and bereavement, and second, the impact of cultural ideas of death and grieving on the child's experience.

What is necessary for a child to grieve?

At the very center of the grief experience lies a list of "necessary ingredients" to help a child of any age move through the grieving process. J. F. Crosby and N. L. Jose (1983:84) offer the following framework. Children need:

1. Space and time to absorb the fact of loss;
2. Help in labeling and identifying the finality of death;
3. Models who can grieve and express the range of emotional response;
4. Someone who will listen to them attentively and with respect; and
5. To express themselves by giving their own account of what happened.

necessary

Developmental differences

Children grow through many different stages of development in their thinking and the way they cope with their emotions. Their relationship to and dependence on a caregiver remains central in their young lives, but their understanding and expression of that relationship changes with their growth in thinking and feeling.

Loss of that central relationship challenges the child with the overwhelming loss of security and stability. This lack of security may bring any child to behavior typical of a younger child (for example: bed-wetting, clinging to adults, sleep difficulties and baby talk).

Reaching into a child's life with a stabilizing hand, however, provides the child the safety to mourn and the security to build new relationships. By understanding how the mourning process differs at each developmental level, caregivers can either educate the remaining family members or provide the necessary care to a grieving child themselves.

Infants and small children, newborn to two years old

The world of an infant centers completely on its own experience. It knows the discomfort of being hungry or tired and the satisfaction of being fed or rocked to sleep. The child does not experience the mother, or primary caregiver, as different from the acts of caring. If the child is separated from the mother, however, the child will have an extreme reaction to the loss. It is natural for the child to act in the following stages (Crenshaw 1990):

1. Shock; the child seems numb from the loss.

2. A desperate search for the lost mother, with loud crying and much physical activity. (We have all held a child crying for its mother and squirming uncontrollably!)

3. Despair, as the child gives up the search and withdraws into him- or herself.

4. Detachment, as the child builds a wall around feelings so he or she does not hurt any more.

Ways to care for an infant

Infancy is the time when children are deciding if the world is a place for trust or mistrust (Erickson 1959). To maintain a sense of stability and trustworthiness for the child, it is important to provide regular, nurturing care as soon as possible (Giacalone and McGrath 1980). Unfortunately, this could prove difficult in a war setting, where chaos and loss affect almost everyone. But maternal care that is as regular as possible will provide the child with another relationship that will help it to feel attachment and trust.

Children who are beginning to talk (about two years old) now have words to express their loss. These children will experience four stages similar to those of infants. However, these children need words, and physical actions, to reassure them. Tell the child, "I will be here to hold you and take care of you," and follow through with regular care. Answer questions about death with simple, direct statements, such as, "When people die their bodies totally stop working" (Crenshaw 1990:44). Children need answers to their questions that meet them at their own level of understanding.

Preschool age children, three to six years old

Security and structure continue to be crucial needs for children in this age group. New thinking and speaking skills, however, may complicate their experience of the loss. These young children have active imaginations they use in play and fantasy, and they continue to hold a sense of personal power that makes it difficult for them to understand the difference between this fantasy and reality (Crenshaw 1990). For example, some children at this age may hold the conflicting ideas of the destruction of a parent's body with a fantasy that the parent is living somewhere else waiting to return (Eth and Pynoos 1985).

A preschool child may also feel extremely guilty, believing that the death of a parent or sibling was the result of their angry wishes. This may be especially true in a culture that holds beliefs in "curses" and the activity of the spiritual realm (discussed below). Young children have also learned the lesson that bad things happen to them when they misbehave; they need to be comforted with the fact that the death was not caused by their behavior (Grollman 1977).

Ways to care for a preschool-age child

Young children need help learning how to label and express their feelings. Drawing faces with different expressions may give the child help with the task of labeling. Reassure the child that angry thoughts without actions cannot make people die.

As you explain death, remember that children at this age cannot think abstractly. Using the description "your mother has gone to sleep forever," will only cause the child to associate death with sleeping, naturally causing more sleep difficulties. Also, sickness or wounds should not be the "cause of death," because most people who are sick or injured can get better. It is better to use the idea that the person's body was hurt very badly, and medicine and doctors were not able to make it work again.

Also, using the terminology that God "took" the loved one can lead to fear, rather than comfort. The idea that the parent's soul is not buried with the body, but is in a special place that God has made for him or her may reassure children (Crenshaw 1990). If possible, young children can benefit by participating in funeral rituals—the community expression of grief can help the death become more real.

Helping the young child through the grieving process requires patient teaching about how to express feelings. The caregiver can use stories and metaphors, or model correct coping strategies. Metaphors (pictures or examples that are easier to understand) about death in the world of nature can be extremely helpful. For example, pointing to the bloom of a flower, we can describe that the flower does die, but we always remember how beautiful it is. Also, caregivers can tell stories about animals or people who experience a death, and the things they do to cope. The caregiver can talk about his or her own sad feelings, and how to find fun things to do to take the mind off the sadness.

School-age children, six to twelve years old

Children at this developmental level begin to have the language and emotional resources to express their feelings of grief and loss. They are more active with other children their age and learn new social skills. During the later childhood years, children also become more able to understand the perspective of another person. School-age children have the new experience of learning and helping with tasks. The death of a parent puts a large hurdle in this time of skill development and self-esteem based on doing tasks well (Erickson 1959).

The child's understanding of death can change quite a bit through these ages. Younger children (around seven or eight years old) may have a frightening view of death as skeletons and ghosts. At about age nine children begin to understand that death is a natural part of every life, but they may still hold the idea that death is reversible (Crenshaw 1990).

Ways to care for a school-age child

In working with children of this age it is important to use clear and direct explanations. It may be helpful to use a natural example, like an animal or plant, to show that once the body has stopped working it does not start back up again. The child needs to hear that the body no longer feels anything or thinks anything, and that being dead means that the body is not of use any more (Ward 1993). This is particularly important for children who have witnessed violent deaths, to know that the disfigured parent will not come back to life in their damaged state.

Encourage the child to talk about the different kinds of feelings they have: love, fear, anger, guilt. They need reassurance that all the feelings do not always make sense together. One way to start this process with a shy child is to talk about the way other children feel (Crenshaw 1990). Conflicting feelings can be defined as normal by saying, "Some children who have lost their mother or father talk about how much they loved them and miss them. But they also feel really angry because their parent has left them." It may take a while for the child to feel safe enough to express all of his or her feelings.

As with younger children, the school-age child will need to grieve in small spans. Do not assume that a child is not bothered by loss because she or he seems unaffected. It is important to recognize that a child can handle intense emotions for only a short time. To cope with the emotional pain, children put the loss away in their minds and do other things (Eth and Pynoos 1985). Caregivers can encourage positive coping by helping the child identify new activities or friendships. For children in a war zone, that may mean a search for sports equipment, or using what is available to create a new game.

A large part of the work for a mourning child lies in the ability to express and tolerate the sadness and longing that come with positive memories about the lost parent. Positive memories play an important part in the mourning process. Children can talk about their feelings, or by experiencing them indirectly through play, drama or art work.

Children use the "distance" between themselves and the dolls or characters they use to stay at a safe place as they experience the pain. (This "distance" is similar to an adolescent getting advice for the problems of a "friend," rather than talking about his or her own hurts.) Caregivers should not rush in to point out that the child is the one experiencing the loss. The child may experience this well-intentioned insight as an invasion on her safety (Crenshaw 1990). Another safe way for a child to work through sad or painful feelings is by drawing pictures. The caregiver can ask the child to draw a picture of himself and the loved one doing something together, or a picture of something that reminds the child of the lost parent.

Teenagers, twelve to eighteen years old

In Western culture adolescence fills a clear definition for the age before adulthood. Non-Western cultures may expect teenagers to fill an adult role much earlier than is expected in Western countries. In either situation, a teenager is in a time of transition to personal responsibility and commitment to the community. Armed with new thinking skills, the teen has a more adult concept of death. A child of this age has more resources to consider issues of personal loss and reality beyond death.

However, with these resources come new pains and worries. In comparison to younger children, a teenager may feel more threatened by the death of a loved one and the real presence of warfare, due to their new ability to grasp the coming of their own death.

Ways to care for a teen

Despite the new independence of being near adulthood, the teenager will still feel intense longing and pain of loss. The first stage of grieving can be extremely intense for the child, and it is important for the caregiver to offer the space for these feelings to be expressed. Trying to "make it better" for the teen may shut down the pain before the right time. Yet, just as younger children, teenagers cannot maintain this level of intense suffering. Caregivers can encourage the teen to take some time to do something fun to get their mind off the grief, and can reassure them that this is not betraying the relationship with the lost parent (Crenshaw 1990).

Caregivers may notice differences between the ways that boys and girls process their grief. Teenaged boys in Western cultures may use drinking or drugs as a way to distance themselves from the hurt. Boys also respond to caretaking with some hostility and anger. Girls may also numb themselves with anger, but caregivers will discover more longing for comfort in grieving teenaged girls (Crenshaw 1990). Girls may also have more caretaking responsibilities thrust on them, threatening the space and time they require for the mourning process (Tallmer 1980).

Working with a group of teenagers together can reinforce the positive effects of their friendships and offer them the place to see that they are not alone in the experience. Groups can discuss what feelings they associate with loss, make up stories or poetry about these feelings, or compose music that expresses their emotions (Ward 1993). Discussions could center on the difficult topics of forgiveness and revenge, life after death, and the "normal process" of grief. Teens also benefit from positive reminiscing by sharing with the group the best memories they have of their lost parent.

Recovering from traumatic death

Caregivers empowered with the knowledge of the developmental issues of mourning will still need sensitivity to the trauma of death in war. Children who have been living in a war zone will most likely have lost a family member or close friend to combat violence. Some will have been told about the death; others will have witnessed the violence themselves. The pain of loss due to the violence of war adds many complications to the child's experience. Children who have lost parents to wars around the world have experienced continuing nightmares, physical problems, suicidal thoughts, hopelessness and hostility (Garbarino, Dubrow, Kostelny and Pardo 1992).

The trauma of witnessing a death

Witnessing the violent death of a loved one drastically

threatens a child's grieving process. As a witness to an act of violence, the child has been put in a helpless position, forced to watch
a horrible thing without any power to make it stop. The nearer the
relationship between the child and the victim, the more we can
expect to see trauma symptoms in combination with the grief reaction (see chapter two on PTSD in children). Witnessing the death of
a parent will be emotionally overwhelming for the child (Pynoos
and Eth 1985).

A young girl who saw her mother shot by soldiers may see
that rifle blast again and again in her mind. Reminders of her
mother may bring that traumatic scene back to her thoughts, rather
than the positive memories important for grieving (Pynoos and Eth
1985). A caregiver can carefully work with the child to fantasize the
process of making the mother's body whole again, allowing the
child to remember the mother in a happy way (Pynoos and Nader
1988).

Children who have witnessed the death of a parent need to
have the opportunity to talk about any fantasies of revenge against
the killer or changing the outcome of the violence. In a war zone,
there will never be the justice of a trial and a prison sentence. It is
natural for a child to have dreams of revenge against the enemy.
This is a child's response to the helplessness of witnessing the acts,
a way to put blame on the murderer, and a chance to fantasize
away any further threat (Pynoos and Eth 1985).

Offering open ears to a child with these feelings may help
neutralize some of the pain. Drawing a picture or play acting the
revenge scene offers the child a way to cope. Some children may
need to be reassured that there is a difference between having the
fantasy and taking actions of revenge, especially in a culture where
spiritual "curses" are considered a natural response to an enemy.

The relationship between trauma and grief

Post-traumatic stress symptoms do hold a strong overlap
with the experience of grief. Both traumatized and grieving children have unwanted thoughts and dreams (intrusion symptoms),
and they will avoid relationships and situations that are reminders

of the person or experience (avoidance symptoms). There is a difference, however, in the quality of the two. For example, thoughts during grieving hold the quality of reunion or relationship with the loved one, whereas traumatic dreams or thoughts will center on the frightening death event. Caregivers can help the children distinguish between the experiences of trauma and the work of mourning (Pynoos and Nader 1988).

Yet even natural mourning reactions can cause anxiety in children. Many school-age children respond with fright when they experience normal dreams of reunion with the lost friend or family member, or "see" that person out of the corner of their eye. Children are not yet able to understand how their minds can "play tricks on them" when they want so much to be with the person again (Pynoos and Nader 1988).

Even a child that grasps the finality of death may believe he has seen a ghost of the person, or that the person has returned from the grave. For example, two young Liberian brothers living in an orphanage described their most frightening experience in the war as seeing their dead mother walking nearby, dressed in a white cloak.

An important reminder in working with children who have experienced a sudden violent death in the family or community is that the traumatic reactions may complicate the grief process. It is difficult for children to find the resources inside themselves to handle both recovery from trauma and the work of grief. Relief from the anxiety and fear of trauma needs to happen first, so that the child has the internal resources necessary to face the process of mourning (Pynoos and Nader 1988).

The pain of "missing" parents

The chaos of war also brings confusion and a desperate hope of seeing loved ones who are missing. Refugee families may be separated during displacement; children may need to scatter into hiding when soldiers come to a village; or parents may need to leave to search for food. Many orphans in Liberia saw their parents leave to look for something for the family to eat, and the parents never came back. Some children heard later that their mother or father had been shot; others never knew what happened to their parents. The children who were left wondering experienced deeper emotional pain than those who knew their mother or father had died. Recognition of the reality of the loss is necessary to begin to mourn.

Anitha Ronstrom has worked with children in Central American warfare. She describes the two different outcomes for children with loved ones that are missing:

> For those children who do not lose their hope, the situation becomes one of permanent anguish and hope. For those who decide that their relative is dead, the decision involves another complication. As long as the death has not been confirmed, it is as if [the child is] symbolically killing [the relative] (1989:150).

An extremely difficult job for a caregiver will be helping a child make the most appropriate decision concerning a missing parent's death. Yet, moving on to new relationships requires letting go of a harmful hope.

Cultural perspectives of death and grief

The trauma of war is not the only added concern of working in a war zone. Cultural sensitivity and understanding will "make or break" any attempts at caring for a nation's hurting children. Much of what is written concerning a child's experience of grief comes from a Western psychological model. Here are a few suggestions for sensitively adapting these insights to a non-Western culture.

Cultural influence on ritual

Keep in mind the perspectives on death and burial that differ from traditional Western thought. John Bowlby (1980) describes three aspects of mourning that occur in almost all societies (yet have particular meaning in non-Western cultures):

1. There is continued relationship with the loved one despite the death of the body.

2. There is an expectation that mourners will feel angry with whomever is responsible for the death.

3. There is a prescribed time limit for appropriate mourning.

The idea of continued relationship has different connotations across cultures. A Western child or spouse may talk to the loved one as though he or she were still present, or visit the grave and tell the loved one family news. Most non-Western cultures, however, consider both the living community members and the dead ancestors as active members in the community (Steyne 1990). For some cultures these ancestor relationships are vital to the continued welfare of the community; elaborate burial rituals and offerings then assure continued aid from this person's spirit (Bowlby 1980). A dead parent then becomes an ancestor in the community, and children may be encouraged to practice spiritualistic rites to communicate with this loved one.

The question of responsibility and revenge runs hot in the minds of many children who have lost a parent to the enemy. In many non-Western societies, murder or war require special rituals, sacrifice or punishment for the guilty person to soothe the spirits of the victims. The evil deeds also point to spiritual activity, and the community may seek to recover balance in the spiritual realm through other rituals (Burnett 1992).

The influence of ritual on mourning

In the chaos of a war zone, special rituals may be impossible, but the meaning behind them is not lost to the community and the children. A special sense of panic or anxiety may exist if the child believes the spirit of a dead parent is restless. Asking the child what he or she has been told about the dead parent's spirit may provide important insight for caring for the youngster. Older children may even believe it is their responsibility to avenge the death, as was the case for many Liberian boys who quickly joined the rebel forces after their parents' deaths.

The cultural idea of spirits may also be used in a harmful way. For example, in one Liberian orphanage, the children were told that if they did not behave, their dead mothers or fathers would come back to punish them. One can imagine how frightened a child would be to then "see" their lost parent. These children would also avoid telling any of the orphanage workers about their experiences, for fear of being accused of misbehaving.

As Christians, we may have very different ideas of death, spirits, and revenge. We find ourselves in a complicated place. It is important not to discount the meaning that these rituals hold for the community. Yet, it is also important to discern the spiritual nature of the ritual, and pray for wisdom in how to use any rituals to bring stability back to the community, and to the child. (We Westerners need to struggle with the reality of the unseen!)

Rituals can be an important commemoration and a powerful way to express the reality of the person's death. Using culturally appropriate rituals with children offers a place for them to put action to their belief of the loved one's death. Through critical thinking and dialogue with Christians in the community, we can use these rituals in a way that honors Christ. Analysis of the meaning of the beliefs and rituals within a community informs the decision on how to contextualize these rites into the life of the church (Burnett 1992). I am not suggesting that this is easy work. Relationships within the community and earnest prayer are invaluable in discerning ways to encourage the expression of grief, with a hope in the resurrection promised by Christ.

Conclusion

Clearly, the journey that lies before a grieving child is complex and frightening. Each age group must struggle through its own understanding of a painful loss, and each must find ways to meet the need for stability and security. The violence inherent in war complicates this path by leaving children with painful and traumatic memories of the loss. Work will take time, as patient caregivers offer themselves as guides to the community and families. Yet, we can empower caregivers with the knowledge of the process of grief, and the faith in God's direction and discernment in culturally sensitive ministry. Those that mourn will be comforted.

REFERENCES

Bowlby, John. *Attachment and Loss, Volume III: Loss.* London: The Hogarth Press, 1980.

Burnett, D. *Unearthly Powers.* Nashville: Oliver Nelson, 1992.

Crenshaw, D. A. *Bereavement: Counseling the Grieving throughout the Life Cycle.* New York: Continuum, 1990.

Crosby, J. F. and N. L. Jose, "Death: Family adjustment to loss" in *Stress and the Family.* C. R. Figley and H. I. McCubbin, eds. New York: Brunner/Mazel, 1983, pp. 76-89.

Erickson, E. H. *Identity and the Life Cycle.* New York: International Universities Press, 1959.

Eth, S. and R. Pynoos, "Developmental perspective on psychic trauma in childhood" in *Trauma and Its Wake, Volume I.* C. R. Figley, ed. New York: Brunner/Mazel, 1985, pp. 36-52.

Garbarino, J., N. Dubrow, K. Kostelny and C. Pardo. *Children in Danger: Coping with the Consequences of Community Violence.* San Francisco: Jossey-Bass, 1992.

Giacalone, G. M. and E. McGrath. "The child's concept of death" in *Bereavement Counseling: A Multidisciplinary Handbook.* B. M. Schoenberg, ed. Westport, Connecticut: Greenwood Press, 1980, pp. 195-212.

Grollman, E. A. *Understanding Bereavement and Grief.* N. Linzer, ed. Yeshiva University Press, 1977, pp. 160-162.

Pynoos, R. and S. Eth. "Children traumatized by witnessing acts of personal violence: Homicide, rape, or suicide behavior" in *Post-Traumatic Stress Disorder in Children.* S. Eth and R. S. Pynoos, eds. Washington, D.C.: American Psychiatric Press, 1985, pp. 17-44.

Pynoos, R. S. and K. Nader. "Psychological first aid and treatment approach to children exposed to community violence: Research implications" in *Journal of Traumatic Stress* 1988:1, pp. 445-473.

Ronstrom, Anitha. "Children in Central America: Victims of war" in *Child Welfare* 1989:68, pp. 145-153.

Steyne, P. M. *Gods of Power.* Houston: Touch, 1990.

Tallmer, M. "Sexual and age factors in childhood bereavement" in *Bereavement Counseling: A Multidisciplinary Handbook*. B. M. Schoenberg, ed. Westport, Connecticut: Greenwood Press, 1980, pp. 164-171.

Ward, B. and Associates, eds. *Good Grief: Exploring Feelings, Loss and Death with Over-Elevens and Adults*. Philadelphia: Jessica Kingsley, 1993, pp. 114-116.

Wilson, R. "The whirlpool of grief" in *Good Grief: Exploring Feelings, Loss and Death with Over-Elevens and Adults*. B. Ward and Associates, eds. Philadelphia: Jessica Kingsley, 1993, pp. 114-116.

4
Breaking Fragile Bonds: What Bonding and Attachment Mean to Children of War

Carole A. McKelvey

Who can forget the images flashing on the television screen? The faces of war-ravaged orphans crying on evacuation buses. Tiny children whose bodies have suffered massive trauma. Little victims starving because they cannot get nourishment.

Orphans? Yes, many have been orphaned. In today's world their numbers grow daily as civil unrest visits such places as Rwanda, Bosnia-Herzegovina, Mozambique, Angola, Liberia, Guatemala, the Sudan, Romania, Lebanon, even Russia.

The statistics[1] as we approach the turn of the century are sobering:

- In at least 20 countries of the world, children as young as 10 have been used in civil war, armies of liberation and even in international conflict.
- More than 50,000 Iranian children between age 12 and 15 were killed on the battlefield as child soldiers in the war with Iraq.
- Worldwide, children's rights are being violated in civil and international conflicts.

Many, many children are the unseen victims of wars when their bonds and attachments with their primary caregivers are torn asunder. They are the faceless victims who may suffer the greatest trauma in a war situation.

Even if they are not orphaned, many of war's children are broken in spirit. There are horror stories: stories about children who have been lost in the confusion of war, who are psychologically abused, neglected and mistreated so that they no longer can love or trust any adult.

The most important thing that can happen to a child in the first two critical years of life—other than having proper nutrition—is attachment to a primary caregiver. For many tiny victims of war, this attachment has been broken. Generally the greatest psychological damage is done to children under the age of two, but older children, too, suffer the consequences of broken attachments.

Annie's story

Annie Wuantee is a refugee from Liberia. Liberia has been torn by civil war for more than five years. More than 150,000 people have died because of this war. Annie is very fortunate—to be alive and out of the war-torn region she once called home.

Annie's freedom came at a price. She has lost her husband, her home, her livelihood, her heritage. Annie has also lost four of her brothers, who died because of ethnic purging.

Annie is a member of the Gio tribe. Her husband was once a powerful politician in a large county in Liberia. The couple had prestige, a nice home, money and a large family. All of that disappeared when Annie's husband was gunned down and their home burned to the ground around Annie.

Since Annie and her husband were Gios, the soldiers of Samuel Doe (then president of Liberia) targeted them for murder. Their crime? Being Gio and being influential and learned.

To escape the persecution and horror that broke her family apart, Annie tried to flee Liberia in 1990. She and her five children, her elderly mother and other members of the family fled to a neighboring country. But in the escape attempt, Annie was thrown in jail.

"They wanted to kill me, too. The soldiers treated me very badly and they said they would kill me, despite my family needing me.

"My daughter had gone to the United States to school and got word that if she brought $3,000 she could buy me out of jail." But Annie's daughter could not get to her in the jail with the money from America, so she had to come back to Liberia to try to rescue her mother.

Meanwhile, the members of Annie's family had scattered, some escaping the country and others unable to find their way to freedom. Annie's two older children were stranded and lost without their mother's guidance.

Even some of the little grandchildren became separated from the family and had to fend for themselves. Lost and alone, children of the Gio tribe in Liberia were targeted for murder by Doe's thugs, Annie says.

"All of the attachments with my children and grandchildren were severed because of the war. This hurt them very badly, because they couldn't see their mother, and their father was dead. They were lost without us.

"Doe's tribe [the ruling Krahn] at one time came and took 3,900 kids from Gio and Mano families and put them in trucks. They carried them to the president of Liberia. Samuel Doe ordered the soldiers to bury the children alive.

"And they did. They took the bulldozers and buried all the children alive; all of the children were Gio and Mano. And they all died—3,900 children!"[2]

The impact of the loss of attachments on Annie's family

As in many cases of war-separated families, the lost children and grandchildren of Annie Wuantee had no one they could count on for help. Annie says it is very bad to be separated from your family. All of the attachments are gone.

"Now we are a poor family. We lost everything to the war. I was the one in the family who had the most. They all looked up to me. Now they are without anything."

Because of the loss of attachments, Annie says her children, even the adult ones, feel at a loss in the world. After her daughter managed to bribe Annie out of jail, three children, some grandchildren and an elderly grandmother did manage to escape finally to Freetown on the coast. It meant a seven-day walk in the bush in hostile territory, constantly fearing for their lives. They finally crossed the river bordering their country and escaped. But much of her family is still missing.

Even children who are not physically injured in a war suffer great losses. When their attachments fail them, children feel lost and do not know who to depend on. This has happened to Annie's adult children and her grandchildren. They are still lost in Liberia, where in mid-1993 the war flared up again after an uneasy six-week truce.

"They are scattered," says Annie. "I know I can't return to my homeland, but I must get my children and grandchildren out. I need help getting my children out of Liberia," she cries. "Can you help me?"

Every other month some lucky refugees from Liberia make it to America. In June 1993, Annie says, an estimated 170 refugees from Liberia made it to the U.S. from Ivory Coast refugee camps. Annie's children, however, are still among the missing.

Children with attachment issues are rampant in the world of war. These unattached children, who may grow up without supportive homes and in the chaotic atmosphere of war, can eventually become tomorrow's sociopaths. This is especially true of children who grow up in the hectic atmosphere of refugee camps within a hostile territory. These children grow up surrounded by war, never knowing peace. Guns and tanks are their playthings and they learn aggression from their elders. When your model is a terrorist, what possible outcome can there be?

When young children become unattached, when that fragile bond is broken with their primary caregiver (usually the mother), children display distinct symptoms. These symptoms can render them unable to love, unable to live a normal life.

The loss of attachment can occur as they are ripped from the arms of those whom they once trusted to take care of them. In the place of trust come fear and anger. When this happens in a war situation, it usually means these tiny victims bounce from one place to another, constantly experiencing "bonding breaks." Many of these children can become what is clinically diagnosed as "character-disordered."

Those caring for them need to know what to look for and what they need to do for a child who may have an attachment disorder.

Symptoms of character-disordered children

Specific symptoms[3] to look for, even in very young children, include:

1. Lack of ability to give and receive affection
2. Self-destructive behavior
3. Cruelty to others or to pets
4. Phoniness
5. Stealing, hoarding and gorging
6. Speech pathology
7. Extreme control problems
8. Lack of long-term childhood friends
9. The caregivers seem unreasonably angry
10. Abnormalities in eye contact
11. Preoccupation with blood, fire and gore
12. Superficial attractiveness and friendliness with strangers
13. Learning disorders
14. Crazy lying

With the diagnosis of attachment disorders comes a new set of behavioral problems. Says specialist Selma Fraiberg:

> When, for any reason, a child has spent the whole or a large part of his or her infancy in an environment that could not provide him or her with human partners or the

71

conditions for sustained human attachments, the later development of the child demonstrates measurable effects. For example:

- The children form relationships only on the basis of need, with little regard for one caregiver over another.

- There is an impairment of the capacity to attach to any person.

- There is also retardation, which continues in follow-up testing. Conceptual thinking remains low, even when favorable environments are provided for the children in the second and third years of life. Language itself, which was grossly retarded in all the infant studies, improves under more favorable environmental conditions, but this area of learning is never fully regained.

- Disorders of impulse control, particularly in the area of aggression, were reported in all follow-up studies of these children."[4]

Experts know that an attachment problem can manifest itself in children who are orphaned or otherwise estranged from their caregiver as small infants. Potential bonding problems in small infants, however, are easier to address than in older children who have suffered bonding breaks before the age of two. With proper intervention, including holding techniques, new caregivers can lead a baby to an emotional attachment to them.

The key, experts say, is having one consistent nurturing caregiver available to the child during the formative first two years, even if those years occur in the middle of a war.

A lack of attachment affects children's ability to form close relationships throughout their lives. It is an affectionate bond between two individuals that endures through time and space and serves to join them emotionally.

Attachment, literally, helps a child to:[5]

- Attain full intellectual potential
- Sort out what is perceived
- Think logically
- Develop a conscience

- ◆ Become self-reliant
- ◆ Cope with stress and frustration
- ◆ Handle fear and worry
- ◆ Develop future relationships
- ◆ Reduce jealousy

We can help many of these children who have attachment disorders with adequate therapy, but the number of children currently receiving adequate treatment is minuscule. Early intervention and treatment are rare and too many substitute caregivers do not understand attachment disorders or recognize the symptoms.[6]

Many mental health problems of children of war come from their removal from their family of origin and their subsequent movement through the system. This is why those working with children of war must be prepared to offer these children stability. The best cure for attachment disorders, other than adequate therapy, is a consistent, nurturing caregiver who is committed to the child for the long term.

Multiple moves, or "breaks," cause the greatest wounds to a child's psyche. These breaks can cause the condition we have been talking about—"attachment disorders."

Among the most difficult children to rear are older children who have suffered from attachment disorders because of their early childhood experiences. These children have not made that critical connection with a primary caregiver that is so important during their first years of life. The result can be severe.

Jason's story

The last few weeks the couple had their adopted son, Jason (not his real name), they actually tied bells to their bedroom door when they went to bed. They feared he would murder them in their sleep.

After more than a year in their home, the 14-year-old Asian boy had driven his adopted mother to the brink of a nervous breakdown. He had also alienated his father and terrorized his sister.

Nevertheless, it was an agonizing decision, his mother says. The family finally decided they had to give him back. They had to relinquish him. There was no choice, for they feared they had unwittingly welcomed a dangerous psychopath into their loving arms.

Family members blamed themselves for the adoption failure, for its disruption. Privately, they also blame their adoption agency. It was the agency, they say, that gave them too little information when they decided to adopt the boy. The medical papers they were given revealed nothing wrong with him, they say.

At first, the adoption of 12-year-old Jason was a dream come true for the Midwestern couple. From the day he arrived, however, their world turned topsy-turvy. He was the second Asian-born child the family had adopted. Before Jason came Sumiko, now 16, who remains with the family and has adjusted well to her parents.

But with Jason it was different. Jason had come from a country torn by war. He was an orphan; he lived on the streets and in the refugee camps on his own; he was finally sent to an orphanage. There the workers had their hands more than full and were barely able to feed their young charges, let alone give them the love and attention they needed.

In the orphanage Jason had physically thrived, unlike the other children who were badly malnourished. Jason learned to steal what he needed. He got what he needed by abusing younger, weaker children. And he learned how to please adults, in a superficial way, to get what he required.

Life with Jason

All of this his adoptive family learned after they adopted Jason. They sought the truth because from the minute Jason entered their home there was not a moment of peace. They did not even have the "honeymoon period" one often finds even with difficult adoptive children.

"For the next one and one-half years we had not one good day," says his mother, listing a string of horrifying incidents. She says Jason:

♦ Told his adopted sister he wanted her dead;

- Physically molested his mother, and the children at his school;
- Was extremely cruel to animals;
- Never did anything his parents told him to do, but only manipulated them;
- Tore things to shreds just for spite;
- Beat up and hurt children in school, interrupting classes; and
- Was "extremely bad" when the family went on vacation trips, disrupting all activities.

At one point his mother says she pleaded with the adoption agency for help, asking, "What do I have in my home? A terrorist?"

This family insists the private adoption agency they went through to adopt their son gave them no support when they needed it. Jason was extremely disruptive in school. His mother says she dreaded to hear the phone ring. She knew it would be the school complaining, or an irate family of another injured or sexually molested child. The school sent home a report that Jason had grabbed the breasts of eight girls.

According to his mother, animals knew instinctively that he was dangerous and "literally went berserk" when he approached them. "[Dogs] often barked and cried and ran away. Any dog he could get to was greeted with a kick or otherwise hurt," she says.

One schoolmate complained that Jason threw him against a fence on the way home from school. School reports sent home contained accounts that said Jason "threw rocks at me and beat me up."

He was also functionally illiterate—even in his native tongue—when he arrived at the home. Adoption reports, however, indicated he had attended school.

After they realized the extent of Jason's challenges and his hostility, the family consulted experts, who advised them to get the boy out of the house as soon as they possibly could, because he was dangerous to them.

After months of trauma the final straw came one day when Jason and his mother were home alone together. She told him to do something he didn't want to do. He began to glare at her with what she describes as "a demonic look . . . his eyes just turned black and he stared and stared at me. Then he flung his chair aside and came at me, his hands in a strangle-type hold.

"I became really frightened, realizing that he was almost as big as me now. He was older than 13 then and had gotten much bigger and stronger since being at our house. I wasn't sure that I would be able to fight him off."

She says she managed to stare him down. When she distracted him, he turned his anger from her to household items. He began rampaging through the rooms, throwing and smashing things. It was this day that his adoptive mother decided something drastic had to be done.

When faced with the deadline to make the adoption final, the couple hired an attorney for an extension. They hoped they eventually could adopt Jason, find help for him, and work things out. It simply was not meant to be.

The family could not resolve their incompatible relationship with this young man. In January 1988, they ordered their attorney to stop the adoption and give Jason back to the agency. Together, the failed adoption and medical bills for the child had cost this adoptive family more than $10,000.

Just what caused such a situation? Why did Jason act so badly and why did the family feel they had to reject him?

It should come as no surprise that children who have endured war and the breaks with their families that Jason had encountered come with histories, many times histories of pain and loss. Children who are abandoned or mistreated will carry with them emotional scars. Some of them will bury these scars deep inside and appear whole. Others, lost in their own confusion, will show their pain in many ways.

Psychologists say young Jason was "acting out" because of circumstances that occurred in his young life. Jason could not love or attach himself to the family that tried to love him and save him.

Many children who suffer attachment disorders due to breaks with their families in wartime build walls around themselves, walls that make them unlovable. They simply do not trust adults any more and many never will, unless intervention occurs. Jason had become attachment disordered.

"In a child's life, a year, even six months, of moving about is too much," says John P. Steketee, a juvenile-court judge.[7] These breaks in attachment are occurring around the globe in countries fighting for survival. Some examples include:

- In the Serbian aggression hunger and disease killed about 1,000 children in Srebrenica, Bosnia-Herzegovina, in 1993. Many more children suffer from the trauma they have endured as their lives have been dramatically and tragically changed.

- Today an estimated 35,000 Jasons of all ages are out there. They long for the day when they will have a real home to come home to.

As an example of what attachment disorder can look like, particularly in a child who has been sexually abused, we present Angie Trenberth. Although not a child of war, Angie suffered through trauma almost as deeply wounding. Her story can help those who work with children who have been abused.

Angie Trenberth

Her name is Angie, as in Angel. This curly-headed, petite cutie, however, turned out to be an angel from hell.

When Gail and Kevin Trenberth first laid eyes on baby Angie, she was a battered eight-month-old infant with wispy blond hair. They were called by Illinois Social Services on the spur of the moment to see if the couple could take in Angie and her two-year-old sister for temporary foster care.

The children's babysitter had called police after the little ones showed up—too many times—battered and bruised. It was after social services fetched the girls that a frantic search began for a home in which to place them.

At the time, the Trenberths were getting ready for a trip to New Zealand with their own four-year-old daughter, Annika. "But we agreed to take them for a short time," Gail says. "We had the two girls for only about three weeks, and then they had to be placed with someone else while we were gone."

Three months after the family returned to Illinois, they were reunited with Angie. They were not asked to care again for the older sister, who was in other foster care.

Baby Angie crawled into their hearts, despite warnings that she had suffered early severe abuse, including sexual abuse. "We were her foster parents for two years and had a chance to see she had problems. But we thought we could help her. We never dreamed how bad it would get, how badly scarred she was," says her adoptive mother.

So scarred was this child of abuse that as she grew she:

◆ Was unable to get emotionally close to anyone;

◆ Was very demonstrative sexually;

◆ At ages four and five, turned the family into virtual hermits, because they could not take her out in public or invite friends to their home; and

◆ Would go up to guests and grab them in their private parts; put her hand down women's blouses; and tried to masturbate on anyone's leg. This was while she was still little more than a toddler.

"She was totally out of control. We didn't know then what we do now—that Angie was an unattached child. We didn't know how to get her the right treatment, and we felt helpless. But we couldn't give up on this child."

The Trenberths, like many adoptive parents of very troubled children, went ahead with the adoption despite the obvious problems. "We just felt if we loved her enough and gave her a stable environment that she would get well," Gail says. They were wrong. Love was not enough.

As Angie grew older and it was time to go to school, her bizarre behavior escalated. It took only three days for her to be expelled from kindergarten. Her adoptive parents turned to an expensive residential treatment center for help, not willing to give up. The other alternative was to relinquish Angie and to see her spend her childhood in a series of foster homes or in an institution.

The Trenberths would not allow this. They had decided they loved this child and they would not give up on her. The couple saw no positive change in Angie after a year in residential treatment. "In fact, she was much worse," Gail says.

The Trenberths' love was about to meet its greatest test. On a field trip, Angie bragged to other children about alleged sexual abuse from her adoptive father.

In what Gail calls a "totally unbelievable" series of events, the couple was brought before authorities and grilled. The accusations devastated the couple. Eventually, authorities declared the couple completely innocent.

The suspicion and threat that the couple might lose this child in whom they'd invested so much love, energy and expense, however, almost cost Gail her sanity. She was so hysterical about the situation that her doctor prescribed tranquilizers and nearly had her hospitalized for a nervous breakdown.

"To this day," Gail sighs, "I suffer from medical problems caused by the stress of that time." For months, she could not sleep a full night: "I would get up and wander around the house, baking bread, washing floors."

Finding help for Angie

Finally, the family found help. A psychologist referred them to the Attachment Center at Evergreen (ACE), Colorado. "I called and talked to Connell Watkins, then the director, about Angie," Gail says. "And for the first time I had hope that she might get help."

As she turned seven years old, Angie began receiving attachment therapy and was placed in a therapeutic boarding program she would attend for two years. At ACE, an internationally acclaimed center, Angie began a therapy program that consisted of a series of controlled "holdings" that brought out her control issues and confronted them.

79

This therapy is confrontational and remains controversial in some areas of the psychiatric community, but has proven very effective for children with such severe attachment disorders as those exhibited by Angie. Many children who have been subjected to sexual abuse, no matter how young, can eventually become perpetrators of sexual abuse themselves. Their anger and rage take them down the road that hurt them so deeply. It is the only way they know how to hurt those around them.

During the holdings, a therapist and helpers held Angie down in a loving way. Unattached children, who cannot stand closeness and touch, become extremely agitated when their control of a situation is threatened. During this agitation these children can be gently guided to confront the rage that boils just under the surface. Why rage? The child is full of rage due to unresolved needs as an infant, when the child felt hopeless, helpless and hurt. War ?

In Angie's case these unresolved needs revolved around severe sexual abuse as a baby. This rage usually erupts during the holding session, when the child has a screaming fit. It is just the opening the therapist is looking for.

Once the therapist has guided the child through this "rage reaction," the child is vulnerable and open to rebonding. During this opportunity the therapist gently leads the child to a bond with the therapist, in a loving way.

Later, after more work on control issues and getting the rage worked out of the child, the therapist can bond the child to a trained therapeutic foster parent. Once a child has bonded to anyone, it is a matter of transferring that bond to the appropriate caregiver.

At the Attachment Center, work on control and bonding issues continues in therapeutic foster homes, with the eventual goal that of bonding the child with the permanent mother, usually an adoptive one. Children with severe problems, such as Angie, often require up to two years in the therapy and therapeutic home before they can reintegrate into their families.

In the Trenberths' case, once Angie was in therapy the family began a "healing vacation" to put distance between Angie and

Gail, her adoptive mother, who was finally able to get some sleep.

"When we returned from vacation we didn't know what to expect," Gail said, "but they included us in the therapy sessions. Angie was a changed child. We couldn't believe it.

"Friends who had known Angie before have said, 'It is Angie's body, but there is another child in there.' We were ecstatic, but scared. I was so afraid I'd never be able to love and trust her again. I had been raised to feel that love and trust come together. But I wasn't sure I could ever trust her."

Watkins soothed Gail, telling her: "The love is always there; the trust must be earned."

How is Angie now?

Angie is now in her preteens and she is a joy. "Oh, she still has a few small problems," Gail acknowledges, "but what child doesn't? But she is well; she is cured."

When it comes to the issue of trust, sometimes Gail still does not have it totally. Most of the time, however, her little angel comes through for her.

"Do you know what she did the other day?" Gail asks, her eyes sparkling, "We were chatting while I cooked dinner. She said, 'Mom, do you know what I want to be when I grow up?'

"I thought, 'Oh, she's changed her mind again on a profession,' so I didn't think too much about it. I asked her 'What?'," Gail says.

Angie turned to her mother and said, "I want to be just like you."

Gail stammers, tears in her eyes, saying, "You know, no unattached child could ever say that! They never want to be like their mothers. I couldn't believe she said that. I didn't know what to say, because I was all choked up. It's so wonderful."[8]

Angie Trenberth is one of the lucky ones. She was a victim of birth parents who did not value children. But she was also a damaged adopted child who found a family who could bond with her and love her, despite the problems, and work through the difficult times.

— *Damaged children of war*

The attachment cycle

Psychologists and psychiatrists are just beginning to realize the crisis created by a lack of attachment. Like little Angie, many children of war have also suffered from abuse—that abuse may be sexual or it may take the form of physical or mental abuse. All these can cause bonding breaks and render a child unattached.

When considering a substitute caregiver for a child who has suffered bonding and attachment breaks, it is important to note that the primary caregiver to a child can take several forms—it can be the birth mother or father, foster mother or father, an adoptive parent, or someone else who can provide consistency in the child's life. The key is to have one consistent caregiver who can stick with the child for the long haul—give that child an anchor in the stormy sea of life.

In a normal childhood in a loving, consistent family, a child gets this anchor during the first two years. It is through the attachment cycle that an infant first attaches to a primary caregiver and, subsequently, to society. This two-year cycle[9] is the key to healthy attachments later in life (see Figure 4.1 on page 83).

During the attachment cycle an infant experiences a *need*—either pain, hunger or discomfort—and expresses that need through a rage reaction that elicits a response from the primary caregiver to *gratify* that need. It is important that the need is gratified with touch, eye contact, motion or food.

It is the repetition of this cycle of gratification, thousands of times during the first two years, without interruption, that results in the formation of a strong trust bond between the child and caregiver. The bond of trust and attachment later enables the child to accept limits and controls as they are imposed by parents.

This bond of trust is a fragile one. It is a bond easily broken and an interruption of the cycle can occur when there is:

◆ Separation from, or change of, the primary caregiver.
◆ Abuse or neglect.
◆ Chronic and unrelieved pain.
◆ Gratification without touch, motion or eye contact.

Figure 4.1: The Attachment Cycle

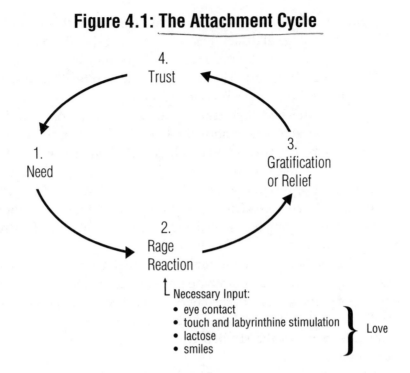

Any one of these interruptions can cause a bonding break in a child in a war-torn country. Children who have experienced interruptions of the attachment cycle during the first two years of life may exhibit some symptoms of attachment-disordered children later in life described above.

A major problem with children is correctly identifying their attachment issues. Dr. Foster Cline of Portland, Oregon, says, "What many people do not understand is that a very disturbed child is unlikable. The disturbance makes it hard to like the kid, even though you love him and want to love him to pieces. And these [unattached] kids know how to play the victim role," he says. "It's always, 'Poor me.'

"So what happens is they really may be victims, but that is no excuse for their behavior."[10]

Psychologist Barbara Rila of Dallas, Texas, says it is important to know the history of a child.[11] With access to the child's history, those working with the child may learn why this child has ongoing psychological disabilities, such as those described above.

In a war zone, obtaining the child's history will be difficult, but it is worth the effort. The history can also offer the therapist clues on how to begin the rebonding process.

An unattached first year of life gets children off to a very bad start. Then, if a person adds the trauma of war on top of that, the result can be very disturbed children with many problems.

A newly released study shows the extent of the damage as found in a group of adopted children who had suffered bonding breaks at an early age. The study looked at deviant behaviors, including the symptoms of attachment-disturbed children described above.

Researchers wanted to find out at what age problem behaviors first appeared. They found the problematical behaviors did not show up significantly until the children reached adolescence. They also believed that deviant behaviors were connected in some way to the adoptions of the studied children and the bonding breaks they suffered.

Although not a clinical study, J. Lynn Rhodes and Ellis P. Copeland found the "roots of the behavior may lie in early life experiences, but the fruit is not produced until adolescence." Although no such study has been done to date on children suffering the trauma of war breaks, I believe this information comparing birth children and adopted children suffering bonding breaks is relevant in any such discussion (see Figure 4.2 on page 85).

Many of the children studied showed significant evidence of attachment disorders that stem from multiple bonding breaks in infancy (probably caused by moves in foster care). It is still not known how many breaks it takes before a child is sure to have attachment difficulties. In a war situation, the author speculates it may not take many breaks, because of the trauma caused by the war itself.

We cannot cure the problems of children with attachment disorders by gentle holding, hugs and kisses. These children need more than love, especially those children who have witnessed war.

Figure 4.2: Survey of dysfunctional behavior in children[12]

BEHAVIORS	BIRTH (%)	ADOPTED (%)
Inability to give or receive affection	3.2	21.3
Phoniness	1.9	15.1
Self-control problems	3.9	26.3
Lack of long term friends	4.5	21.9
Lying	3.9	25.7
Rejection of authority	1.3	30.0
Refusal to follow parental guidelines	3.2	25.8
Manipulation of others	2.6	23.8

Many unattached children need intensive long-term therapy—such as the kind described in Angie's story—related to the rebonding process. In therapy it is important to bring out the behaviors that resulted in the attachment disorders. Then the therapists can deal with specific causes and help the child to begin to heal.

"Traumatic incidents have a direct and concrete result in subsequent traumas and the child's emotional behavior," says Dr. Barbara Rila, a founder of the national group, ATTACh (Association for Treatment and Training in the Attachment of Children).

"A second major reason to know the past," she says, "is that children base later relationships on the earlier model of the original family."[13] If sexual abuse is suspected in a child torn by war, it is even more important that the child's caregivers know this information. Children with attachment disorders based on sexual abuse often become perpetrators themselves, because of the abuse.

With the help of a qualified therapist, the caregivers can help a child cope with the aftermath of abuse. "What works with one child may not work with others. We need to empower parents and professionals to parent children with attachment issues," says Rila.[14]

Child therapist and specialist in attachment issues, Connell Watkins, M.S.W., of Evergreen, Colorado, says continuity is the key to helping children so traumatized.

"Continuity and a stable place to call their own, a place they can go back to and get special treatment is so important. But the basic need is the continuity," says Watkins.[15]

Author's suggestions

It is particularly important that those deciding the fate of such a child consider specific guidelines regarding child development and rule accordingly. These guidelines include:[16]

- The emotional state of the child
- The nature of the attachment between the substitute caregivers and the child
- The nature of the attachment with the birth parents
- The environment that will best match the needs of the child

The goal should be to provide stable, caring, supportive parents for these needy children.

Only with the early intervention of a committed, nurturing caregiver can a child avoid the horror of attachment disorders. Those who work with children in war need to allow for this. Good parenting and a positive environment seem to help children overcome bad beginnings to become all they can be, despite the influence of war and other abuses.

With older children who can transfer their bond to another caregiver when separated from their families, this is a healthy sign and one to be encouraged. For when a child has bonded with one caregiver it is possible to transfer that bond, even in the middle of the chaos of war, to another.

The author urges parents and professionals alike who are working with an emotionally challenged child to get to know as much as possible about the child's background and any genetic factors that may be influencing the child's behavior. With proper professional guidance it is possible to rescue a badly challenged child.

Cautions

Some pitfalls for caregivers to avoid in war include:

Children placed randomly and repeatedly. A system that shuffles children and babies from place to place with little regard for the outcome must be corrected.

The system must keep track of children and plan permanent homes from the minute it is determined they are orphans. Parents, adoptive and foster, must be given the tools they need—in matching and pre- and post-placement counseling—to stay with a challenged child.

It will be up to substitute caregivers, and social and adoption workers, to keep track of the children and hasten this permanency planning. They must also be the advocates for their young charges.

Inadequate knowledge among professionals. In another arena, often the therapeutic community is undereducated when it comes to bonding and attachment issues; many do not recognize or properly diagnose damaged children. Additional educational efforts are needed to give therapists working with children traumatized by war the tools they need to provide help.

What happens over time when these war-ravaged children finally find a secure place? What solutions are there for those substitute caregivers who discover, over time, that the children they have brought into their homes suffer from the effects of attachment disorder?

These parents with very difficult children may have to use strict parenting methods. They may have to handle the children in a hard way (such as "tough love") to make them responsible in the future.

Most of the children mentioned in this chapter suffered the consequences of being thrown into a war situation. Those who have not are used to explain attachment issues.

These children are real and although their names may have been changed, they have taken a journey along a path that has shocked and shaken their very foundations.

During this journey, with its multiple bonding breaks and moves, many of these already hurting children develop emotional disabilities and mental challenges. Making the situation even worse is the inability of substitute caregivers to respond. Clearly every child needs a permanent, safe home:

◆   A home where they can be matched to parents[17] and feel nurtured, safe and loved.

◆   A home where they can heal and grow.

One of the effects of war is that many children have come to mistrust others. The older children are the ones agencies have had trouble fitting into a family.[18] These children (ages 9 to 19) must be placed in a predictable, positive environment. A reliable attachment figure must be present.

If a child *must* be moved it has been found that records on the child can make all the difference.

◆   The agency can keep histories with pictures recording the child's feelings while in their care.

◆   Using these records, substitute families can help the child understand the real reason for the placements and remove hurt feelings acquired along the way. Many children from broken families in war or not, come to feel they are in some way to blame; this causes guilt the child needs help in resolving.

An estimated 100 million people, many of them children, have died in the 207 wars of this century.[19] Untold thousands beyond that number have suffered the traumas of war. It is time for this tragedy to stop.

NOTES

1   The Center on War and the Child, Eureka Springs, Arkansas, U.S.A., Summer 1993.

2   Annie Wuantee, personal interview, New York City, U.S.A., 1993.

3   Foster Cline, *What Shall We Do with This Child* (Evergreen, Colorado: Youth Behavior Program, 1979).

4   S. Fraiberg, *Every Child's Birthright: In Defense of Mothering* (New York: Basic Books, 1977), pp. 51-54.

5   Ibid., p. 28.

6   Magid and McKelvey, *High Risk: Children Without a Conscience* (New York: Bantam Books, 1988).

7   Berman, *Redbook*, December 1987, pp. 221-238.

8   Gail Trenberth, personal interview, Boulder, Colorado, U.S.A., June 1991.

9   Carole A. McKelvey and JoEllen Stevens, *Adoption Crisis* (Golden, Colorado: Fulcrum Press, 1994).

10   Foster Cline, personal interview, January 1991.

11   Dr. Barbara Rila, personal interview, Atlanta, Georgia, U.S.A., July 1991.

12   J. Lynn Rhodes and Ellis P. Copeland, *Dysfunctional Behavior in Adopted Children: Behavior Differences Between Adopted and Birth Children* (University of Northern Colorado, November 1991). Reprinted with permission. A survey conducted with a Christian adoption group that had placed more than 900 children in the past twenty years. The 388 adopted children and 290 birth children tested lived throughout the U.S.A.

13   Rila.

14   Ibid. Rila says that is the basis for the group ATTACh (Association for Treatment and Training in the Attachment of Children), of Dallas, Texas, U.S.A.

15   Connell Watkins and Associates, Evergreen, Colorado, U.S.A., provides therapy, consultation and training regarding attachment issues.

16   Magid and McKelvey, p. 334.

17   For information on matching and the SAME (Stevens Adopt Match Evaluator) matching instrument, write to Dr. JoEllen Stevens, P.O. Box 1133, Oakview, California, U.S.A. 93022.

18   For more information on adoption of children who have suffered attachment disorder, see *Adoption Crisis* by Carole A. McKelvey and JoEllen Stevens (Golden, Colorado: Fulcrum Press, 1994).

19   The Center on War and the Child, Summer 1993.

5
Moral Development

Perry Downs

Children must learn right from wrong, and be willing to do right. Indeed, the health of a society rests to a large degree on its capacity to live according to principles of right and wrong. When the moral base of a society is lost, the society is doomed to failure.

Children who have been brutalized by the effects of war, and by the direct actions of warriors, find it especially difficult to determine right from wrong. Treating children in unjust ways eliminates their capacity to understand the difference between right and wrong. How do we know right from wrong, and how can we help children learn right from wrong? What can we do to help children recover the ability to sort out right from wrong and make moral decisions based on what is right?

BASIC DEFINITIONS

Before we consider how to help children, we must be clear on definitions. Clarifying what we mean will help us do a better job of working with children in the area of their moral behavior.

Moral judgment and moral behavior

Moral judgment is how a child *thinks* about a moral issue. It is concerned with how a child decides what is right or wrong. Moral behavior is how a child *acts* concerning a moral issue, despite how he or she thinks about it. A common problem is that children's (and adults') moral behavior is not always consistent with their moral judgment. We are all prone to do things that we think are wrong, or fail to do things we think are right. Therefore, how we think and how we may act are two separate issues.

Moral choices and moral decisions

Moral choices are concerned with *what* a person believes to be right or wrong. Sometimes called "moral content," moral choices deal with the content or substance of a moral belief. "Killing is wrong" is a statement of moral content because it states what a person believes to be right or wrong.

Moral decisions are the basis of moral choices and are concerned with *why* a person believes a specific content. Sometimes called "moral structure," the decisions are rooted in a specific kind of moral reasoning. "Killing is wrong *because it hurts other people*" is a moral content supported by a reason or structure. In working with children we must understand the reasoning behind their moral choices, because it is in the reasoning that the potential for growth resides. Therefore, helping children develop morally is concerned with both *what* is right or wrong, and *why* it is right or wrong.

Morals and ethics

Morals are rules of behavior that are related to any society. They change from society to society, or can change over time within a society. Things that may be considered immoral in one society may not be immoral in another. For example, certain clothing styles may be acceptable in one culture, but be offensive in another. For a woman to bare her arms in most Western societies is not immoral, but would be considered immoral in many Muslim contexts. Morals are rooted in society and therefore change as society changes.

Ethics are principles of right and wrong that are always the same in every context and are not negotiable. They are "above" cultures and society and are always binding in all contexts. People may disagree on what these ethical guidelines should be, but that they should exist is generally seen to be true.

The immense difficulty in working with children who have been brutalized by war is that they have virtually lost their capacity to see and respond to either moral or ethical guidelines. Because these moral and ethical restraints have been violated in the lives of these children, they have difficulty understanding that they even exist. Even the broader, more basic ethical guidelines of human living are lost so that the child cannot make even the most basic of moral choices. Basic behavioral limits such as lying, stealing, or even killing can become acceptable behaviors to persons without moral or ethical principles operating within them. We must teach these children to think and behave with moral guidelines controlling them.

THE CONNECTIONS BETWEEN KNOWING AND DOING

Helping persons grow morally is more than a matter of teaching them right from wrong. The simple teaching of moral content (what is right and wrong) will not necessarily change behavior. As we all know from our own life experience, knowing and doing are two different things. How does a person move from right thinking to right action?

First, a child must know right from wrong. We cannot expect children to do that which they do not know. There is a place to teach children moral content so that they might know right from wrong.

For children who have been in a context without any moral teaching, this is a critical step. We must teach children that right and wrong exist, and that "we" (the group with whom they are related) have standards and beliefs about what is right and wrong. We must communicate the truth of right and wrong.

Teaching moral content is best done in relationship. If there is an emotional bond forming between the child and an adult or group, the child will more easily accept the moral standards being taught. If children are loved, and can receive that love, they will be more likely to learn the values of the persons who love them. Children must feel related to a society in order to accept the morals of the society.

But knowing right from wrong is not the same as doing the right thing. It is perfectly possible to know the right thing, but not be willing to do it. We can all remember times in our lives when we knew what we should do, but we simply did not want to do it. It was not a matter of moral knowledge, but a matter of moral will. Children must not only know what is right—they must also be willing to do what is right.

It is not true that all people are "good" and always want to do right. The brutality around us shows the great evil of which we are all capable. The corruption of our moral will is more than a matter of what the people around us have done to us; it is also a matter of human personality. We do not always want to do what is right. All human hearts have a rebellious spirit that may choose to do evil.

Helping children grow morally concerns the desires of their hearts as well as the information in their minds. Moral training that helps children must deal with their desire to do right along with the knowledge of what is right.

But it is possible for a child to know the right thing, want to do the right thing, and still not have the strength to do the right thing. They may lack the emotional or inner power to act on what they know and feel to be right.

The apostle Paul described this condition in his own life when he wrote, "For what I want to do I do not do, but what I hate I do" (Romans 7:15). It is frustrating not to have the moral strength to act upon our own moral convictions.

The strength to act on convictions independently will be very weak in abused and victimized people. Strength to act on what they know is right comes more easily in a group than in individuals. If an entire group can be moved to behave in increasingly moral ways, the individuals will also be strengthened.

STAGES OF MORAL REASONING

The research in moral development suggests that there are three primary levels of moral reasoning through which each person

North american 94 Prisoners sometimes brag about + encourage detachment in themselves + others.

will normally progress as he or she moves toward moral maturity. If he or she is in a context that does not hinder moral development, the *structure* of moral reasoning will develop through three predictable stages. Although children in war have probably been in a context that does not allow them to develop normally in their moral reasoning, it is helpful to understand what a normal pattern of development looks like. That will help us understand which level of moral reasoning we want to see the children get to as they begin to heal from the traumas of war.

Before they reach the first level of moral reasoning, very young children are pre-moral or simply not concerned with moral issues. Babies are not aware of any moral issues when they cry to be fed. Their only concern is their hunger. They do not consider any moral dimensions to their actions, and this is how it should be. They should be free to be babies, not yet concerned with issues of right and wrong.

As children move into early childhood, however, we expect them to have a sense of right and wrong. We expect behaviors from them that are in keeping with basic expectations of our society. We expect them to obey, to tell the truth, and to be kind to those around them. If a child or an adult remains in the pre-moral state of infancy, we have a right to be concerned. Such children and adults are threats to society because they have no internal limitations on their behavior. This is the kind of person who can injure or kill another person and never feel remorse. It is not good for a person to remain at the pre-moral state.

Level one judgments

The first level of moral reasoning, called *pre-conventional*, focuses only on self and personal concerns. "Good" is that which serves me well, and "bad" is that which causes me pain. An individual determines right and wrong based on how these concerns affect them.

For example, the moral content "It is wrong to steal," is supported by the reasoning that says "It is wrong to steal because you can get in trouble if you steal." The main consideration is not concern for others, but only concern for self. What makes stealing wrong is the fact that you could get in trouble for doing it. The only real consideration is the effect upon oneself.

But the content can easily change with this kind of reasoning. If a person decides that if they steal they can get good things, and probably not get in trouble, the obvious conclusion is that it is good to steal. If the only consideration is what happens to you, *jail!* there will be no moral absolutes other than self-interest.

Many people remain at this level of moral reasoning for their entire lives. All they ever consider is self-interest, and all of their moral decisions are made in reference to themselves. While such reasoning is appropriate for a child, it is not good when youth and adults reason this way. There are others to be considered besides ourselves. Moral development means growing in the way we reason about moral issues.

Level two judgments

Level two morality, called *conventional*, thinks about others as well as oneself. Level two thinking concerns itself with rules and regulations, and wants to obey the law. A person at level two understands that society is more than self, that there are others to consider, and that individuals must obey rules and laws for the good of all.

Level two reasoning will explain that stealing is wrong because it is against the law. Stealing is against the civil law of the country, or against God's law in the Bible. Either way, what makes it wrong is that it violates a law.

In its simplest form, this reasoning concerns itself with pleasing others who are important to me. I will not do those things that displease those who are important to me, and I will do those things that please them. Later, this level recognizes that rules and laws are the expressions of those things that please a society.

Yet those to whom the person is committed control this level of thinking. If the person is trying to please a morally mature person, this level of reasoning can be quite good. Many Christians, for example, are concerned with doing what pleases Jesus. But if the commitment is to a criminal, the behavior will follow accordingly. In the mind of the child, he or she is doing right because it is pleasing to the person to whom he or she is committed.

It is normal for children in later childhood or adolescence to move into this stage of moral reasoning. The authority for their moral decisions rests outside themselves, and they depend on others to sort out their moral issues for them. Level two is more mature and better than the self-centered reasoning of level one, but it depends on completely external influences.

Level three judgments

Level three reasoning, called *post-conventional*, is concerned with ethical principles. It can judge the rules and regulations of a person or society, and decide if they are in keeping with universal ethical principles. Even if everyone else is doing it, if I judge it to be naturally wrong, I will not do it. Stealing is wrong because it violates the rights of others.

Level three morality is in touch with the law God has written in our hearts (Romans 2:12-16), and understands that universal ethical principles are more important than self-interest, or even the laws and expectations of a community. Persons who function at level three can look into their own hearts and know right from wrong internally.

The most important ethical principle is *justice*. Level three reasoning seeks the best for all people, and is aware when injustice is being carried out. Above all else, at level three persons make their moral decisions around issues of justice.

The Bible is greatly concerned with justice. Condemnations of people and societies who were unconcerned with matters of justice fill the Old Testament. The opening chapters of Isaiah make this clear. Justice is an issue that is close to the heart of God, and should be close to the hearts of God's people.

All persons begin in the first level of moral judgment. As a child first begins to make moral judgments, these judgments will be made according to the structure of the first level. As moral reasoning begins to mature, the second level will become more controlling. Finally, if moral development continues, thinking will progress into the third level. The levels, however, are always achieved in the same order.

APPROACHES TO MORAL EDUCATION

Teachers have long been concerned with how best to help children develop morally. Several different approaches to the problem have been tried. A brief overview of these might be helpful.

Teaching moral behavior

The most basic approach is concerned with getting children to behave properly. By rewarding good behavior with praise or even prizes, the teacher attempts, in effect, to "buy" good behavior from children. This approach is very popular in some forms of public education, and does work to keep children under control. Children will learn to behave in the ways the teacher wants, if the rewards are good.

The problem with this approach is that the long-term effects are not strong. If someone with a better set of rewards comes along, the children can be easily led astray. In addition, this approach does nothing to help the child develop any internal moral strength.

There are times when God teaches us in this way. The biblical teachings of obedience leading to blessing and disobedience leading to cursing is clearly a system of rewards and punishments. There can be a place for this approach, but it is limited in its usefulness.

When children have been traumatized and corrupted by war, this may be the place to begin. Rewarding good behavior and ignoring or punishing bad behavior may be the only language of moral education they understand. A careful system of rewards for doing right can be a good starting place to rebuild the moral understanding of children.

It is much more powerful to reward good behavior than it is to punish bad behavior. Children who have been abused by adults do not need more punishment. Positive rewards will do more than punishments to help correct behavior.

Teaching moral content

A second approach, common in religious groups, is to focus moral education on the question of *what* is right and wrong. The teacher has a specific set of beliefs regarding right and wrong, and these beliefs must be passed on to the students. The role of the teacher is to tell the children what is right and wrong so they can do it.

This approach recognizes that moral and ethical guidelines exist, and they should be taught to children. There are clear and firm guidelines that children must know.

This approach fails to recognize, however, that knowing is not the same as doing. Children can learn right beliefs about moral issues and yet never do them. While it is important to teach moral content, this approach alone is not adequate.

Children who have been raised in a context where no moral content has been taught must learn that right and wrong exist. There is a place to teach them the rules and regulations of a society. Any school, home or other institution must have rules of behavior, and these should be taught to the children. Children must know what to expect if they act according to society's rules and regulations.

The Bible contains God's truth regarding moral behavior and is essential for moral development. We do not need to teach God's truth as a set of rigid laws we must obey or God will punish us. We can teach that God's laws are his gift of love to us, showing us how we should live. But there can be no moral growth without the teaching and learning of moral content.

Moral truth is best taught in the context of relationships. Level two reasoning is an extension of relationships, where children want to please others who are important to them. If the teacher loves the child, and the child can receive that love, the child will be willing to accept the moral beliefs of the teacher.

Jesus taught this truth when he said "If you love me, you will obey what I command" (John 14:15). He linked the acceptance of what he taught to relationship with his students. If children know that an adult loves them, and the adult tells them truth they should believe, children will believe it. The context for teaching is that of a loving relationship.

Modeling morality

A third approach to moral education is demonstrating what is expected. Children are very sensitive to the examples set by other people. Especially when they see other people "succeeding," they will want to imitate that behavior. Strong leaders set examples for others to follow, and children naturally imitate those they respect.

Moral educators must be aware of the examples set before children. Their first concern must be that teachers "practice what they preach." That is, the teachers must be examples of what they are teaching. Children must both hear and see moral messages from their teachers.

The apostle Paul wrote, "Whatever you have learned or received or heard from me, or seen in me—put it into practice. . . ." (Philippians 4:9). People will do as we do, not just as we say.

Moral values are as much "caught" as they are "taught." Children imitate those around them, and naturally follow the example of others. Moral education must include regular setting of examples for children to follow.

This principle is most difficult to follow when children are surrounded by examples of immoral behavior. If they are in a setting where the primary behaviors are not good, they will learn to follow those examples. The Bible correctly teaches "Bad company corrupts good character" (1 Corinthians 15:33). So it may be necessary to remove children from the influence of the surrounding community. This is why some groups set up residential schools, so that the children will not be exposed to the bad examples of a society.

The just moral community

A final approach to moral education is called the "just moral community." This method is especially helpful with people who have little sense of morality, but it is also a very difficult approach to maintain.

The school or institution becomes a community, and the focus of the community must be that all people are treated with justice. The children will normally be functioning only at level one, thinking almost exclusively about themselves. Such moral reasoning naturally leads to problems, because what is good for one person may not always be good for another.

Teachers lead discussions with the children, helping them discover the problems with thinking only about themselves. Such discussions take time, and must be conducted regularly. The point is to help them discover that the rights of others must be considered.

As their thinking matures, the group will begin to establish rules of conduct for their community. They will tend to become very legalistic as they attempt to establish more and more rules to control their behaviors. They will discover that rules and regulations are a necessary part of living, and that rules and laws make things better for everyone.

As this process continues, however, they will discover that they cannot establish rules for every situation. The rules of the community become so detailed and specific that they cease to be of real help. They will begin to discover the principle of justice that is the foundation for their rules and will learn that principles and not laws can control our behavior.

Prisons and schools with very disadvantaged children in the United States have used this approach successfully. It is time-consuming and difficult to do, but it also has the best long-term results of any approach to moral education.

No single approach to moral education is the best. Each has strengths and weaknesses, and each can be used in combination with others. The key is to understand that we must consider both the "whats" and "whys" of moral issues, and that there is a clear progression of thinking that we can encourage.

The natural order of development of moral thinking is through the three levels of moral judgment. Hearing how children reason about moral questions helps us understand their level of moral reasoning, how we should teach them and how they need to grow.

GUIDELINES FOR WORKING WITH CHILDREN

There are no guarantees with working with children, especially with children who have been abused by war. But the following suggestions can assist us in helping children develop morally.

1. There is a place for rewards.

Children will respond to rewards, especially in the training of moral behavior. Because children reason moral issues first in relation to themselves, it is appropriate to reward correct behavior. Prizes for doing right and not doing wrong can be an important first step to moral education. The reward must be something the child values, but it does not have to be costly. Even words of praise from a respected teacher or leader can be an important reward for a needy child.

One useful approach can be the use of a chart or record of good performances. Each time the child does right, he or she receives a star on the chart. When a child earns a certain number of stars, the child receives a prize. In this way prizes are not given out all the time, but only as a child shows consistently good behavior.

2. Ask "why" questions regarding moral issues.

Teachers must not be content that children can give the right answer regarding moral issues. Children must also be able to discuss why a behavior is right or wrong. Teachers must be concerned with structure as well as content in children, seeking to understand the reasoning that is supporting a moral choice. Not only must they know that "stealing is wrong," but they must be aware of why it is wrong.

This does not mean that we must tell the child the right answer regarding "why" questions. It means, rather, that we must hear their reasons why. This will tell us the level at which they are reasoning, and give ideas about how we must work with them. Children who reason only at level one will respond to rewards; but they must also learn that there are larger issues than how it turns out for them.

Issues of justice.

102

3. Provide opportunities for moral problem solving.

Children learn best, not from teaching or telling, but from their own experiences with moral problem solving. As they experience the effects of their choices on themselves and others, and are taught to think about what has happened, they will mature in their moral reasoning. Lectures on moral issues are not particularly powerful for children; but discussions about moral issues and experiences with moral dilemmas help moral growth.

The wise teacher will watch for opportunities to discuss moral questions with children. Life is filled with moral issues as we relate to others, and these all provide opportunity for moral education. Teachers must be ready to discuss conflicts with children as a means of helping them grow.

4. Treat children with respect.

A climate of respect will greatly enhance moral development. Adults must respect children as people, listen to them and speak to them with respect. Because moral development is concerned with justice, an environment where justice prevails will make growth much easier.

If only those in authority have power, and they have all the control, moral growth will not be enabled. There must be some freedom for the children, and some room for them to make decisions. Respecting children requires giving them some control over their lives. It means that adults must ask them, not tell them, and treat them as persons, not as objects.

Clearly there is a proper respect that we reserve for adults and those who are older. But we must treat even children with respect, because it is in a climate of respect that they will learn to respect others. And respect for others is at the heart of morality.

6
Disabled Children

Sue H. Enoch

Children's war-related experiences, including exposure to shelling and combat, can result in serious physical injuries and permanent disabilities. Some children are severely disabled through participating, either through coercion or voluntarily, in dangerous acts of war.

Severely injured children not only have to cope with amputations, loss of sight or hearing, severe burns, and other crippling injuries, but also with the ensuing rejection that comes from being "different." These children are in desperate need of love and acceptance. Parents also need help in coping with their grief, anger and guilt, along with struggling to accept their children's loss.

The impact of disability

At the same time that parents are coping with all the practical mechanics of living with a disabled child, they are also struggling with their own emotional responses. Guilt, anger, and fear are often near the surface. They experience grief, real and long-lived, as the limitations imposed by the disability replace the dream of what their child might have become. The death of that dream brings real grief with its anger, denial, and (it is hoped) finally acceptance. We cannot minister to a disabled child without understanding this chronic sorrow and also ministering to the child's family.

The disabled child is faced with a limited range and variety of experiences. The parents may limit experience because of fear for the child's safety. A child who has been ill for long periods often remains at risk in the family's mind. Parents of a disabled child may unnecessarily protect their child from teasing by other children and other similar threatening experiences. Because most of a young child's learning takes place through experience, the impact of such limitations is great. Disability is a crisis that causes the child not to function within the expected norm; it is long-term and ongoing.

Society imposes a great number of restrictions on disabled persons. Everything we do is designed for able-bodied persons. Whether in building design, entertainment or transportation, accommodation for persons with disabilities is a low priority. When confronted by a child who is unable to function within these guidelines, we quickly become frustrated and confused. Our reaction is to retreat so that maybe the problem will go away. Our first question is, "Can't something be done?" Our deep need is to heal the disability, to make things whole and right again. When we cannot fix it, we leave it alone. In this case "it" is a person, a child of God. Our own helplessness defeats us at the very point where ministry should begin—acceptance.

The first impact of disability is isolation. Usually, the disabled child is left to play alone or to sit in the company of adults. Other children, or their parents, are often afraid to come near. This forces the disabled child and its parents to withdraw from public places to avoid pain. The disabled child must constantly struggle for the right to participate in society. It becomes the role of parents, friends, and caregivers to be the child's advocate.

Disabled children have great difficulty in developing peer relationships. Parents trying to compensate for this become so child-centered they have no adult relationships. The cycle perpetuates itself and no one in the family can maintain healthy socialization. Anger, frustration, and overdependence, on the part of both the child and the parent, become a major problem.

Many people assume that disabled children always function below normal mental expectations. This is not true. Children with visual impairments or physical disabilities function well within normal intellectual limits. A particular disability may limit communication, requiring additional effort to share the child's thoughts, but the reward is frequently a bright, alert mind. No generalizations are adequate about the level of intellectual functioning possible for any disabled child.

The psychological impact of a disability becomes evident in the family and in the disabled child. As children become aware of the differences their handicaps make in their lives, several things may occur. Isolation may begin to cause loneliness. "Normal" children, who initially tolerated the difference, suddenly become impatient with doing things with someone who cannot do them well. Outwardly, visible indications of the disability become targets for teasing and name-calling. Children can be cruel to each other, and the disabled child may respond with withdrawal, self-pity, or anger.

As disabled children recognize differences resulting from their disabilities, they often experience and interpret these differences as negatives: places they cannot go, things they cannot do, schools they cannot attend. Often, this results in a very low self-esteem: "If I cannot do all the things the other children can do, I must not be any good." Their feelings of worthlessness are intensified when other persons refuse to let them try. Disabled children may soon believe they really cannot do anything, and give up.

Being different may also create strong feelings of anger. Disabled children begin to ask why they are different, why others don't want to be with them, why they cannot become what they want to become. The anger may manifest itself in withdrawal and a refusal to attempt any activity, or in defiance, resulting in unrealistic goalsetting and a refusal to accept any limitation caused by the disability.

Needs of the disabled child

The needs of a disabled child will vary according to the severity of the disability, the amount of early intervention provided and whether the disability is present in isolation or in combination with other disabilities. Some general characteristics are the same for all disabled children.

The need to be treated as a child, not a disability.

Disabled children are more like other children than they are different from other children. It is important that we remember and emphasize their childhood rather than focusing our energies and efforts on their disability. They are children who need love, want to have fun and are eager to learn and try new things.

Disabled children are not necessarily intellectually limited. They must be allowed opportunities to use their abilities in as many ways as possible. They should be respected as capable individuals, emphasizing the things they can do rather than the things they cannot do.

The need for acceptance.

Whatever the disability, these children need affirmation of who they are—members of the family of God on earth. Their pain, sorrow, joy and success are ours also. They are people of worth who have gifts to share with everyone. Disabled children should be included in all the activities available for their peers. This may mean adaptation of the activity, but it will be worth the extra time required.

The need for community and communication.

It is easy for disabled children and their families to become isolated. A hearing impairment establishes barriers to the community due to the lack of expected communication modes. Both the natural family and the church family should participate in whatever language teaching model is used to encourage language development.

The community should provide appropriate materials for the disabled child, whether it is amplification for the hearing impaired, enlarged visuals for the visually impaired, or accessibility for the physically impaired. The important thing is to consider the child's needs and adapt the materials to meet that need.

108

The need for independence.

Disabled children need to develop as much independence as possible. They need to try things and fail, as well as to succeed. They need discipline. They need to be left alone sometimes. They need established limits and goals. They need to be expected to do their best. In other words, they need to be treated like any other child of the same age in terms of behavior and development. The adaptations for their specific disabilities must not impede their growth as independent persons with socially appropriate behaviors and self-care skills.

Visually impaired children must be able to travel safely and feel secure in their surroundings. Their independence is increased when a sighted person learns proper sighted guide techniques.

Faith issues

The faith issues for disabled children will vary according to the nature of the disability and how it was acquired, and the amount of reasoning ability and language a child possesses. The issues are going to be more advanced for a visually impaired child of normal intelligence than for a multihandicapped child with limited ability. The issues seem to group themselves into three categories.

The first issue for disabled children may very well come with the awareness that they are different from other children. They begin to ask, "Why me? Why did God let this happen to me?" The question most often finds us without an answer. I cannot reconcile the God who loves and cares for me with the image of God choosing to make or allow a child to become disabled. It is too presumptuous, too uncaring. The presence of disability in the world and in the life of a particular child is as difficult to understand as the presence of any suffering in the world. It simply exists; it is a part of life. Disability is a reality of the child's life. What is most important for children to know is that their disability or handicap does not separate them from God's love and care.

The child may ask, "What have I done wrong? What did my parents do wrong?" Jesus answered that question clearly in his interaction with the blind man in John 9:1-38. When his disciples asked whether the man's sin or his parents' had caused the man to be blind, Jesus answered, "His blindness has nothing to do with his sins or his parents' sins" (John 9:3, TEV). The disability is clearly not a punishment for wrongdoing. I do not know why some children have to become disabled, or why disabled children must endure pain and frequent medical treatment. I do accept Jesus' word that the disability is not a punishment, and I do know God loves those children.

The New Testament is rich with stories that illustrate Jesus' acceptance and care for people who were different. He healed the slave of a Roman soldier (Luke 7:1-10), he accepted the despised tax collector (Luke 19:1-10), and he forgave the Samaritan woman (John 4:5-30). When Jesus visited the synagogue in Nazareth to preach his first sermon he named himself an advocate for disabled persons (Luke 4:18-19). The encounter with the Gerasene demoniac illustrates his willingness to cross barriers that isolate in order to heal (Mark 5:1-20). Each encounter demonstrates inclusion of people in the family of God who were not the norm for their society. It is this acceptance that is important.

Disabled children may also question the image of God as a good God. They may become confused as the stories of God the Creator and their own disability seem contradictory in their minds. The Genesis account repeatedly tells us God was pleased with what he made (Genesis 1:25, 31). The beauty of the world around us, and the love of family and friends are all good creations of God.

Disabled children are loved and cared-for creations of God with gifts and abilities to share with all of us. It is in helping these children to recognize the goodness and love within themselves that we can lead them to recognize the goodness of a God who loves them. Daniel Day Williams helps us understand God's image not as physical form or intellectual capacity but our capacity to be in communion with another, or our capacity to love and be loved.[1]

The third confusing faith issue for children may come in the stories of the miracles of healing. In Matthew 9, Jesus healed a paralyzed man (vs. 1-7), two blind men (vs. 27-31), a dumb man (vs. 32-

34), and many others during his earthly ministry. The children may ask why Jesus does not heal them now. We teach them to pray for what they need, and they may feel they need healing. We can base an honest discussion of seeking God's comfort on Matthew 7:7-12. All of us must ask, in faith, for the strength to live with or change those things we feel are wrong with our lives. God knows how to give us the good gifts we need. They are not always the gifts we want, just as parents and teachers do not always give us what we want. We should help disabled children develop trust in a loving God who is faithful to care for all of us.

The issues of faith for disabled children have no easy answers. The questions offer opportunities for caring adults to admit that simple answers do not exist. We can continue to demonstrate our own trust in God despite suffering and imperfection. Helping children understand that they are not separated from but are loved by God as people of worth is critical to the development of a strong, healthy relationship with God and the church family.

Suggestions for ministry

The discussion of the impact of disability and the needs of specific disability groups provides some guidance for ministry with disabled children. We can summarize these in the following areas.

Family support

Living with a disabled child is living in chronic sorrow. The constant challenges, both medically and educationally, can easily deplete the resources of the most stable family. Others can give support in several ways.

Take time to listen to and share the concerns of the disabled child's parents and siblings. Just having someone to talk to will help decrease their stress levels. Accept, in a nonjudgmental way, whatever anger, grief, and confusion you may hear. Listen carefully for ways to intervene.

Become a referral source. Learn who does what in your community and learn about referral agencies. Trying to locate

111

needed services can be a frustrating and frightening experience. Help the family through this complex problem.

Establish a network of respite (provision for rest). Parents of disabled children are often reluctant to leave the child. Find, or become, someone they can trust with care of the child so they can get away from the constant caregiving and supervision. Provide special activities for siblings so they can have extra attention and feel special.

Friendship

Disabled children need the accepting, loving friendship of other adults. Become that significant adult who they can depend on for support and counsel.

Guided integration

As a caregiver to a disabled child, you set the tone for the church's acceptance of disabled children. Educating the church family about the ways they can help and the needs of disabled children is vital. Help the church family develop Jesus' attitudes toward the disabled. He was not frightened by them, he took time for them, he accepted them as they were, and he affirmed their ability to care for themselves.

Help the church practice acceptance of the disabled in all educational, recreational, and social programs. Lead children's workers to become knowledgeable of, and sensitive to, the adaptations necessary for disabled children to become fully participating members of the church family. Remember that ministry should be with disabled children, not to or for them. The church family should accept them as equally participating members of the church ministry.

Pastoral care through medical crises.

Because they have more medical crises than others, disabled children are sometimes forgotten when they are patients in the hospital. The caregiver's understanding and support through each hospitalization is important.

Guidance in faith issues

As you develop a relationship with both the family and the disabled child, they will find you more approachable. In addition to the child's faith issues, the family is also dealing with guilt, anger and rejection. Your presence and acceptance can bring those issues into focus. It is typical for parents of disabled children to carry a great deal of guilt about their children. "Surely there was something I could have done to prevent this. Why didn't I protect them better?"

The guilt can lead to compensation by overprotecting and doing everything for the disabled child. As the child remains dependent, anger surfaces, directed at the child because of its lack of independence. Then guilt over the anger arises because, after all, the parent was responsible for the disability. This cycle can continue for years unless your gentle intervention helps parents deal with the guilt.

The family members also need assistance in dealing with their grief over the death of a dream and in learning to live with reality. The intervention is not unlike that needed for any grieving family, except that the grief of a family with a disabled child does not end.

Advocacy

In social, educational and religious settings, disabled children need persons who will speak up for them and seek to lead the institutions to change. As a caregiver to disabled children, your knowledge can lead to wider acceptance and positive action.

Ministry to disabled children is ministry that seeks to include all persons within the family of God. Its motive must be genuine love for, and acceptance of, children with disabilities. Disabled children are children first, much loved by God.

[Adapted from *When Children Suffer: A Sourcebook for Ministry with Children in Crisis*, Andrew D. Lester, ed., (Philadelphia: The Westminster Press, 1987), pp. 138-147.]

NOTES

1   Daniel Day Williams, *The Spirit and the Forms of Love* (New York: Harper and Row, 1968).

7

A Healing Environment for the Sexually Abused

Ann Noonan

During times of war children are traumatized in a variety of ways through violent acts of sexual abuse. The trauma from their sexual abuse is often intensified by other humiliating experiences surrounding the events such as forced acts of incest, initiated to break down a people's strongest cultural taboos and thus the very core and fabric of their culture.

Young boys, hungry and homeless, consent to engage in homosexual acts with soldiers in exchange for food—often just the scraps left on the soldiers' plates; young girls are forced into prostitution as their only hope of obtaining money for desperately needed food for themselves and their younger siblings. The random, widespread raping sprees of soldiers are often accompanied by capturing young girls to take back to their barracks where they are forced to serve as "wives" for the soldiers.

The extent of psychological problems that such violent acts of sexual abuse, usually initiated to crush a person's spirit, cause for children is immense. One must also remember that in times of prolonged warfare, many children enter early adulthood without having received any help in dealing with their trauma. While there has been little documented research on the treatment of children suffering trauma from war-related sexual abuse, it is certain that these children, and young adults, are in desperate need of a "healing environment" as described in this chapter.

Children who have been sexually traumatized have learned two extremely important and sad lessons:[1]

1. The world is not a safe place.

2. I do not have control over my life.

This chapter is designed to help the reader better understand what the sexually abused child has lost and what needs to be present in the therapeutic (healing) relationship for the children's restoration to psychological health to occur.

Relationship

It is within a relationship that a child is hurt and it is also within a relationship that restoration can occur. The destructive relationship is one that usually views the child as a thing or less than a developing human being. Perpetrators (persons committing the sexual abuse) use children to express their personal power and control and do not consider the children's needs for safety, security or connection. The good news is that it is also within a caring relationship that the child (or adult) can experience healing.

Losses due to abuse

The two major losses for the sexually abused child are the loss of personal power and the loss of connection. Abused children are without power and are temporarily disconnected from protective and nurturing adults. They become disconnected because of their deep feelings of guilt, humiliation and shame; feeling they are "damaged goods" abused children withdraw from caring adults instead of seeking the healing environment they could provide. This is particularly true for children who have been traumatized due to the atrocities of war. Healing for those individuals is based on the empowerment of the survivors, within the context of a new connection (i.e., within relationship). It cannot occur in isolation and can only occur within healthy relationships.[2]

Vocabulary

In working with children who have been sexually abused, it is important to refrain from calling them "victims." It is more helpful to use the term "survivor" and by that draw upon and acknowledge their strength. By doing this, you can instill an impression of personal strength to the injured. This also gives the survivor a sense of respect and esteem.

Symptoms or characteristics of an abused child

The difficulties experienced because of childhood sexual abuse are vast. The Crime Victims Research and Treatment Center of U.S.A. researched the issue and discovered some painful information. I should note here that the researchers conducted this study on children in the United States and not in a war-torn country.

The findings suggest that children who had experienced rape as part of their sexual abuse show significantly higher lifetime rates of psychological problems than a group that has not experienced violence, and have a 75 percent greater risk for major depression occurrences, five times greater risk for agony (suffering or distress), six times greater risk for obsessive-compulsive disorders, have social phobias (fears), a 50 percent greater risk for sexual disorders, a 50 percent greater risk for thoughts leading to suicide and are three times more likely to have made suicide attempts.

Children who are abused by family members, those who witness a high level of violence in the abuse and those who are sexually abused show signs of great emotional distress.[3] Many warning signs that alert one to possible sexual abuse in children closely resemble the symptoms children display when traumatized by other war-related events.

One must also remember that war-related sexual abuses are not usually "hidden" from others as they often are in more normal life situations. War-related sexual abuse is often widespread and affects most of the women and children in a whole village or area instead of as a series of isolated events. Also, often the abuse is conducted openly. "Gang rape" is a common occurrence in wartime. Knowledge of the events that have occurred in an area, and the

117

presence of several symptoms listed below, could be an indication that a child has been sexually abused.

Behavioral and emotional indications of sexual abuse

Karen Johnson[4] lists the following symptoms of sexual abuse.

- Fear of specific persons or situations, or of strangers (always on guard, never quite relaxed)
- Nightmares, waking up during the night sweating, screaming or shaking
- Withdrawal (social or emotional)
- Begin wetting the bed, or a change in sleep patterns
- Personality change
- Loss of appetite or other eating problems without a logical explanation
- Unprovoked crying spells
- Clinging to significant adults
- Excessive washing or baths
- Poor self-image, low self-esteem (feeling of worth)
- Changes in type of fantasy play
- Fear of being alone
- Refusing to go to school
- Running away
- Attempting to control environment, fear of unknown
- Early sexual precociousness (knows too much about sex too soon, as exhibited in the child's talk and actions)
- Difficulties with impulse control
- Depression (feelings of discouragement and despair)
- Expressing thoughts about death or suicide (killing oneself), or displaying suicidal actions
- Self-destructive behaviors, for example drug or alcohol abuse, suicidal gestures

- One child being treated by a parent in a significantly different way from other children in the family
- Poor peer relationships (boredom with their activities)
- Masturbating excessively
- Extreme fear of undressing
- Regression to behavior the child has already outgrown
- Suddenly not performing as well in school

Physical indicators of sexual abuse

- Complaining of pain while urinating or having bowel movement, indicating infection
- Symptoms indicating evidence of physical trauma (abrasions or lesions) to the genital area
- Somatic complaints: Develop frequent unexplained health symptoms, for example: returning stomachaches, headaches and pains in muscles and bones that have no logical cause or possible indicators
- Abnormally early physical development
- Difficulty with the menstrual cycle
- Symptoms indicating pregnancy
- Bouts of asthma, choking, and gagging, possibly recreating the sensation of oral rape

Sexual abuse can result in other emotional problems, such as:

- Anger
- Trust difficulties
- Lack of feelings of safety
- Lack of autonomy (independence)
- Lack of initiative (ambition or motivation)
- Decreased competence
- Loss of identity
- Inability to have intimacy (affection or tenderness)

119

Anger

Anger is always present when someone has been abused. It may be masked (hidden) or even repressed, but there is always an angry child inside every abused survivor. If the anger is masked, it may even look like a wonderful, happy child who is anxious to please. This could be the student who makes all A's and is considered at the top of the class. Or the anger may be repressed and buried deep inside. This may be the depressed child who is the quiet and very sad child in the corner. It may be the hostile child who is inappropriately aggressive. The anger of such children is easy to see, for they wear it clearly on their faces and in their body gestures and actions.

Trust

The abused child has usually had his or her ability to trust crushed and so finds it very difficult to reestablish a trusting relationship. Children always experience an intense feeling of betrayal when they discover that someone on whom they were vitally dependent has caused them harm. During wartime, children experience betrayal of another kind. The authority figures—whether teachers, local leaders, or military personnel—who have been role models to them, those they have learned to trust and respect, all have repeatedly violated the expected moral standards of behavior and inflicted intense suffering upon them.

Empowerment and control

Children who have been sexually abused have lost their personal power and sense of control over their lives. The need to restore control to the traumatized child has been widely recognized. Martin Symonds, working with hostages, describes the principles of treatment as "restoring power to the victims, reducing isolation, diminishing helplessness by increasing the victim's range of choice, and countering the dynamics of dominance in the approach to the victim."[5]

A worker can offer the survivor encouragement, care, advice, support, affection, and even the context for healing, but not

120

the cure. Survivors need to believe they will get better, that their future can improve and that, in the process, they will gain a sense of personal power over their lives.

Safety

Sexually abused children have had their sense of safety violated at the deepest levels. In recovery a sense of safety must be restored. Children need to grow in their ability to experience a shift from unpredictable danger to consistent, reliable safety. Abused children need to learn who "safe" people are and when and where they can experience safety and protection. A safe person is someone who is consistent, respectful, has a good sense of self and has healthy boundaries.

Boundaries and autonomy

Autonomy or a sense of separateness is an important aspect of healing. Being separate is different from being isolated. Separateness is an individual's ability to know his or her personal boundaries—that is, where their space ends and someone else's begins. Abuse victims have had their sense of separateness crushed and do not understand healthy privacy. Isolated victims build impenetrable walls around them that keep others out and themselves in.

Hearing the survivor's story

Developing autonomy or separateness restores a person's sense of control. A helpful way this can occur is by validating the survivor's experience. There are many ways to do this. One inevitable way is hearing the survivor's story without recoiling at the atrocities and allowing the survivors to tell their stories using their language—allowing the children to "name" whatever happened to them. It is important to help the children to say what happened (appropriate to their age), such as "my parents were brutally murdered," instead of "my parents went to be with Jesus." To force the children to use language that is more acceptable to the worker invalidates their stories and forces them again to conform to another's idea of acceptability.

HELPFUL BEHAVIORS OF WORKERS

Listening to the story

The worker can show respect and provide a caring environment by allowing the children to tell their stories as they experienced them. The survivor in a caring environment can experience acceptance of another person who imparts the message that they are important and they do not need to continue to live in isolation.

Children will feel respect when the adult worker allows them to find their own sense of readiness to relate. The children can usually let the workers know if they do not feel safe and if the trust level is low and undeveloped. By honoring the children's resistance to talk, the helper is allowing them to feel their personal power and to take control over themselves. Relating to children is very different from relating to adults. Asking children direct questions about abuse can cause them to suppress the memories further into their subconscious. A worker cannot overemphasize the elements of safety and protection, for both were badly crushed when the abuse occurred. It is more effective to use an art, play, or music experience to ease the children's sharing of their experiences (see chapters ten and eleven).

Restoration of control

Restoration of control is a primary need for the abused person. The helping adult is in the role of a facilitator or ally (partner)—assisting the wounded in the healing process by allowing them to assume appropriate control of their lives. A simple yet profound way to do this is that the helper should not be obvious in assisting the children to express their feelings. The helper needs to have good listening skills and be able to ask questions that bring more than one-word responses, questions that allow the content to originate in the children the worker is helping.

Examples of such questions are:

- "Are you hurting?" (Bad)
- "What are you feeling?" (Better)

◆ "Describe what you want me to know." (Even Better)

◆ "Tell me what you'd like to tell me." (Best)

Boundaries of the worker

Abused children not only need to learn to establish their boundaries (separateness, autonomy), but also to respect the separateness of others. This can be a particular annoyance to helpers who find their space, time and emotions intruded on and perceive an apparent unawareness by the survivor. When this happens, the worker needs to be direct and clear about what is acceptable and unacceptable.

Having healthy boundaries is very important for anyone working with the sexually abused. The sexually abused are a population who have not known any line of demarcation between themselves and the rest of the world. Without healthy boundaries the helpers will find themselves pulled into painful situations and incapable of setting caring limits that are an essential part of the healing process. Helpers with unhealthy boundaries are in real danger of burning out or, even worse, possibly reabusing the ones they want most to help by contributing to the confusion that is already present.

The worker's support system

Because of the horrendous information to which a worker is exposed when working with the sexually abused, it is essential for the counselor to have the support of others who can share this burden and listen to the worker's personal pain. It is also helpful to have an accurate view of God and to know that Jesus' mission on earth, as outlined in Isaiah 61:1-3 (TLB), gives the hope of healing.

> The Spirit of the Lord God is upon me, because the Lord has anointed me to bring good news to the suffering and afflicted. He has sent me to comfort the broken-hearted, to announce liberty to the captives and to open the eyes of the blind. He has sent me to tell those who mourn that . . . he will give: Beauty for ashes; Joy instead of mourning; Praise instead of heaviness. . . .

It is essential that the workers believe God is the healer and can cause healing to occur. We must also remember that God usually uses relationships with his people here to bridge the future relationship between himself and the wounded.

Applying the principle of the sower

John 4:34-38 contains another biblical principle we need to practice. That principle is "one sows and another reaps." This can be a great comfort to those working with severely abused or traumatized youngsters. We need to realize that we may be only a small part of this young person's healing and be willing to be just that.

CONCLUSION

In conclusion, I would like to share a survivor's drawings. These drawings depict the negative messages that resonate within a survivor, the lack of personal identity that can occur during the healing process and later, a restored view of self.

I need to note that this young woman continues to spiral back to the abusive messages, but as healing progresses she can more easily find her way through the doubt to the restoration. This young woman was sexually abused by a person she especially trusted—her youth pastor—from age 11 through 13. This resulted in further spiritual problems for her. She continues to struggle today with her understanding of God.

The first illustration (see Figure 7.1 on page 125) was drawn when she had no hope, only tears and negative messages. One of the things she wanted during her childhood was for someone to play with her and take an interest in her.

The second illustration (see Figure 7.2 on page 126) was drawn when she was midway through the healing process. She knew she wanted to get rid of the negative messages, but did not know how or what was now true about her. Notice that her eyes are now looking up in hopeful anticipation. In our counseling we talked a great deal here about getting up in the tree and writing her own positive messages, based on what God said about her identity and who she was in Christ.

Illustration three (see Figure 7.3 on page 127) was drawn some time into therapy and after some very hard work on the

Figure 7.1: No hope, only tears and negative messages

young woman's part to put positive messages about herself into her thinking and belief system. One day she came in with this delightful drawing and so many positive messages she had to draw a picket fence! This illustrates the depth of damage and restorative work required for healing. It also expresses the process of healing; children can often go from "bad" to "worse" before "better."

The healing relationship

As already stated, the two essential areas of damage for the sexually abused are the loss of power (often called control) over themselves and the loss of connection with significant people.

Figure 7.2: Midway through the process

Figure 7.3: Positive messages return

Healing is based on restoring the children's sense of personal power and enabling them to reconnect with others.

A Rapha booklet (*rapha* is the Hebrew word for "healing") lists some "Do's" and "Don'ts" for those in relationship with a survivor[6] (see page 128). I found them useful.

It is helpful to remember that in the children's renewed connections, they recreate or repair psychological faculties (or abilities to perform an action) that were damaged or deformed by their traumatic experiences. These faculties include the child's basic capacity for trust, autonomy, initiative, competence, identity, and intimacy.[7]

THE DON'TS

Don't say to the victim:

1. I don't believe you were ever abused.
2. Why can't you just forget it?
3. That's in the past. Why keep bringing it up?
4. Can't you just let go? It's not happening now.
5. Why are you making such a big deal? You were only three.
6. Just pray about it. Give it to God.
7. You are the problem, not what happened.
8. Why didn't you stop it?
9. Stop thinking about it. It's a sin. The Bible says to think on things that are good.
10. What did you do to cause it to happen?
11. Why can't you hurry up and get over it?
12. Paul said to forget the past and move on toward the future.
13. You're not forgiving. You have to forgive or God won't help you.
14. I am so sick of this, what about me?
15. You have got to quit feeling sorry for yourself.

THE DO'S

Do stand ready:

1. To give support.
2. To give acceptance.
3. To give love.
4. To give time.
5. To give understanding.
6. To give interest.
7. To give forgiveness.
8. To give help.
9. To give belief.
10. To give prayer.
11. To give encouragement.
12. To give hope.
13. To give honor.
14. To give trust.
15. To give validation.

You may struggle with the destructive acts of the destroyer and become part of God's healing and restoration to the children. May you be a channel for God's healing light in the darkness of our fallen world.

Beware of hateful or vengeful feelings towards the perpetrator.

NOTES

1   Henry Cloud and John Townsend, *Boundaries: When to Say Yes and When to Say No* (Grand Rapids: Zondervan Publishing House, 1992).

2   Judith Lewis Herman, *Trauma and Recovery* (Basic Books, 1992).

3   Sandra L. Brown, *Counseling Victims of Violence* (Alexandria, Virginia: American Association for Counseling and Development, 1991).

4   Karen Cecilia Johnson, *Through the Tears: Caring for the Sexually Abused Child* (Nashville: Broadman Press, 1993).

5   Herman.

6   James Mallory Jr. and Cynthia Kubentin, *Learning More About Sexual Abuse* (Dallas: Word Publishing, 1992).

7   E. Erikson, *Childhood and Society*, second edition (New York: Norton & Company, 1963).

Part 3

Principles for
Intervention Planning

8

An Introduction to the STOP Sign Model

Phyllis Kilbourn

The STOP sign model presented in this section is an attempt by child psychologists and researchers to arrange systematically their knowledge of the psychological and social effects of war on children. Psychologists and researchers then use this knowledge to formulate the main principles for intervention planning.

Building this model starts with the premise that to understand the children's psychological needs resulting from their war-related experiences, and then devise effective intervention plans, we must understand the differences in the state of emotional health between (a) healthy children, (b) healthy children in war, (c) children of war that show symptoms of emotional problems, and (d) children of war who show no symptoms of emotional problems. Discovering what children in each of these groups are like will help one understand the various ways children in war can be affected in their thinking, feelings, and behavior.

The healthy child

The starting point is understanding what a healthy child is like—a child who is healthy not only from a medical point of view, but also from a psychological and social perspective. One must

133

remember that crises, conflicts, anxiety, fear and aggression belong to children's normal development in all circumstances. War, however, changes the context and the meaning of these for the children's emotional health.

To understand how children change in their ways of thinking and behaving because of their war-related experiences and traumas, we must look first at how healthy children think, how they feel, how they express their emotions, and how they interact with others. The circle in Figure 8.1 below represents the healthy child.

In healthy children the outside shell of the circle is transparent or mirror-like, allowing you to see inside the children's thinking. You can understand much of what the children are thinking by listening to what they talk about, by observing their reactions to people and situations, and by noting the content of their play. Healthy children can also communicate their true feelings and genuine thoughts directly to people, especially to those they trust.

Figure 8.1: The healthy child

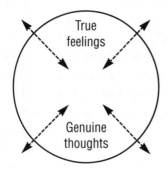

Figure 8.2: The healthy child in war

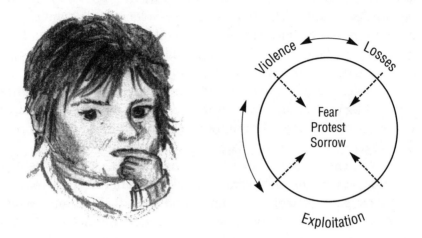

Healthy children are part of a family with strong personal links to parents and other persons important to them—extended family members, teachers in both school and church, or other community figures. As members of a society they are included in a network of relations and security systems. They know society is prepared to protect them the very day their families fail to do so. The children not only enjoy feeling that they are a part of their families and communities; belonging also brings them a sense of safety, security and well-being.

The healthy child in war

What happens to a healthy child in war? First, we should remember that war is not a single, consistent event that all children experience in the same way. Rather, war consists of a series of events that affects children in different ways. From a child's point of view, however, the experiences of any war can be divided into three categories: *violence, losses or separations* and *exploitation* (taking

135

unfair advantage of the children in their situation). The circle in Figure 8.2 on page 135 represents the healthy child in war.

Most children in war experience and become victims of *violence*. This violence is expressed in many ways. Some children may be tortured or killed intentionally, or the violence may be more randomly directed against places where children are. For example, a grenade may land in a school yard while the children are playing, or a boy tending cattle may be blown up by a land mine.

Even more common for children is experiencing violence directed against adults. In war-afflicted areas most children have witnessed the apparently unmotivated shooting of adults, sometimes even relatives or friends.

As children grow up in this landscape of violence, the violence usually results in severe *losses* or separations. Children may lose their parents, siblings, homes, and even their country when they are forced to flee from violence. Consequently, they must often live as refugees or street children. They also may suffer physical losses resulting from the violence inflicted on them. These losses include health, appearance, or body parts, causing them to become crippled or disabled for life.

These are tremendous losses, but when children actually observe the violence they can in a limited way comprehend what is going on because they see these tangible results from the violence. Sometimes, however, the losses are less discernible or concrete and can be even more devastating to a child. For example, a father may disappear suddenly without any explanation. Such situations are difficult enough for an adult, but almost impossible for a child to handle.

All these losses can lead to yet another tremendous loss for children—the loss of faith in their parents' ability to protect them and to keep them safe. To realize as a small child that the parents have no chance of protecting the family if a group of armed men appears means that the child's faith in the loving care expected from adults breaks down at an early age. When this happens, the loss affects the deepest attachment bonding a child experiences. The loss of trust in an adult's ability to care for them, to provide for their needs and to protect them has damaging effects on the way children think and behave.

Perhaps the deepest loss for children in war is the loss of their basic right to be a child, with limited responsibility, protection by adults and a secure freedom to explore and discover their world. They may lose all the open senses of the curious, innocent child.

When a child's parents are killed or missing, many have to "grow up quickly." Taking responsibility for other siblings and assuming other adult roles deprives them of a normal childhood as described by the UN World Declaration on the Survival, Protection, and Development of Children:

> The children of the world are innocent, vulnerable, and dependent. They are also curious, active, and full of hope. Their time should be one of joy and peace, of playing, learning, and growing. Their future should be shaped in harmony and co-operation. Their lives should mature, as they broaden their perspectives and gain new experiences (*The State of the World's Children*, 1991).

But, doubtless, the worst form of violence for children is when they are forced to commit violence themselves—often against those who are the very ones that provide nurture, love, and security for them. In the children's world of experiences, *exploitation* becomes a combination of violence and losses. Through violence, the children are forced into actions that are not compatible with their actual needs. As the children are forced, their losses become even greater.

Children are exploited in various ways during war. Many boys and girls—some as young as five years old—are used in the army as child soldiers. Some adult soldiers are quick to assert their beliefs that children do not yet fully know or appreciate the value of life, so killing will not be too harmful or traumatic for them. These soldiers have even claimed that the act of killing causes less damage to children than it does to adults. Consequently, children often are made not only to shoot and kill, but also to engage in such activities as disposing of the dead bodies—dragging them into pits or throwing them into rivers.

Another form of exploitation is using the young girls as prostitutes to earn money for the soldiers, or giving them directly to the soldiers for their own sexual exploitation. At other times children who have to live on the streets are forced to serve as prostitutes in a desperate attempt to earn some money for themselves or their families.

Experiences of violence, losses, and exploitation are interrelated and often strengthen each other, rotating in an extremely destructive and vicious circle. These experiences of war are very hard for children and result in three basic *psychological reactions: fear, protest and sorrow (or sadness).* Children live in constant *fear* of all that can happen to them. Their biggest fear is that their parents or siblings will be killed. Research shows that most children fear the death of significant persons in their lives more than their own deaths. They fear there will be no one to care for them; that no one will be able to provide food for them; or that they will never go to school again. All that they have witnessed and experienced in the war magnifies their fears.

Children also *protest* against the war-related events that have affected them. They have at least a limited sense of fairness and justice and know that senseless killing, looting or other forms of brutality are not justified. The whole idea of war with its confusion—the little they can understand and the vastness they cannot understand—results in frustrating anger. They can see no reason for soldiers rushing into their villages, killing their parents, taking their siblings and friends and forcing them into the army, or into sexual exploitation. This anger can greatly affect the emotional well-being of children.

Then there is a *sadness* over the losses that have already occurred and, in most instances, can never be replaced.

These reactions are normal, healthy reactions and necessary cornerstones for the children as they work through their experiences and losses, seeking to reconstruct what has been damaged. Healthy children in war, represented by the circle in Figure 8.2 on page 135, are children who are still protected by their families or who have significant persons in their lives as caregivers. These trusted adults are there and can help the children contain their feelings and reflect on their thoughts and feelings. The clear mirror-like shell depicted in Figure 8.1 on page 134 is still transparent and the children are still able to communicate from the inside, in one way or another, what they have experienced.

The triangle of chaos

A more dangerous threat for children in war is what Lars Gustafsson (1986) terms the "triangle of chaos"—a threat he perceives as even more dangerous than the isolated war events themselves.

The triangle of chaos reflects confusion on three different levels. First, there is the *chaos within the children* themselves resulting from the fact that the war, from the children's point of view, makes no sense. It is impossible to understand the real meaning of the war, and nobody can really provide any meaningful explanation. This is especially true for small children who find it hard to understand why people are so angry and hurting each other, nor can they comprehend why several different armed groups are fighting each other year after year. The children are constantly afraid of something they cannot understand or control.

The second side of the triangle represents the *chaos in the family*. Often the family and home are no longer able to function as the safe, supporting structures that they were in the past. The children's faith and trust in the parents' ability to care for them has been frustrated. There is fear and anxiety that parents are no longer in control.

These traumatic events have hurt the children's basic trust and attachment bonds. This breaking of trust within the family also inhibits the children's capacity for trusting themselves and others, therefore destroying their capacity to enjoy life and feel secure. Trauma victims of all ages report difficulty reestablishing trust after a traumatic event. Children appear especially vulnerable, however, to the collapse of "basic trust."

The third side of the triangle represents the *chaos within the community and society*. Often all the people in a village or community must flee for their own safety. The children find themselves living in strange surroundings as refugees. Food is no longer easily obtainable. The children no longer have the familiar community structures surrounding them: school, church, markets, or the familiar palaver hut or other structure that represents the center of community life.

Examples of modifying or mitigating factors (factors that make the situation or the trauma less severe or painful) are the children's ability to understand what is going on, or the presence of important structures in their lives such as the family and the school. When these mitigating factors do not function properly, the triangle of chaos establishes itself in the child. The triangle of chaos limits the space available for creating incoming information about violence, losses, and exploitation. The triangle of chaos blocks the children's abilities to communicate their true feelings and it conceals what is really going on inside the children.

Figure 8.3: The child of war with symptoms

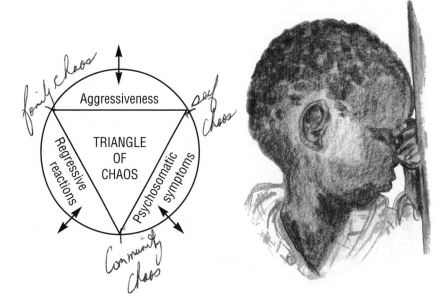

When approaching these children, one cannot be sure of getting in touch with their fears, protests or sorrows. One just knows that they must be there, somewhere. There are two possibilities one may encounter on approaching these children: meeting a child with symptoms or a child that does not express any symptoms.

Children with symptoms, represented by the circle in Figure 8.3 on page 140, will react to this confusion with aggressive behavior (hitting, kicking, screaming, breaking things); with signs of regressive behavior—behaving in ways commonly found in younger children, thus losing some of their latest steps in maturity for some time (bedwetting, clinging, "baby talk"); or with physical symptoms (headaches, stomachaches, loss of appetite).

The child, parents or caregivers, teachers and even doctors regularly misinterpret these symptoms. For example, many times when the children express physical symptoms, they are not actually sick. But these symptoms often are the children's last desperate attempt to communicate when all other channels of communication are blocked. What the children really are trying to communicate is their need for someone to understand that they are hurting, that they are sad, that they are afraid and that they are protesting. Children have a tolerance level for just how much sadness they can deal with before the body reacts.

These symptoms can be healthy if caregivers are alert to discern what is happening with the children. Their reactions can provide an important clue that something is wrong with the child, and dealing with those symptoms can provide an opportunity for children to talk about how they really feel. While there are symptoms, there is hope.

Far more serious problems surround the children who, because of the severity of their trauma, display no symptoms. The circle in Figure 8.4 on page 142 represents these children.

Caregivers must be very alert to recognize these children who are suffering the most severely and are in the greatest need of help to prevent long-term or ongoing effects from their trauma. With these children the shell has become completely opaque, or

141

Figure 8.4: The child of war without symptoms

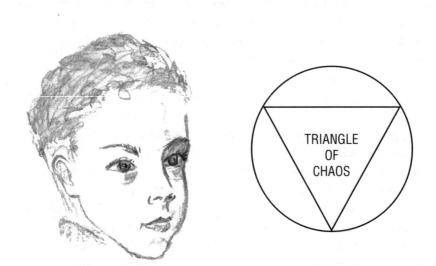

TRIANGLE
OF
CHAOS

dark. The triangle of chaos has become so dense that they have lost all ability to communicate their true feelings, thoughts and emotions to the outside. The soul of the child is silent.

One knows that these children have lost their families' protection and security networks. Yet the child seems to be more like an adult, a mature or perhaps more intelligent child with an air of resignation. They appear more tired than aggressive, more competent than regressive, with no medical complaints. They firmly deny any sense of fear, anger or sorrow. They appear self-sufficient with the attitude, "Oh, life is just like that; I can handle it"; and they display a decisive attitude of "Don't bother me, I'll take care of myself."

These children are regarded as "strong" or even "admirable." Yet one knows and must remember that they have experienced a considerable amount of violence, loss and exploitation. From a psychological point of view, these children are suffering the

142

greatest degree of trauma and usually will need more long-term care than the children described in Figures 8.2 and 8.3. Caregivers must enable these children to communicate their true feelings and thoughts.

For all these children we, as members of the body of Christ, must discover meaningful ways that the church can play an active role in the children's "extended family" network. We must help them understand the fear, protest and sadness they are experiencing and provide ways for them to work through these feelings so they can be restored to emotionally healthy children.

Caregivers helping such children must also try to stop the devastating process of chaos—strengthening the mitigating factors—through planned interventions. A basic strategy, symbolized by the "STOP sign," is used here to explore ways to accomplish this task. Each letter of *STOP* represents an important action for helping children overcome the psychological traumas they have experienced in war. The four cornerstones in this basic strategy are: structure, talking and time, organized play (various forms of play therapy), and parental support.

"S" = Structure

The letter "S" represents the children's need for structure. Confused children desperately need structure in their lives. The structures that surrounded and supported their lives before the war are no longer in place: community, school, church, friends and age-mates, and a normal, healthy family life. As family and church members we need to decide which structures we can reestablish for the children, or perhaps we will need to create some new ones until the restoration of the former ones.

"T" = Talking and Time

Talking to someone about what has happened to them is the starting point in the children's healing process. The children need someone who is ready to listen to them. In war, parents and other adults often are so preoccupied by their own fears and sorrows that they reject or neglect the children's stories. Other parents believe that allowing the children to talk about what has happened disturbs the children too much.

Allowing and even encouraging children to talk and express their feelings and real thoughts are an important part of helping the children overcome their feelings resulting from the traumas they have experienced. But it is also important to understand that the children need time and a person that they can trust, a person who is ready to listen to and to hold to what he or she has heard.

Kathleen Lentz (1985) stresses the importance of enabling children to express their sufferings in ways that are meaningful to them. Telling their story enables children to reorganize the pieces of their now broken lives by exploring and discovering new meaning—or a new design—that can come from that brokenness.

Children need to have the security to share their stories in the context of the faith community. Hearing adults and caregivers sharing their stories in the faith community will help them to enter new experiences of community, and give them a broader perspective of their own situations, traumas and sufferings. The faith community can also help the children find new meanings to what they have experienced in the war that will be a necessary step in their healing. The children will be unable to resolve their problems concerning their experience by relating only to the old frames of reference. Finding new meanings will help them reorient themselves and find new purpose in their lives.

Kathleen Fischer (1988) suggests that reading the Scriptures with an open attitude of participation in the text and discovering how their own story connects with the scriptural text can also help children in the telling of their stories. Children can be presented with stories of suffering, wholeness and healing, imagining themselves living out the experience of a character in the story. Children can be encouraged to celebrate these faith stories through the rituals of the community and then to carry the celebration into their daily lives.

The church needs to determine which adults, along with the pastors, can best help the children in this way—especially for those children who no longer have parents. The pastors also need to think about training those people who have time to give to the children and who can guide them in their story telling in ways that will facilitate their healing.

"O" = Organized Play

Play is important for a child's normal development. Children regard playing activity as real, and it is their way of gaining life experiences. Lars Gustafsson, A. Lindkvist and B. Bohm (1987) noted that children from war affected areas are lacking in constructive and meaningful forms in their playing. One reason for this is that when children are surrounded by adults experiencing fear and grief, they do not feel that they dare play and enjoy themselves. Play would also bring the children into touch with their feelings and to the children these feelings seem too dangerous to handle. So the children keep quiet.

This lack of play suggests that the children affected by war are losing valuable aspects in their development that are decisive for ongoing normal psychological development. When the children do find the opportunity to play, war and violence often heavily dominate their games. Interpreting children's actual playing behavior is one of the tools used in psychotherapy for children. Role playing and artwork provide meaningful ways for children to express the horrors of their experiences and thus experience a release of their emotional tensions both verbally and in actual behavior. These are especially helpful for those children who are not able to express their feelings in words. Play also restores and preserves the cultural traditions, thus helping the children to regain a sense and feeling of normalcy.

"P" = Parental Support

The influence of parental support is considered the most important factor for all children whether in war or in peace. If contact between children and at least one parent or caregiver is not maintained during war, a child's actual and future psychological development will be even more disturbed (Ressler, Boothby, and

145

Steinbock 1988). A young child will consider even a short separation from parents as a permanent loss.

Therefore we must be careful to ensure that all our efforts to help children traumatized by war include the parents or other significant caregivers. The church needs to examine ways that it can actively provide strong support to the children's caregivers. We must provide children with a sense of belonging.

[This chapter and the circle illustrations are based on principles from "The STOP Sign—A Model for Intervention to Assist Children in War" by Lars H. Gustafsson, prepared in conjunction with Agneta Lindkvist. From *Action for Children: NGO Forum—Children in Emergencies* (New York: Radda Barna Report, April 1986).]

REFERENCES

Fischer, Kathleen R. *The Inner Rainbow.* New York: Paulist Press, 1988.

Gustafsson, Lars H., prepared in conjunction with Agneta Lindkvist. "The STOP Sign—A Model for Intervention to Assist Children in War" in *Action for Children: NGO Forum—Children in Emergencies.* New York: Radda Barna Report, April 1986.

Gustafsson, Lars H., A. Lindkvist and B. Bohm. *Barn i kriq* [Children in War]. Stockholm: Verbum Gothia, 1987.

Lentz, Kathleen A. "But these little ones: Reflections on the suffering of children" in *Religion and Intellectual Life* 3:(1), Fall 1985.

Ressler, E., N. Boothby and D. Steinbock. *Unaccompanied Children: Care and Protection in Wars, Natural Disasters, and Refugee Movements.* New York: Oxford University Press, 1988.

UNICEF, *The State of the World's Children,* 1991, p. 53.

9

"S" Equals Structure

Phyllis Kilbourn

The letter "S" in the "STOP Sign" model represents the children's need for interventions that provide *structure*. Children need the daily activities and routines that provide structure to enjoy a normal, healthy childhood. Interactions with parents or other significant adults, or the ritual, routines or schedules of family and community life normally provide structure for young children. Older children get much of their structure from the school context.

The need for order and predictability in a safe, disciplined—but not rigid—environment is essential not only for children who have been deeply traumatized by war, but also for those children who show some degree of resilience in handling their trauma. A structured environment promotes healing. It also provides children with a routine that places limitations on their behavior, providing them with a natural form of discipline. Such discipline provides children with a sense of security and well-being.

Children who become confused by ongoing, chaotic war-related events are in desperate need of having meaningful structure reintroduced in their lives, thus making this an important intervention ingredient. Lars Gustafsson (1986) says that the first task in all programs aimed at assisting children in war must be to reestablish structure or, if needed, to create new, temporary or substitute structures.[1]   *North American prisons?*

War destroys vital structures

Often in wartime the predominant structures of the children's lives disintegrate. The structures that were so important to them before the war are suddenly no longer in place for them: community life with its activities and rituals including school and church, and a normal, structured family life. After the destruction of the children's home and community structures, children often find themselves living in unfamiliar surroundings as either internal or external refugees. Missing family members can also disrupt the order and routine of family life. Through the loss of these important structures the children, to a large extent, lose control over the events of their daily lives.

When familiar structures are removed from the children's lives, their world becomes filled with chaos. They find it extremely difficult to handle the loss of security, routine and discipline that the familiar structures helped to provide, especially those relating to their family and community. Even as adults, with mature coping mechanisms, we are aware of the intense frustrations we can experience when our daily routines turn chaotic.

As caregivers we need to quickly determine which structures we can restore—or temporarily create—for the children. These structures will help them to piece together, from within their own inner confusion, the bits and pieces of their experiences and construct new meanings for the events of their lives.

Adults are very important to children trying to establish those cognitive structures that are decisive for future development. Children need adults to take responsibility for the structure they so desperately need in a world that, for them, has become filled with violence, fear and chaos. Children need the assurance of adult support and concern in their struggle to find that which will give them new meaning, identity, self-respect and a hope for their future.

Family and community structures

Children are very dependent on family for security and a sense of well-being. In emergencies it is important to try to preserve the family structure as much as possible. The social closeness of their community also strongly influences the children's reactions to war and disaster. While sometimes difficult, the immediate family (parents and siblings) should do as much as possible to try to maintain not only the child's support, but also that of the extended family, the child's school and other institutions the child relates to.

If a family becomes fragmented through death or by separation during flight, a substitute family or other stable attachment figures should be provided as soon as possible. Immediately initiate reunification programs to reunite families that have become separated in war.

Ongoing routines and daily activities following stressful events give children a sense of stability and security. Encourage

149

and instruct parents or caregivers to establish and maintain daily routines in their homes for: children's chores (such as carrying water first thing every morning); family prayer times; regular meal-time and sleep schedules; free time for play and fun with their friends; and time for educational and community activities.

Community leaders need to restore a similar likeness of for-mer community life whether in a refugee camp or hometown situa-tion: worship and activities, schooling in some form, rules and guidelines to govern the community life, and assigned individual and family responsibilities. The emotional development of children is closely connected with the safety and nurture (care) provided by their environment.

Participation in community projects and activities such as restoring the community's facilities or the distribution of food or other relief goods also can provide valuable forms of structure. Family and community structures help foster a sense of belonging, self-worth and hope that are important to traumatized children who have suffered enormous losses, especially the loss of impor-tant people in their lives. Such activities can also help adolescents feel a sense of control over their lives by taking positive action.

School and other structured learning activities

For children, structure particularly includes school—schools in which instruction, discipline, social activities and rela-tionships are coordinated to provide a secure environment. School programs support the children's need to have some control over their otherwise chaotic lives, and provide them with a daily oppor-tunity for learning and growth to continue a somewhat normal developmental basis.

Education also functions as a sort of surviving mechanism for children living in areas surrounded by war. Going to school and meeting teachers and peers helps children who desperately try to cope with chaotic, confused learning structures caused by their insecure situations. School represents an organized and predictable environment with clearly defined and consistently enforced stan-dards, rules and responsibilities. Daily activities fully occupy the children in school settings, and school attendance often gives them the opportunity to experience more secure environments than those around their homes.

An organized school situation also has significance as a social context for caregiving as well as learning. Where children have lost the significant caregivers in their lives, programs that support the establishment of strong relationships between a teacher and child enhance the child's sense of protection and safety. School attendance provides children with an opportunity to develop strong relationships with adult role models in a "nurturing setting that combines warmth and caring with a clearly defined structure . . . and explicit limits that are consistently enforced" (Werner 1990:113).[2]

Often in war situations using methods and plans from the traditional formal classroom format of education is not a possibility. Any number of nonformal methods of education and teaching, however, can provide significant structured situations for children—even if classes are taught under a tree, without books, and with parents or community leaders providing the instruction.

In refugee situations, it is almost certain that there will be some teachers among the refugees. These teachers need to have a task to occupy their time and doubtless will be glad to contribute their time and skills toward helping the children.

Parents, elders in the community and religious leaders can transmit a wealth of valuable information to the children during informal learning sessions: story telling for enjoyment; elders sharing the country's culture and history; explaining folklore and proverbs; instruction in the functions of the local and national governments; age-appropriate discussions on the background and effects of the present war (history in the making) and how one can arrive at peaceful, instead of violent, solutions to problems; participation in drama (a natural with most children); teaching crafts, such as basket weaving or pottery; sewing classes; child-care classes; basic health instruction; agricultural knowledge; and church leaders can provide Bible teaching, Scripture memorization, choirs, Bible clubs—the ideas are endless! And, of course, recreation and sports programs must also be included.

151

Personnel from relief groups working in war-torn areas bring with them a wealth of expertise that they are glad, time permitting, to share in community situations: teaching basic health-care measures, music classes, literacy training, and many other skills. Some have even been responsible for starting educational and recreational programs as well as drama clubs.

Having nothing meaningful to do will destroy the morale and development of any individual. This is especially true when people have too much time on their hands to spend thinking about the tragedies they are experiencing. Therefore, try to engage as many community members as possible in the programs planned for children. For example, the teens would be happy to assume responsibility for the younger children's sports program and could also assist the younger children with their lessons; the church or school choir director could form a community choir (adults and children); or a local health nurse could share basic preventive medical procedures. Find out what skills various individuals have to share.

The Child-to-Child program

An exciting, proven program that involves children in the vital role of a family and community resource person is the International Child-to-Child program launched by Professor David Morley from the Institute of Child Health and colleagues from the Institute of Education, University of London.

As Morley and his team became aware of the central role of the growing child in the community—who often become the first literate members of their communities and are competent at caring for younger siblings—they saw the potential of using children as health care workers and educators.

Morley developed the Child-to-Child program around the concept of providing and sharing information and ideas that would enable the children themselves to improve health, development and the well-being of their brothers and sisters and children in their communities. Child-to-Child is a method of teaching about health that encourages children to participate actively while learning and to put into practice what they learn.

Children are encouraged to participate in such activities as caring for younger brothers and sisters or other young children in the community (Child-to-Child); influencing other children in their community, especially those with fewer opportunities and education (Children-to-Children); spreading health ideas and messages within their own communities (Children-and-Community); and sharing information within their families (Child-with-Family).

Child-to-Child has trained children to work in such fields as personal and community hygiene, safety, helping children with disabilities, food and nutrition, and prevention and cure of disease. They have recently introduced a new category for training children to help other children—children in difficult circumstances.

Four new activity sheets and teaching tools have been devised to assist children in this category: children who live or work on the street; children who live in institutions; children whose friends or relatives die; and children who have experienced war, disaster or conflict. (Chapter 15 is an example of a Child-to-Child activity sheet.)

Through participating in a program such as Child-to-Child, children help to better their families and communities while having their minds diverted from the atrocities and war-related events surrounding them. Perhaps more important, such involvement can provide children who often have been deeply humiliated through war-related events with a renewed sense of self-worth, dignity, purpose and hope.

Vocational training

Creative vocational training programs will perhaps represent one of the most needed forms of education for children in ongoing war situations. Prolonged war situations usually leave children with little hope of ever returning to a formal school situation. The loss of education represents a loss of financial support and a loss of hope for the child's future. These fears are intensified by the fact that many children have also lost the caregivers who provided their support.

Liberia is now past its fifth year of civil war—a war that has almost totally devastated the country. Many children have not been in a formal schooling situation since the war began. Liberian social worker Thomas Teage, executive director of CAP (Child Assistance Program), discovered a valuable and culturally relevant way to provide education for some of these children. It is an educational plan that provides structure and hope—both for the present and for the future.

Teage and his staff took over a vacated school and began training children—boys and girls—from age eleven. These children include former street fighters and combatants, and those left homeless when parents and caregivers were killed in the war. The goal of CAP is to provide a year-long training program for the children that includes literacy training, co-operative skills, animal husbandry (pigs, rabbits and poultry) and agricultural skills.

After one year of training the children will form co-operatives. They may choose to specialize in agriculture or animal husbandry. CAP hopes to provide each child with a plot of land or an animal to get them started in the business of their choice. The children will govern themselves, making their own rules and decisions—how to spend money, what to plant or what animals to buy. Staff will intervene in their problems or decisions only if the children have difficulties they cannot resolve.

The children work diligently in the program, appreciative of a hope for their future as well as meaningful engagement that keeps their minds off the horrors of the vicious civil war that engulfs their country.

Teage's theory of using co-operatives as a framework for training and employment stems from the children's gang experiences and knowledge obtained through their war-related experiences as street kids. Many children who had lost their parents or caregivers were former street fighters, combatants or had taken to the streets as the only option for existence. These children know how to "pull together" to support and encourage one another.

At another site CAP offers the children an alternative program that focuses their training on manufacturing handicraft items that the children can market. At the time of this author's visit, almost 500 children were involved in this project.

Programs that provide children with structure also offer a variety of opportunities for caregivers to assist the children: counseling, provision of basic physical needs, recreation and other meaningful forms of family and community structure.

The key

The key to all activities that provide structure for children is to make sure they have value—and sense! Do not involve the children in activities simply for activities' sake or to "babysit" them; too many of their important developmental needs are at risk. Children need meaningful activities that stem from an ordered, predictable and safe environment and that provide cognitive stimulation, a form of discipline and a general feeling of security and well-being.

NOTES

1 Lars H. Gustafsson, prepared in conjunction with Agneta Lindkvist, "The STOP Sign: A Model for Intervention to Assist Children in War," *Action for Children: NGO Forum—Children in Emergencies* (New York: Radda Barna Report, April 1986).

2 E. E. Werner, "Protective Factors and Individual Resilience," *Handbook of Early Education*, S. J. Meisels and J. P. Shonkoff, eds. (Cambridge University Press, 1990).

10

"T" Equals Talk and Time: Reaching the Troubled or Traumatized Child

Josephine Wright

A five-year-old child sits huddled in a corner of a playroom. She was admitted to the hospital the night before, having suffered from burns and alleged sexual abuse by her "father." Since her arrival she would not speak to anyone, would not eat and screamed when touched. In desperation, the staff asked for my help. "You will know how to get her to talk," they said confidently. Me, a newly qualified child psychologist!

I had been off-duty so I was wearing slacks. I changed into a long, flowing dress and asked everyone else to go back to their usual duties. Then, holding a child's drink and a cup of coffee for me, I quietly stepped into the playroom on the opposite side to the little girl. All I knew about the little girl was what had happened to her and her name, Sara.

I sat at a low table at an angle to the little girl. I did not look directly at her. I felt her body stiffen as I arrived. I started drawing pictures, nice pictures about quiet picnics and story times. I talked myself through the picture stories.

I never looked at the little girl but frequently looked up at the window as I sipped my coffee. Slowly I felt the little girl move closer. I pushed the crayons around the table, having left big sheets of paper all over the table. I drew a girl. Quietly I said to myself, "I wonder what color to do this little girl's dress?" A green crayon rolled across the table. I did not look up. "Okay, let's make it green. All green?" I asked. A red crayon rolled across the table. "Let's put some red on it too then," I said. Slowly, I drew the picture.

"This little girl could go for a walk, I suppose, to the park or the swings," I quietly said as I carried on with the picture. Slowly I was aware of the sound of scribbling coming from the other end of the table. Sara was drawing flowers, flowers that could have been drawn by a three-year-old. Slowly I rolled a few crayons across the table toward her. She stopped drawing and tensed up. I did not look up. Slowly she relaxed and continued drawing. Then she picked up her drink, watching me all the time as she drank.

After an hour I quietly said to myself, "I am hungry. I wonder if I can get a biscuit or a sandwich—would that be a good idea?" A quiet "yes" came from Sara. Slowly I got up and collected some sandwiches. We ate in silence as we drew our pictures. Sara began to look tired. "I think I am going to have a sleep," I said. "Shall I come back later to do some more drawing?"

Still I did not look at her. This was the first time that I had spoken to her directly. Sara went and curled up on the cushions. As I passed, she put out her hand. I gestured "goodbye" to her with my hand. "Yes," she said quietly. I looked at her for a moment and smiled. "Okay," I said, "I'll come back when you have had your sleep."

The counselor's role

When I was asked to write this chapter, I smiled at the title, "Talk." In my work as a child psychologist, there are colleagues, parents and caregivers who often ask me, "How can you help us to talk to our children better? I never know what to say to them."

In Liberia the request was the same. Caregivers recognized that the children's war experiences troubled them and that the children needed to talk about their hurts. This basic assumption and desire to help children are certainly valid. We have to be aware, however, of two basic principles:

1. Children do not always talk using words.
2. Often we do not need to worry about what to say, but what not to say.

Troubled children often revert to the behavior and understanding of a much younger child. Thus children who are usually able to express themselves quite well verbally may find it hard to talk about their feelings about the trauma. Adults and children often find it hard to put into words what has happened to them, since by doing so they make the trauma a reality—a reality that may be too difficult for them to deal with. Furthermore, older children are often very sensitive to the needs of their caregivers, so they may not want to describe their experiences in order not to upset their caregivers or to avoid risking rejection from their caregivers.

Our role as counselors is to enable children to explore and gain mastery—a sense of control—over their feelings and to make sense of their experiences (Ayalon 1988). This role is basically a listening one. In the example of Sara that I described at the beginning of this chapter, the counselor's success in beginning to build a relationship with her was helped by the way the counselor said relatively little.

Helping a Child Talk

Looking at Sara's case example helps us to see what helps a child to talk. The counselor needs to build a trusting, safe relationship with the child and so must provide:

a) Time

Often in a disaster situation, time is a luxury. Distressed children and adults surround us. It is difficult for us to give a child one and a half hours as I gave to Sara that day. Both from my own work and from the experiences of other therapists working with child survivors, however, (e.g., Yule and Williams 1992), the importance of giving a child reliable unhurried time is essential so that they can begin to share their story.

If you are unavoidably called away while meeting with a child, it is important to acknowledge to the child that you recognize that this is unacceptable. Ask the child's permission to leave or apologize to the child and set up a new time to meet with him or her.

Most therapists would recommend between half an hour to an hour for a listening session with a child, since you will spend at least ten minutes of each session reestablishing your relationship (you will need more time in the early sessions). You need to be careful not to rush a child or push him or her in your enthusiasm to help. One characteristic marks all new counselors—they try too hard to use all the techniques they have learned, and to find solutions for their clients' distress. As a good counselor you need to try to stop and give the child space to be silent or to talk. Let the child do the "work." Healing is often a slow process, so do not think that slow change equals no change.

b) A safe place

If you are going to be successful in encouraging a child to talk and to help the child to let down his or her defenses, the place where you talk must be safe, both physically and emotionally. Often a child will find a place where he or she feels safe, such as a bedroom, under a particular tree, or behind a building.

If the place is not physically safe or is a location where you will be interrupted, it is often useful to go to a place the child has chosen. We need to ask the child's permission to join him or her. In Sara's case, I made sure that my hospital colleagues, and especially Sara's father, were kept out of the playroom while I was there with her. I did not invade her part of the playroom until she gave me permission to do so.

In Liberia I spent many hours sitting, often in silence, under the palm trees by the sea with bereaved and troubled teenagers. They were using the sound of the sea to soothe their pain and the beach to remind them of their loved ones whose murdered bodies often lay badly buried under our feet.

c) A safe space

Emotional safety is as important as physical safety in a counseling situation. Most children in normal situations see adults as figures of physical safety, but will often reluctantly share their normal fears and worries with them. They are more likely to talk to their peers. Traumatized children are even more likely to perceive adults as "unsafe," because often adults will have been responsible for causing their trauma, such as by raping them or torturing or killing their parents. Children are also often wary about how confidential an adult can be with their stories. It is essential to clarify with children if you can keep their stories confidential, and in what circumstances you would have to break this confidentiality.

Later in this book there is a discussion of the issue of your needs as caregivers. I must emphasize the need to give yourself space to resolve and work with your own pain. We will only let a child properly explore what we ourselves can explore. For example, if you have been sexually abused or lost loved ones, it is difficult for you to hear and hold the feelings that a child with similar experiences may have. Children are often very adept at detecting how emotionally "safe" a person is, whether an individual really wants to or can hear their hurts.

Both children and adults have defense mechanisms that are conscious, and more usually subconscious, ways of defending ourselves psychologically from being hurt. For example, when you hear some bad news you often initially feel very numb. This numbness protects you from fully realizing what has happened. This is a useful biological mechanism, because it enables you to escape or to cope initially with the situation. As discussed elsewhere in this book, however, if we do not feel safe we may build up our psychological defenses to such an extent that we either detach ourselves from our experiences and appear not to care, or we may become very distressed and unable to cope with everyday life.

The children we are counseling in war situations have often been holding their pain for a very long time. They have not had the opportunity for what is called "critical incident debriefing"—an opportunity to talk about the experiences and to normalize feelings immediately after the trauma. Such a debriefing appears to reduce greatly the development of post-traumatic stress disorder (PTSD) (Dyregrov and Mitchell 1988). We need to gently encourage children to feel safe enough to reveal their pain.

d) Reliability

A principal feature of PTSD is a sense of feeling vulnerable and out of control. One of the primary purposes of therapy or counseling is to help children regain a sense of being in control of their situation, feelings and reactions. To assist in this, it is important that the persons involved with helping the traumatized child are reliable, that is, they keep counseling appointments with a child or let a child know if they cannot keep an appointment.

e) A clear role

Often people who are caring for children have to adopt several different roles such as caregiver, teacher and counselor. The role of the counselor is to provide the child with an accepting, listening environment, and offer the child unconditional love. It is helpful, therefore, if the person who is a child's counselor is not also the child's teacher, or seen in a disciplining role. Also, counselors ideally are not involved both in counseling the child and in helping the whole family. Otherwise it is difficult to decide who should be your priority.

Families in crisis often generate a great deal of emotional conflict. Unless counselors are clear about their role from the beginning, they can get entangled in these emotional conflicts and demands, feeling very hurt or "scapegoated" (inappropriately blamed for everything that is going wrong or hurting the family, and becoming "vessels" or containers for the family's anger and guilt). "Scapegoating" occurs because, when we are troubled, we look for a reason for our pain and— even as Christians—we look for someone to blame.

Unless a counselor has a clear role and proper support, the family may blame him or her for things that are not the counselor's fault (such as the family's homelessness or someone's death). The counselor may feel very hurt as a result. It is important to clarify with the children and their families what your role is before you start to help them. Children are very much influenced by their family's reactions to disasters, so it is essential to assess the family's reaction as well as the child's.

A counselor may talk to the child about God's discipline and forgiveness, to help the child restore his or her relationship with God and release the child from the burden of guilt and anger. The counselor's primary role, however, is to "be there" for the child, to accept and not judge. This can be particularly difficult if the child was a soldier, and may even have killed people whom the counselor loved. Providing regular support, supervision and opportunities for individual help for counselors are essential to prevent them from projecting on the child their anger about the tragedy.

f) Respect

Many people think that respect is a proper attitude we should have toward adults or elders. The counseling situation demands that the counselor give such respect to any counselee (person receiving the counsel), whether adult or child. The counselor's role is not to make the child talk. A counselor must encourage the child to express distress, disquieting thoughts and feelings, but also to respect the child's need for silence concerning a particularly painful memory or embarrassing incident. The counselor must be non-judgmental, not just in their response to what the child has done, but also to what the child finds distressing.

g) Trust

The characteristics of the counselor and counseling situation discussed so far affect the degree of trust between a counselor and a child. Trust is the most important quality of a counseling relationship; it cannot be bought. Both counselor and counselee must nurture it, and it may take a long time because wars often reveal how unreliable and selfish adults are.

In a disaster, trust is frequently abused. Social norms and taboos are often overturned, either deliberately or accidentally. To a young child, a parent is totally trustworthy, all-powerful and all-caring. Since a parent is often unable to fulfill these demands in a war, children often find it hard to trust them again and to regain a sense of the normal social order.

h) The counselor's knowledge of the trauma

When beginning to help a traumatized child, it is useful to try to gain an idea of what has happened to the child. This information may have to come from the child, but it is useful if caregivers or other reliable witnesses can also provide it. This information will enable the counselor to ask the child appropriate, sensitive questions and yet not invade the child's feelings too harshly by asking hurtful questions inadvertently. For example, in the story of Sara, my knowledge that her father had abused her in her bedroom enabled me to change into a feminine dress and not to mention fathers or bedrooms until she began to trust me more and was less afraid of me.

Knowledge of the effects of PTSD (described in chapter two) enables the counselor to assess the child's severity and type of

164

trauma, the child's recovery and the effects of counseling support. It can also help to highlight a child's particular problems, such as specific fears. It is often difficult to sort out which part of a disaster a child is reacting to, since disasters result in both fear and loss, and so a child's response is usually a trauma, a fright response and a bereavement response (Terr 1981, 1991). Clarifying a child's response and needs requires sensitive listening and counseling, because children themselves often do not know what is troubling them.

i) Support systems

A question children often ask me when they come for counseling concerns what they should do if they want to talk and I am not there. They have previously hidden their pain behind a big psychological wall or defense system. If we are encouraging children to talk about their fears and distress, we may be unlocking a great volcano of pain and tears. This can feel very frightening and make a child sense that they are out of control.

As a responsible counselor, it is essential to help the children identify several people they can go to for support. These may be other caring adults, or they may be other children who have had to cope with similar traumas. Such self-help support groups can be very effective in helping children cope with disasters and find healing in their pain.

j) Responsiveness, a listening ear

The role of the counselor is to listen and respond to the child's needs and hurts. Unlike many social situations, the counselee (the child) is ultimately in control of the progress in a counseling situation. It is useful to establish certain ground rules at the beginning, particularly if the counselor is using play therapy techniques. The following describes some basic ground rules for being a good counselor, and gives techniques for dealing with common, difficult emotions that children often experience:

- See that no one gets hurt (play or fantasy hurt is allowed);

◆ Assure the child that what happens in the session stays in the session, or that counselors will keep confidential what the child shares with them;

◆ Be sure that the session only lasts for a set period.

These rules help children feel safe in the session and enable them to regain some sense of normality. For example, a child who spent most of his childhood as a child soldier may find it difficult to relate to another child or adult, and to know what the difference is between really hurting someone and play hurting.

After establishing these ground rules, it is also important to check that the child's basic needs (food, water, shelter) are being met. If a child is hungry or has nowhere to sleep, he or she is not unlikely to be able to concentrate on her feelings.

The main role of a counselor is to provide a listening, loving ear for a child. That sounds so simple and deceptively easy. It is very easy for the adult counselor, however, to try to take control of the situation and start advising the child what to do.

This is a natural response. When faced with a crying, hurting child, we want to try to make the pain go away; we become anxious and we search for solutions. It is very difficult to give children what they need: an accepting, listening silence. We find it difficult to cope with silence. We often feel we are failures as counselors if a child does not talk. But it can be incredibly healing for hurting children if you will just sit quietly and let them slowly try to put their feelings into words.

k) Creating a loving atmosphere

Children are usually in touch with their environments. Infants will touch, throw or smear their food as they taste and eat it. They are not usually being naughty, but are simply exploring their environment with all of their senses. When children are in distress, their physical and emotional environment is especially important. Children perceive an environment as friendly, loving or hostile based on nonverbal communications and the tone of peoples' voices, more than whether comfortable equipment and seats fill a room.

We need to be aware of how our voice tone may sound to a small child or troubled teenager. Our body language can enhance or contradict the message that we give to a child by the tone of our voice. Body language is specific to a person's culture. For example, folded arms and legs can suggest defensiveness and possible hostility. A tilted head, arms relaxed across the body, legs crossed just at the ankles usually suggests an open, inviting, listening counselor.

We need to look and listen to those postures that are emotionally important in a culture, especially when viewed through the eyes of a child. For example, an abused child I once worked with preferred that I sit with my hands clasped together until he came to trust me; then he knew that he would not be held, interfered with, or hit. He knew where my hands were. We must use physical contact with care so that the child perceives it as holding and nurturing instead of invading and abusing. For a very troubled child, it may be better to use your body language to suggest intimacy rather than actually touching the child.

In the story of Sara, we had three sessions together before we had any physical contact—which Sara initiated. It consisted simply of her touching my hand. I did not return her touch until the next session, but I smiled in response to her touch to encourage her and to let her know that it was okay.

In Liberia I saw two children who had been separated forcibly from their mother and were desperate for physical contact from a mother figure. They followed me everywhere, holding onto my skirt. Part of the counseling for these children was nurturing them, enabling them to slowly separate from me and work through their feelings of abandonment and rejection so they could learn to understand a normal, loving relationship, and not be open to abuse in their driving need for affection. *Co - dependency*

We need to listen to, and try to meet, an individual child's needs. The danger in a disaster is that we feel overwhelmed by the sheer number of children in need, and we assume that they all have similar needs. We need to allow children to have and to enjoy their individuality. It can be helpful to put children with similar needs

167

together to support each other, but we must also allow children to regain a sense of their own needs and identity.

l) Facilitative materials

Often in a disaster we have very limited resources, such as play materials and relaxing chairs. Very simple gestures or resources, however, can transform counseling situations.

I saw a child in Liberia who felt very uncomfortable when we spoke to each other while seated on the upright chairs provided in the schoolroom. The chairs faced each other in a formation that suggested aggressive combat or disciplining. The child associated the setting with discipline and learning. We went outside in the yard and spread a blanket on the ground that we could sit on. The blanket created a "safe world" in which we could talk, despite the noise of other children and the traffic around us. By coming down to the child's level, by my willingness to go to a place where he felt safe, I found he could begin to talk about his painful memories and allow himself to cry. Another child preferred to talk in my room or in the jeep, where he felt that others could not hear him or see him cry, and where his emotions felt more contained and safe.

The next chapter explores how you can adapt various play materials for your use in talking with children; you do not need Western toys. Watch children in the street after a disaster. They will create what they need to explore their memories and feelings.

Besides these general factors that help a child to talk, there are certain basic counseling or listening skills that a support worker or counselor can use to encourage a child or teenager to say what he or she needs to say.

Helping a counselor or support worker listen

There are various techniques you can use to encourage children to talk, and to show them that you have heard them. This second part of the counseling conversation is very important if children are to feel emotionally held, and to know that you want to hear their pain. Both children and adults recognize very quickly when someone is only listening out of duty. A powerful technique is reflecting to a child some of what he or she has just said to you. The following conversation illustrates how to do this.

Child: . . . and then the soldiers got her; there was nothing that I could do.

Counselor: There was nothing you could do.

Child: Yeah, I couldn't get to her. They were hurting her; I should have stopped them; I couldn't—

Counselor: So you felt very helpless.

Child: Yeah, and I still feel like that, I mean you should, I should have been able to save her so I—I'm meant to be a big man now (he was eight years old), I mean I've looked after my two sisters, but they got my mama (cries).

Counselor: (Sits still in silence, hands child a handkerchief.) That sounds like a horrendous situation to have to cope with, and it still hurts. (Child nods.) You seem to have felt so helpless and guilty that you couldn't—

Child: They were so big; there were five of them—(cries).

Counselor: So if you had tried to rescue your mama, they would probably have gotten you, too, and you wouldn't have been able to care for your sisters.

Child: I never thought of that. Yeah, they were too big for me, and mama shouted at me to look after my sisters.

Counselor: So you are doing what she asked you to. She would be proud of you.

Child: Yeah, (suddenly smiles) she would. Would Jesus too?

Counselor: Yes (smiles, pauses, and prays briefly for the family).

Child:	Do you think Jesus is looking after my mama? She used to talk to him each night. She would have forgiven those soldiers. I can forgive them, but those big men. They did wrong.
Counselor:	It's okay to feel angry with them. Jesus will help you forgive them when you're ready to. (Silence. Child prays. Pause.)
Child:	I'm hungry!
Counselor:	We'll go and get some food then. How are you all coping?
Child:	We got a place; my friend's auntie, she gives us some food; we go to the center if we need medicine.
Counselor:	And the sleeping?
Child:	The nightmares still come and I jump all the time. I can hear her screaming but they are less when I talk to you.
Counselor:	Shall we talk about them now?
Child:	No, I'm hungry!
Counselor:	Do you want to meet this time next week?
Child:	Yeah, and I'll bring my diary. It helps me when you're not here to talk to.

A listener may reflect back to a child what the child has said or what he felt.

A listener can help a child to feel *understood and affirmed* (valued, thought well of) by statements such as these. We must be careful not to tell a child what she or he is feeling or thinking. We *offer* her or him our interpretations or ideas: "It seems to me that . . . ," "It sounds like . . . ." This enables the child to reject what you have said. It is hard for a child to do this under normal circumstances because children usually perceive adults as all-powerful. This is especially true in a counseling situation when the child often feels very vulnerable.

If a child is telling you a difficult or complicated story, you can check your understanding of the story by occasionally *summarizing* parts of what the child has said, and offering him or her new ways of thinking about the situation, especially his or her response to it. The counselor must take care to be sensitive when making such interpretations because a child may need the guilt or anger, and not be ready yet to give it to Jesus, or to reinterpret it.

The counselor can also help the child cope with the intensity of the feelings by allowing the child to decide when she or he has talked enough for one session and needs his or her basic needs met. Arranging the time for the next session and giving the child a choice about it enables the child to feel in control of the session. The counselor in the preceding reflecting example used several *open questions* to ask how the child felt.

An open question is one that a child cannot answer "yes" or "no" to, and so encourages the child to talk more openly. Questions using the words *how*, *why*, *what* and *shall* are open questions. Asking a child *do you*, *can you* or *did you* questions are closed questions. Closed questions can be useful for gaining specific information from a child. Do not encourage children to talk if they do not want to, however, because they can be polite and reply by nodding or shaking their heads.

Unless it is inappropriate because of the child's spiritual orientation, it is helpful if the counselor prays with the child at the end of each session. This helps the child feel that Jesus is with the child and is holding the child's pain. It is also helpful to encourage children to give Jesus the people they have lost, so they can feel that he is looking after them. Just as children and adults need to feel that their loved ones are safe and cared for, so they can also release themselves from caring for them and from feeling guilty about them.

As counselors we try to stand in the child's shoes, hear the child's pain and understand how the child feels, thinks and behaves about what has happened. In the example given on pages 169-170, the counselor never told the boy that she understood. You can never really understand. You can only try to hold, hear and, through Jesus, heal their pain.

Specific techniques

The most valuable part of any therapy for a child is for the child to share his or her story and to feel that someone listened to them. Yule and Williams (1990) and Yule (1991) found with children they studied that such sharing, either with their peers in an emotionally safe environment or with a counselor, greatly reduced the children's symptoms of PTSD.

Terr (1983) says that in her view talking is an essential part of therapy even for young children. Playing is not enough. Play therapy (combining play, drama and counseling techniques) is more helpful. A child needs the verbal exchange with a caring listener to help process or sort out the experiences in the child's head (Rachman 1980). A child can let herself or himself forget, or at least not remember as vividly, what she or he has experienced. Then the child can get on with life in the here and now.

An approach where children remain relaxed while slowly learning to confront situations more like the trauma they experienced is called "systematic desensitization." Good, sensitive counseling is vital during this process. Offering a child new ways of understanding the trauma or encouraging the child to develop his or her own understanding of it enables a child to "cognitively restructure" or rethink the trauma and releases them from the paralyzing emotions it produces. You will often need to follow up such individual work by working with the family to help the family release the child from the role the child developed in the disaster (that of a pseudo [false] parent or an overprotected invalid), and so can develop as normally as possible (MacFarlane, 1987).

Most counselors or therapists working with traumatized children focus on the trauma itself instead of exploring the child's pre-trauma experiences (Pynoos and Nader 1988). Time and resources sometimes do not permit any other approach in a disaster situation. After a disaster it is most urgent that children talk about their experiences as soon after the event as possible (debriefing). With many children that you are working with, that will not be possible. Even if it is delayed, however, counseling and support can be invaluable for many children.

Some children will probably never be released from their trauma and pain. They have been too badly damaged and may find it too frightening to talk through their distress. For many such children—including teenagers—structured play therapy and drama techniques, explored in the next chapter, can offer them an invaluable emotional release. But of all the techniques and insights that you may learn, the greatest gift we can offer a child is ourselves—loving, holding, helping them to talk, listening, accepting and hearing their distress.

We can be instruments of Jesus' love for them here and now as they relax into his arms and open their hearts and minds for his healing.

REFERENCES

Ayalon, O. *Rescue! Community Orientated Preventive Education for Coping with Stress.* Haifa: Nord Publications, 1988.

Dyregrov, A. and J. T. Mitchell. "Critical Incident Stress De-briefing." *Norwegian Journal of Psychology,* 25:1988, pp. 217-224.

MacFarlane, A. C. "Family functioning and over-protection following a natural disaster: The longitudinal effects of post-traumatic morbidity." *Australian and New Zealand Journal of Psychiatry,* 21:1987, pp. 210-218.

Pynoos, R. S. and K. Nader. "Psychological first aid and treatment approach for children exposed to community violence: Research implications." *Journal of Traumatic Stress,* 1:1988, pp. 243-67.

Rachman, S. "Emotional Processing." *Behaviour Research and Therapy* 18:1980, pp. 51-60.

Terr, L. "Psychic trauma in children: Observations following the Chowchilla school bus kidnapping." *American Journal of Psychology,* 138:1981, pp. 14-19.

Terr, L. "Play Therapy and Psychic Trauma: A Preliminary Report." *Handbook of Play Therapy,* C. E. Schaefer and K. J. O'Connor, eds. Chichester: Wiley, 1983.

Terr, L. "Childhood traumas: An outline and overview." *American Journal of Psychiatry*, 148:1991, pp. 10-20.

Yule, W. and R. Williams. "Post Traumatic Stress Reactions in Children." *Journal of Traumatic Stress*, 3:2 April 1990, pp. 279-295.

Yule, W. "Working with children following disasters." *Clinical Child Psychology: Theory and Practice*, M. Herbert, ed. Chichester: Wiley, 1991.

Yule, W. and R. Williams. "The management of trauma disasters." *Child and Adolescent Therapy*, D. A. Lane and A. Miller, eds. Buckingham: Open University Press, 1992.

11

"O" Equals Organized Play: A Necessary Method for Helping and Healing

Mickie Heard

The ever-present questions, especially from workers in countries where children are physically and emotionally traumatized by war and violence are: "What permanent damage has been done?" "How do we help these children?" and "Can these children ever recover and become mature, responsible adults?"

Since we know from research that abused children have a high tendency to become abusive adults, it is imperative that those who minister to traumatized children do so in a way that helps to keep these children from becoming adults who in turn abuse others. In this chapter I will suggest that child-centered play therapy is one of the most powerful ways to help children recapture what was so violently taken from them: control, power, safety and hope.

Why play therapy?

Play is the child's rehearsal or practice for life, and it is through play that the child finds the root of future successes. During play children can switch roles, control situations, and experiment with a variety of scenes where they can be the author, star and director of their world. Research has shown that if children can play well, they will adjust well as adults.

Play also tells us much about a child's life. Play is the "language" of the child. Play can tell us how children think, feel, believe; it can tell us of pain, conflict and security. When children are playing, they can feel powerful, have a sense of control over their world and can create, reenact and recreate situations in a way that helps give hope for the future. When we honor and value the play of children, their play will tell us things about them that we could not know otherwise.

Those who value the personhood of children should also value the play of children. I must note, however, that playground play is not "play therapy." (Therapy refers to a method of treatment used to facilitate healing and the therapist is the person helping in the healing process.) Play therapy gives a child the right and privilege to play with an adult. The child is in control of the play, and once the therapist and the child have established a safe relationship, the child will begin to go directly to his or her area of pain and concern through the play.

The importance of the therapist-child relationship

One of the most important aspects of effective play therapy is the relationship between the child and the one working with the child. Special training is not necessary to assist a child in a play situation if there is an open respect for children and their play, and if the adult does what seems or feels helpful for the child and *the child alone.*

It takes two sessions to become a helper to the child, because children need time to learn to trust and to believe that you will not be like other adults and violate their personhood. Traumatized children have been violated and abused, and have lost confidence that they will receive what they expect from the world of adults: safety, protection, comfort and respect. Their experience has often proved just the opposite: "Adults hurt me. I am powerless to defend myself. I have no control. I am worthless. Adults use me."

The younger the child, the more likely the child will interpret these abusive relationships as her or his own fault. The child may also feel more conflict concerning the basic need for nurture and the inability to receive that nurture from an adult. Trust is almost completely erased from the child's experience.

The therapist-child relationship then becomes increasingly important as the child moves toward healing. What happens in the relationship is that the adult therapist begins to provide security, protection, safety, validation, respect, trust and hope for the child. As children move toward expressing their area of pain and concern, they will continue to check to see if the adult remains someone they can trust.

It is important for the person helping the child to honor what the child gives at the level it is given. For example, if the child tells a fantastic story it is important for the helper to respond to the story in a manner that helps the child realize that no matter what the child says, he or she is an important person and is to be believed.

Correcting the story the child gives, or asking questions to clarify the fantasy, puts the helper in control and the child will stop genuine communication. Traumatized children have had an experience of adults who have misused power. The moment the adult helper uses power over the child during a play session, that child will stop the play, stop communicating, and may even retreat into a position of defense and aggression.

Defining play therapy—theories

I will describe play therapy and discuss such questions as: Where do I begin? What do I need to "do" play therapy? How do I observe child's play and make some interpretation? How do I talk empathically to affirm the child? But first let us look at some different theories of play therapy that will help us better understand the concepts.

Child therapy is different from adult therapy because it is not based on a cognitive model. Children trade *experiences* for learned knowledge. In their play they are telling you, "This is what it is like to be me."

For traumatized children, playing puts them in a healthier environment. This is an essentially complete environment where pleasure can be independent of external rewards (separate from the frightening situation from which they came) and where they can express themselves as persons instead of objects abused and used by others. Play is person-dominated, not object-dominated.

One of the most important things to realize is that "play is a process of development of a child" (Schaefer 1983:95). When we recognize how important playing is for the development of the child, we can recognize the need for providing traumatized children a place to play, an opportunity to play, and things to play with to help them reenter their developmental cycle, which has been so violently interrupted. It would seem that the sooner we can intervene *with play* in the life of a traumatized child, the sooner the child can appropriate the healing effects of the playing environment and the sooner hope will reenter the child's world of experience.

Play has been alternately depicted as a mechanism for developing problem solving and competency skills, a process that allows children to mentally digest experiences and situations, an emotional laboratory in which the child learns to cope with his or her environment, a way that the child talks, with toys as his words, and a way to deal with behaviors and concerns through playing it out (Gil 1991:27).

Some people view play activities as the main therapeutic approach for children because it is a natural medium for self-expression, it facilitates a child's communication, it allows for a cleansing release of feelings, it can be renewing and constructive, and it allows the adult a window to observe the child.

Psychoanalytic play therapy

There are two different ways to look at the purpose of play in this kind of therapy or treatment. One advocates using play mainly to build a strong positive relationship between child and helper. The other is to use play as a direct substitute for verbalizations. The goal here is to "help children work through difficulties or trauma by helping them gain insight" (Schaefer and O'Connor 1983).

A. H. Esman (1983:19) describes the focus of play in psychoanalytic child therapy this way: "It allows for the communication of wishes, fantasies, and conflicts in ways the child can tolerate effectively and express at the level of his or her cognitive capacities." He goes on to say that the therapist's function is to "observe, attempt to understand, integrate, and ultimately communicate the meanings of the child's play in order to promote the child's understanding of his or her conflict toward the end of more adaptive resolution."

Structured play therapies

A more goal-oriented therapy, known as "structure therapy," comes from the belief that play itself is cleansing in nature. The therapist's active role is to be the guide of what should occur in

Play therapy is information gathering
— releasing + expressing emotions

the therapy session. Structured play therapy has been considered best for extremely traumatized children as long as the therapist's structure *does not become intrusive*.

What is usually meant by the word "structured" is that the therapist helps the child recreate the traumatic event through play. The therapist puts only certain kinds of toys in the room and guides the child to recreate his or her trauma. The therapist may tell the child what to draw or paint or what toys to use. The goal of this type of play is to help the child assimilate the negative thoughts and feelings associated with the trauma by reenacting it repeatedly.

It is important to be certain that a strong relationship exists between the child and the helper before structuring sessions in this manner. The dynamics of reenactment can be very powerful for the child, and it is essential that the child feel completely safe and secure with the helper as the child begins to express needs and feelings during this structured play. Also, it is important to be ready to intervene during this reenactment when it seems that the child is overcome by strong emotions and cannot assimilate them.

Relationship therapies

Otto Rank and Carl Rogers were key leaders in the area of relationship theory. This theory is based on a personality theory that "assumes that an individual has within himself not only the ability to solve his own problems but also a growth force that makes mature behaviour more satisfying than immature behaviour" (Schaefer 1980:101).

Relationship therapy promotes the complete acceptance of the child and stresses the importance of the relationship between the child and therapist. Clark E. Moustakas (1959), another prominent leader in the field of child therapy, emphasizes the importance of the therapist's genuineness as key to the success of therapy. Virginia Axline (1969) calls the relationship between therapist and child as the "deciding factor" in the success of the therapeutic process.

Group therapy

S. R. Slavson (1947) experimented with group situations, guiding latency-age children through activities, games, arts and crafts designed to help them "release emotional and physical tensions." In 1950 Schiffer developed what began to be known as "therapeutic play groups," in which children could interact freely with minimal intervention from those assisting. The unique aspect of this type of therapy, according to Schiffer, is that "the child has to learn to share an adult with other children."

We can see this approach may be very beneficial to workers in war-torn communities who need to work with many children at a time. Group therapy, however, requires more energy and effort from the therapist because of the number of children the therapist must observe. It is not only important to observe each individual child's behavior but also to observe the interactive behaviors of all the children simultaneously.

Group therapy requires the commitment of two or three adults who can be present consistently. Effective group treatment must contain the following elements:

> Leadership, preferably with male and female co-therapists, involves developing cohesiveness, identifying goals for the group, showing the group how to function, keeping the group task-oriented, serving as a model, and representing a value system. In carrying out these tasks, the leader may offer clarification of reality, analysis of transactions, brief education input, empathic statements acknowledging his own feelings and those of members, and at times delineating the feeling states at hand in the group (Kraft 1980:129).

Group therapy needs more structure and is therapist-directed. Some concerns are that group therapy sometimes lacks clear goals, can go on for indefinite periods, and often suffers from inconsistent and inexperienced leadership.

If group therapy is the necessary method of treatment, it will be important to have an understanding of developmental psychology and group dynamics, have consistency in leadership and have clearly stated guidelines and goals with a specific time frame for the sessions.

Group therapy can be done along with one-on-one therapy as part of the whole healing process for children. The therapist should place children in a group with others of approximately the same age. If there is a wide diversity of ages (6-14 years for example), the group dynamics change as the younger ones model the older ones. The need for approval by the older children may threaten or prevent the younger children's honest expressions. It may also keep the older ones from facing their own fears and needs as they focus on trying to protect or harass the younger children.

Directive versus non-directive play therapy

The simplest way of describing the types of therapy used with children is to make a distinction between directive and non-directive styles of play therapy. Non-directive or child-centered play therapy, promoted by relationship therapists, is non-intrusive. Axline (1969), credited with the development of this specific kind of play therapy, distinguished between non-directive and directive therapy by saying, "Play therapy may be directive in form—that is, the therapist may assume responsibility for guidance and interpretation—or it may be non-directive—the therapist may leave responsibility and direction to the child."

In non-directive play therapy, the therapist allows and encourages the child to choose the toys he or she will play with and the child has the freedom to develop or end any particular theme or subject. The therapist is the observer in the room and joins in the game or scene if, and only if, asked to do so by the child. The child may "ask" in different ways. She or he may say, "Will you play with me?" or "Here, you do this!" or may simply begin to use the therapist as part of the scene.

It is essential that the therapist allow the child to take the leadership of the play and respond only when invited. The therapist is not really a "playmate" who interjects personal imaginative ideas and suggestions. The non-directive play therapist observes the child's play and affirms observations verbally. Non-directive therapists give the child concentrated attention and refrain from answering questions or giving directives.

The basic difference between the non-directive and directive approaches rests in the role of the adult therapist.

> Directive therapists structure and create the play situation, attempting to elicit, stimulate, and intrude upon the child's unconscious, hidden processes or overt behavior by challenging the child's defense mechanisms and encouraging or leading the child in directions that are seen as beneficial (Gil 1991).

Non-directive therapists are "actually controlled, always centered on the child, and attuned to her communications, even the subtle ones" (Guerney 1980). A directive therapist may ask the child to draw something specific or use the puppets to act out some specific scene. The non-directive therapist will have drawing materials and puppets equally available to the child and will then wait to see if and how the child uses these "tools."

In my personal practice I have seen the value of using both directive and non-directive therapy with children. I find, however, that non-directive therapy seems to yield a deeper, more complete healing for the child. I believe this is because an assumption of non-directive therapy is the belief that the child knows what he or she needs for healing.—+ *will eventually tell you*

I also believe that the child feels more personal affirmation through self-discovery than through adult-controlled or directed discovery. It is also important to know that different children in the same family, or children who have suffered the same traumatic event, will experience the event differently.

It is important to recognize the uniqueness of each individual. While play therapy research can give us some general principles, only a close examination of each individual and discovering how each individual responds to the traumatic event will reveal how best to work with that particular person.

Basic components of a play therapy session

Now that I have talked *about* play therapy, let me *describe* play therapy and answer some of the questions presented earlier. I will give personal examples from case studies to help strengthen the understanding of the components of play therapy.

Where do I begin?

Begin with a prayerful heart and a love for children. Any adult who respects the personhood of a child, recognizing that the child—at any age—is made in God's image and deserves respect, can be helpful to a child in a play setting. For the Christian worker, it is also essential to spend time in prayer for the child before, during and after every encounter.

Axline (1969) outlines eight basic principles of play therapy:

1. The therapist must develop a warm, friendly relationship with the child, establishing good rapport as soon as possible.

2. The therapist accepts the child exactly as he is.

3. The therapist establishes a feeling of permissiveness in the relationship so that the child feels free to express his feelings completely.

4. The therapist is alert to recognize the *feelings* the child is expressing and reflects those feelings back to him so that he gains insight into his behavior.

5. The therapist maintains a deep respect for the child's ability to solve his own problems if given an opportunity to do so. The responsibility to make choices and to institute change is the child's.

6. The therapist does not attempt to direct the child's actions or conversation in any manner. The child leads the way; the therapist follows.

7. The therapist does not attempt to hurry the therapy along. It is a gradual process and is recognized as such by the therapist.

8. The therapist establishes only those limitations that are necessary to anchor the therapy to the world of reality and to make the child aware of his responsibility in the relationship.

When beginning your work with a group of children, it is important to let them know immediately that you respect them. You may use the format of the following example to introduce yourself to the children to let them know what it is they are about to do. I usually start by saying something like this:

> Hi, my name is Mickie and this is a room where children come to play and to talk to me. Sometimes I talk to the children about their feelings and sometimes we just play. We can do whichever you want. Would you like to look around?

In this opening statement, the therapist tries to establish rapport and place the sense of control with the child. Forcing the child to enter the therapeutic process can feel like reabuse for the traumatized child. It is more helpful to mirror the child's feelings and actions so that the child feels understood by the therapist. This will be much more satisfying for the child and will allow the child freedom to continue to express feelings without fear. Children are so perceptive (aware or discerning) that they already know that this is a place where things are different. Sometimes they are very eager to enter the process because they already have a sense that this "therapy" will be helpful.

One young boy who had been traumatized by the death of an older brother was having nightmares, fears of abandonment, hysteria and loss of appetite. His parents had talked to him, prayed with him, tried to reassure him that "God would never leave him," and encouraged him to "give his fears to Jesus." But this approach, which they thought was biblical, did not seem to "fix his problem." So the mother said, "If your behavior doesn't change we will probably have to take you to see someone; we are at our wit's end!" The son then replied tearfully, "Well, maybe that's what I need." What the parents had intended as a "last resort," the child viewed as a relief. Someone else may be able to help him sort this all out.

One of the first things children experience on entering a play therapy session is that there is an adult interacting with them who is not *forcing* them to do anything. From the beginning the child has some options and some control of the situation. Some children will begin asking questions about the rules, others will ignore you and go right into a play scene. Either way they will be looking to read your reaction to them. When you, as the adult, do not force yourself on the children by telling them what to play, or by giving a list of dos and don'ts, and do not insist on "being in charge" yourself, the children will begin to relax and trust you.

It is important, however, that during the first few sessions you do give a few "ground rules." For instance, you may say, "You can play with anything you want, anyway you want to. This is a safe room. It is safe for you and for the toys. So we will keep the toys safe by not breaking them and we will keep you safe by not hurting yourself." Another time you could say, "All the toys stay in this room and whatever you do or say in this room will be private. If someone is hurting you and you tell me about it, I won't say anything unless I ask you first for permission. We may need to tell someone about it so that we can keep you safe. But that will be a decision that you and I will make together."

When a child believes that you respect his thoughts and privacy, the child can be more open. It is not wise to promise that you will never tell anyone anything, because that usually is not true. Sometimes, for the child's protection or to obtain needed assistance, we must report what has been shared. We need to respect the child's need to be ready to face the abuser or the problem, however, before we disclose too much. Confrontation too early in the child's treatment may endanger your trust relationship with the child and may even send him deeper into himself.

It is sometimes helpful at the beginning to obtain some information from the child to help you understand her or him better. The following are some questions that you may use to initiate conversation, especially with an older child:

- Who is your best friend? What do you like to do together?

- If you could change something about yourself, what would it be?

- Do you get angry with yourself? About what?

- What kinds of things are you afraid of?

- Can you tell me a good night dream you had? A scary one?

- Begin a story and have the child finish it. You can do this to lead into the subject of the child's fears, but save it for a time when you and the child have established a firm relationship.

Because violent abuse is an intrusive act, it is important that the healing relationship is one that is non-intrusive. We need to allow the child plenty of room for physical and emotional space. Abuse invades a child's private space; it blurs the boundaries between the child and the abusive adult. The child "feels too much" of the other person and loses that needed personal control or power over herself. The therapist, therefore, should not initiate physical contact with the child.

The younger the children, the more they feel that whatever an adult insists on doing is the right thing to do, and the more the children view themselves as an *object* rather than as a *person*. As the play therapist, you need to wait for the child to approach you. Since the child has had experiences with adults that are physically intrusive, he needs to know that you will not violate him in any way.

What do you need to "do" play therapy?

You need a room with toys—that's the beginning. It is just about as simple as it sounds, and yet it is also very complex. When the child enters that room, it becomes an extension of the child and that child's world of experience. The room becomes the place where the child can act out aggression, pain, hatred, joy, success and power without being violated or hurt. From the successes that take place in that room, the child will, we hope, transfer the experiences into the world outside. The children will return to that room each time to try out new things, take new risks and spend time reenacting the successes and failures of their experiences in the outside world. Soon they will not only feel safe in that room, they will also know how to keep themselves safe outside that room.

What kind of toys are helpful? A child's imagination can use just about anything, but the following are a few toys that others have found useful tools in the play therapy room:

> Baby bottle, ball, blanket, animals (domestic and wild), cars, clay, safe medical items (such as empty pill bottles or bandages), foam blocks, dolls, doll house, family figures, guns, rubber knife, paints, pillow, paper and crayons, stuffed animals, toy telephone and puppets.

Each cultural setting will need to adapt this list so that the toys represent the actual situation of the children you are helping.

Some may disagree with the aggressive toys—guns and knives—but these are some symbols of the real world, especially for children in war-affected areas. Part of the children's play is to use these items to reenact their real-life experience or trauma, to create different endings to the trauma and, in some way, begin to make sense of the violence that they have experienced. Whenever possible, however, use foam or rubber for this kind of toy. In this way, the children cannot hurt themselves or someone else as they act out any aggressive behavior.

Sometimes children will use whatever is available to recreate and gain control of their situation. For example, I was seeing one young girl whose traumatic experience had been intensified by a recent move to a new home. Here is how she worked it out during a session (names and situations have been changed slightly):

During one of our sessions, the play therapy room had a distinctive odor that Monica did not like. We were limited to using this space in spite of the smell because of other meetings in the building at that time. She announced that we would use markers to draw on large sheets of col-

ored paper. I began to draw. Apparently the smell in the room bothered Monica and she wanted to go into our "old room."

Monica:	I don't like it in here. It smells bad. I want to go in the other room.
Therapist:	You want to go where we cannot go. You don't like being stuck in here.
Monica:	I hate it here. It stinks.
Therapist:	You can leave if you like, but this is the only place we can be today.
Monica:	*(No response.)*

Later, we were not talking about the room anymore. Now we were discussing her situation. She turned to the wall and stomped her feet. As I colored, Monica stomped around the room stepping on the large pieces of colored paper, wrinkling and ripping them with her feet without saying anything. I responded occasionally by reflecting verbally what she was doing, putting a few actions into feelings and setting some boundaries:

Therapist:	You feel like leaving. You want to rip up all the paper. You like to stomp around. You feel angry when you can't go where you want to go. Monica, you may stomp and rip all you want as long as you do not stomp and rip on my papers. This is your time; you can decide to stomp your feet and rip your papers if you want.

After 15 minutes of ripping and stomping . . .

Monica:	I'm going to color now.
Therapist:	You have decided to color now.
Monica:	Yes, and then let's rip up all the papers and throw them into the air.
Therapist:	You want to color the paper, tear it up and throw it into the air.
Monica:	We will make beautiful confetti *(small pieces of colored paper thrown at each other during joyous celebrations.)*

189

> Therapist: You want to turn all these ripped papers into something beautiful.
>
> Monica: Yes, and let's save them forever!

It seemed to me that Monica's stomping and ripping exercise was her safe way of protesting against her current situation. In the play therapy room she was in an environment where she could express feelings of anger and frustration without fear of the consequences from an angry, disapproving adult. At the end of her protesting time, she decided to turn something bad into something good. She wasn't afraid to keep the confetti for it would be a reminder that she can face her fears and be successful.

One note: it is important to schedule into your session a cleanup time so that the next child comes into a neat playroom instead of into someone else's reality.

How do I observe child's play and make an interpretation?

Watching children and making an interpretation does take some skill and the layperson should do it very tentatively and prayerfully. I highly recommend checking over your interpretations with another adult to lessen the possibility of making interpretations based on your own bias (way of viewing the situation). Here are a few ideas for watching a child at play that can help in making an assessment:

- ◆ Watch the way the child enters the room. Does the child stay by the door or does he or she move toward a particular corner each time?

- ◆ Watch for repeated behaviors.

- ◆ Note the child's attitude and approach to the toys. Does he or she approach the toys with confidence? Is there any hesitation when picking up some toys and not others? Does the child change toys and games frequently and sporadically? Are there any particular toys that the child avoids consistently?

- ◆ What words or sounds do you hear being said or repeated with the toys?

◆ How do the children touch the toys? Are they creative in the way they use certain ones? Is there aggression, energy or passiveness?

◆ Do the children seem to be able to play? Or are they just investigating?

Then check to see if the play behavior is appropriate for the child's age. Look for repeated themes in the play. Do you notice anything unusual?

At first you may not see any particular pattern to the play behavior. If at the end of each session you write a few notes, however, after a time you will begin to see patterns that are clues to this particular child. Do not write things down while the child is in the room. Your full attention must be on the child and on being with him or her in the "adventure." Carrying a notebook distances you from the child. It is acceptable for you to play with clay or color on your own, making statements of fact while watching the child explore the room: "I am going to color. I will use bright colors." In this way children realize that you are not going to intrude on their way of using the room nor are you going to hurry them along in any particular direction.

The play of a traumatized child may be a reenactment of the traumatic scene with the use of dolls and toys. The child may set up the reenactment identically, almost ritualistically, each time. The potential benefit of this kind of play is that while the child is recreating frightening memories, the child is moving from a passive stance to an active one in which the child is now controlling the reenactment. Previously the overwhelming event happened *to* the child, while he or she was powerless to do anything about it. Now, however, during the reenactment the child is in control of the event and is recreating it in a controlled and safe environment. It is suggested that the child then gains a sense of mastery and empowerment from this type of play therapy.

There is very little you need to do during this kind of play other than sit and watch, unless the child invites you to participate. When children invite you to play, be sure to let them tell you and

191

direct you to what they want you to do. Do not make the mistake of getting carried away with your own imagination because you are "playing" with a child. In a play therapy setting, your involvement—at the child's request—is to be what that child wants, not what you think might be fun or interesting.

What about children's drawings?

When observing children's drawings, notice the kind of strokes used, the colors and the size of objects. Look for repeated objects or actions in the drawings.

In one picture drawn by a verbally and emotionally abused girl of nine whose parents were divorcing, the paper was first divided in half by drawing a line across the middle of the page. On the bottom half she drew herself and her brother. Then she turned the paper upside down and drew a picture of her mother and father at opposite sides of the paper. She had drawn her father as very large and her mother much smaller. She drew a broken line under her parents' feet and another line across the page that went through their necks. She then turned the paper upside down again to draw a line underneath the picture of herself and her brother.

It is easy to interpret a little of this picture. Her father is the larger influence in her life. In this new scene his leaving has turned her life and her family upside down and he has hurt them all. Her mother is not big enough to fix the situation.

How do I talk to affirm the child?

In non-directive play therapy the therapist's talk is reflective, often rephrasing what the child is saying. This allows the child to feel heard, perhaps for the first time. The therapist offers no interpretations, judgments, compliments, questions or advice. The therapist uses factual statements and repeats phrases the child has used. For example, a child enters the room and says, "I'm going to break all these toys!" The therapist puts these words into a feeling statement, "You feel like breaking all the toys" without any tone of opinion.

A child has a difficult time disagreeing with what an adult says. Therefore, interpretive statements by parents and other significant adults may be viewed as the only interpretation of reality for the child, even if that interpretation does not match the child's experience. By repeating the child's own thoughts and putting some of those actions into feeling statements, the therapist validates the child's words, thoughts and feelings. When the therapist offers no "correction" to the children's talk, the children feel free to continue to express themselves verbally.

Empathic listening allows the child to speak even more, and eventually the therapist will recognize that the child is beginning to reveal more inner thoughts and feelings. The caution here is to restrain our own words so as not to become intrusive with our language and interpretation, which will hinder the children's freedom to express themselves. Empathic listening is reminiscent of James 1:19, ". . . be quick to listen, slow to speak . . ."

Some experts have suggested that children begin to tell you about themselves and their pain as if they were drawing a large circle around themselves. The more validated they feel by your acceptance of their words in their outer circle, the more they will begin to bring you into their inner circles, and finally into the inner core of their life experiences and pain (Byron and Carol Norton 1991). Children will often begin revealing themselves and this "outer circle" by telling you stories and fantasies. If, by your empathic listening, you value the child's story, the child will believe that you are an adult he or she can trust, and soon the child will draw you into the child's inner circle.

The important thing is to remember not to make value judgments about what the children are saying, or to correct them, but to just go along with them. If they can trust you with their fantasy, then they will trust you with their truth. If you judge this outer circle story and say, "Now, that's not really true, is it?" after they have begun to weave a fantasy, they will feel they cannot trust you, that you always have to be right and that your being right is more important than your listening to them.

For example, if a child were to say to you, "I love to play with my lion and put my head in its mouth," an improper response could be, "You don't really have your own lion, do you?" This will invalidate the child, and she will decide not to tell you very much. The proper response might be, "You like to play with your lion and put your head in its mouth." Now the child can take you further into herself with more disclosure.

I am not suggesting that we lie to children by telling them in words, "I believe you when you say that you have a real lion and you put your head in its mouth." The child will wonder about *your* connection to reality. What I am suggesting is that by empathic listening and reflective speaking we enter into the story with the children, validating their experience of telling the story and showing them that we are someone who values the uniqueness of their thoughts and feelings.

Conclusion

Non-intrusive and child-centered play therapy can be an important tool in the hand of the adult who has a passion and concern for abused and traumatized children. This chapter gives some insights into the necessity of using play therapy as a way of empowering children to trust an adult, regain some control of their lives and then see that they can also trust God.

Children will be more ready to accept the idea of God's unconditional love for them when they have experienced it from God's representative here on earth—a caring, significant adult. It seems logical that the method to use for rebuilding trust in these abused and traumatized children would not be through an intrusive model, that is, a strict, disciplined schoolroom setting. Instead it would be through an unintrusive model—a meaningful interaction with a caring adult who is interested in encouraging children to rediscover their sense of self through play and to empower the children by providing them with a safe and protective environment. In this safe and expressive environment the child can feel validated and respected.

Playing in an environment of mutual respect, children can begin to heal themselves. And we have the privilege of their invitation to accompany them on their healing journey. It will be on that journey—as non-intrusively and respectfully as possible—that we can point them to Jesus Christ, the one who knows their pain, shares their sorrows and wants to touch them with healing power so that they can be whole again. How better to accomplish this than through the medium of play, the developmental language of a child's world.

REFERENCES

Axline, Virginia. *Play Therapy.* New York: Ballantine Books, 1969.

Gil, Eliana. *The Healing Power of Play: Working with Abused Children.* New York: Gilford Press, 1991.

Esman, A. H. "Psychoanalytic play therapy." *Handbook of Play Therapy,* C. Schaefer and K. O'Connor, eds. New York: Wiley, 1983, pp. 95-106.

Guerney, L. F. "Client-centered (non-directive) play therapy." *Handbook of Play Therapy,* C. Schaefer and K. O'Connor, eds. New York: Wiley, 1983, pp. 95-106.

Kraft, I. A. "Group therapy with children and adolescents" *Emotional Disorders in Children and Adolescents,* G. P. Sholevar, R. M. Benon and B. J. Binder, eds. New York: Spectrum, 1980, pp. 109-138.

Moustakas, Clark. E. *Psychotherapy with Children: The Living Relationship.* Original copyright 1959. Greeley, Colorado: Carron Publishers, 1992.

Norton, Byron and Carol. This is a concept heard at their play therapy seminar (1991) in Chicago, sponsored by Colorado State University.

Schaefer, C. E. "Play Therapy" in *Emotional Disorders in Children and Adolescents.* G. P. Sholevar, R. M. Benson and B. J. Blinder, eds. New York: Spectrum, 1980.

Schaefer, C. E. "Play Therapy." *Handbook of Play Therapy,* C. E. Schaefer and K. O'Connor, eds. New York: Wiley, 1983, pp. 95-106.

Schaefer, C. E. and K. O'Connor. *Handbook of Play Therapy.* New York: Wiley, 1983.

Slavson, S. R., ed. *The Practice of Group Therapy.* New York: International Universities Press, 1947.

12

"P" Equals Parental Support: Caring for Children During Times of War

Marlys Blomquist

Parental support is the most important factor in the rehabilitation of children who have suffered, whether they live in war-affected or peaceful societies. During times of war, the family always comes under special attack because families become fragmented: fathers and older siblings leave to fight in the war, mothers and children often become separated while fleeing danger and parents and other significant adults in the children's lives are killed. It is crucial to give children who have lost their parents or caregivers the opportunity to form an attachment with at least one adult. All children have needs, and caring adults have the key to meeting many of those needs.

The power of war on the family

War is a perversion or corruption of the need for respect; it is a destroyer of beauty; it forces itself in hostile form onto the lives of people living in community. The enemies of life disturb, attack and threaten out of existence the powerful form of family life.

As the perversion of war spreads, it often shocks families into life-preserving struggles. War creates endless fear and anxiety by producing chaos, extracting the family from its roots of security and forcing it to survive with limited resources. It holds the family in a state of bondage, knowing cruelty will strike but not knowing when. The unexpected force of embattlement and brutality keep the family exhausted and in a constant state of readiness to react quickly.

Fear creates more fear, which can deplete the energy needed for life. War also pointlessly consumes human energy and suppresses creativity, natural expression and the advancement of productive living. The ravaging reign of war can erode or explosively destroy the path of normality in children's lives.[1]

The power of vulnerability in children

Unfortunately, war brings out the tendency in people to become more competitive and self-absorbed.[2] Such tendencies, although adaptive during war, can be all-consuming and may cut

198

off or limit adult nurturing of children. Children are vulnerable and therefore greatly affected by changes in their nurturing environment. When affection, praise and smiles are restrained and the consistency of everyday life is shattered or interrupted, children are unable to understand with clarity that diminished attention to their needs is because of conditions outside themselves.

The younger they are, the more children live each day as it comes and have a limited sense of the future. What they know with certainty is what is directly happening to them. Children's thoughts are broader, more general and limited in scope. They are not like adults, who have a multitude of life experiences that allow a clearer idea of what is happening and a vision of a possible future.

Consequently, children can quickly feel threatened and anxious if they feel trusted adults are in danger or are behaving in a less responsive way toward them. They begin to feel that they are not all right—that something is wrong with them as persons; they become shy and insecure, clingy or whiny. Since the number of trusted adults in the lives of children is small, their concerns about trusting adults are critical to them.[3] The deaths of any of these adults are exceedingly crucial to children who depend on them for their physical and emotional survival.

Helping children maintain a trusting relationship with their parents or caretakers is crucial to their development during wartime. Their resulting sense of security enables them to cope with the harshness of their lives and to rebound from it later without lasting pain.

Parents can lessen the erosion of children's trust of them, and consequently of the world, by responding as consistently as possible to the needs and nature of children. Children need the constancy of nurturing in their lives and they are spontaneous in their expression of feelings and thoughts. Their parents need to find ways to respectfully attend to this expression of self. As parents provide these, children's spontaneity and development of independence, self-confidence and love of self and of others will not be suppressed.

The power of parents or caregivers

As adults in times of thoughtless social upheaval, we have an added responsibility in how we relate to ourselves and others. Additional strengths, formerly hidden within us, are called forth and further developed, to model integrity and a sense of hope to children. To identify with one's own strength, in spite of the many wounds of war, is to diminish feelings of woundedness.[4]

Children, who look to us as their protectors, will absorb our attitudes—whether they are of a will to struggle onward or that of lasting despair. Knowing that healing can arise out of the most chaotic of circumstances can be the most powerful inspiration you can give a growing person.

If we persevere with courage, we reflect the idea that the most terrible of deeds and circumstances will end, that there are means of healing and a meaningful future to behold. If we suffer but are not broken by our injuries, our strength increases and can be used with wisdom to help us go beyond our wounds. Adults who reflect calmness, confidence, honesty and an attitude of taking charge in spite of adversity will help children retain their grip on reality and strengthen their reactions to it.

Because children are often victims of war, they need the help of parents and other caregivers for their healing. Without help, their suffering from traumatic experiences may be long-lasting. They need to be able to make sense out of their experiences so they can again predict how their world will be and not feel helpless to act for themselves; they need to feel safe again in their homes.[5] By recognizing when children need support and approaching them in specific ways, we can help them to penetrate the fear of their experiences and feel strength, self-worth and a growing sense of integrity.

The power of children's feelings

As we come to understand the development of feelings and how they influence us, even long after they may be forgotten, we learn increasingly the importance of attending to feelings. Attending to the feelings of children is the key to healing their wounds of despair, futility (sense of hopelessness and uselessness), anger, terror, anxiety, uncertainty and a missing sense of themselves. When any one of us experiences an event, the images and feelings about it become embedded within us as memories.[6] It is like having a taproot within ourselves that receives all of our images, perceptions, feelings and interpretations of our experiences. Memories may be forgotten or remembered, may be good or bad, but all are stored within us and form a part of our inner life.

When our experiences have been frightening and negative, we may want to forget them, or at least avoid feeling the intense pain of what happened to us. Consequently, we try to hide, suppress or subdue these memories to shut off the pain. We use forgetting as a shield, or cover, to protect us from the painful experience. This holding back separates us from the pain we once felt so deeply, and it can lead to a total loss of memory—a repression of what once happened now completely erased from our everyday awareness.

These forgotten painful memories, however, live within us in hidden form and have a life of their own. They have an energy that will influence how we act in our everyday life, although we often are not aware of it. We may feel an impulse to act in ways that result in destructiveness to ourselves or to others. The force of the stored energy now arising within us can be so strong that our everyday reasoning cannot hold off its influence.[7]

Unknown to us, we are in bondage to the energy of the painful memories that are now forgotten or partially submerged. Times of duress or chaotic circumstances can especially release this hidden energy, becoming destructive to ourselves or others. Children can easily be victimized by the feelings of their frightening experiences when such feelings are left unattended. When children have experienced paralyzing fear, they can eventually become emotionally numbed: they feel nothing and may then seek out dangerous risks to gain a sense of feeling.[8] When such children are with other children, the buried feeling can emerge in feelings of panic or despair.

As children continue to experience war, we now know that it can become a part of their inner life that influences how they act and how they view themselves and the world around them. To avoid the tragedy of children becoming self-criticizing, worrisome, anxious and sometimes angry and violent adults, parents must tend to their war experience in an ongoing, respectful way.

The power of home

The children's own home, especially during war, must provide them with a refuge from the outside world. As they feel the protection of hugs and soothing words when they feel frightened, their fear will quiet and a sense of calm will take over. Knowing that at home their names will be heard with affection, their wounded feelings will be attended to and they are emotionally safe will enable them to manage conflict outside the home with greater strength.

The power of self-expression

One of the most caring and healing ways to help children avoid the destructive burial of feelings is to have them express their deeply felt feelings of insecurity, anxiety, fear, terror, distrustfulness and unhappiness produced by the impact of major disruption, violence and other experiences of despair. Just as physical wounds need caring treatment through time, so emotional wounds need as much caring attention and time to heal.

Children need encouragement and guidance from parents and caregivers to help them express their feelings in a protected and safe environment. Children feel a sense of protection when they are with adults who allow the spontaneous expression of their experiences and feelings and offer interest, acceptance and an understanding of these expressions. Given this opportunity, children will not hurt themselves.[9] Especially in times torn apart by strife, violence and disorder, children who have the opportunity to express their experiences become stronger and more resilient and can recover from the destruction caused by war. Children who are listened to and whose feelings are acknowledged by others begin to feel more secure, valued, loved and loving.

The power of listening

We help heal children by listening to them, encouraging them to express their impressions and feelings of what is happening in their lives, waiting patiently for their willingness to express themselves, respecting all that comes from them and having a non-judgmental approach toward them.[10] When children know that someone is listening seriously to them, they become more trusting and accepting of themselves. They relate to themselves in ways that help reveal their strengths.

The most important thing adults can do is to quiet ourselves when we listen to children. The position or stance of our body and the gaze of our eyes can signal our readiness and interest to listen. When we move to the place where children are sitting, standing or playing, our message of showing interest increases. With most children, being physically close to them prompts a feeling of security and an eagerness to talk. When we want children to listen to us and follow our requests, a gentle move toward them before we calmly speak our request will produce more willingness from them to oblige.

The power of words

War conditions can limit the amount of time adults can listen to children. This can decrease children's natural spontaneous tendency to talk. When the opportunity comes to listen intently to children, we can help them feel better about themselves by the way we respond in words to what they are telling us. There are two ways we can respond: by commenting on what they are saying—the content or facts and descriptions; or commenting on how they appear to have felt or are now feeling about what they are describing.

If we respond in a conversation with children to what we believe is happening on a feeling level, instead of remaining at the level of content, then we help them become aware of their feelings and recognize the importance of those feelings. If we continually relate our understanding of feelings to ordinary, everyday happenings ("That must have made you feel good"; "I hope you feel proud of yourself," and so on), it helps children to be comfortable with discussing feelings and more able to talk of their fear, anxiety and distraught feelings during times of crises. We can express acknowledgment of their feelings in many ways: a nod of the head, a knowing look, and most important, the reflection of feelings through words.

The following are some examples of effective comments that mirror what children may be feeling as they describe a frightening experience:

- ◆ "I believe I understand how you must be feeling."
- ◆ "How scary; I would have felt scared."
- ◆ "How frightening! But now you're safe."
- ◆ "I'm so sorry that happened to you; that must have been awful."

If we respond to them in this way, children will learn to interpret the truth of their feelings about what happened. Without such help, children may deny that they felt scared because of thinking that they may appear childish or inadequate for feeling frightened. When children release and acknowledge negative feelings, the force of acting them out disappears. We can help children know that no feeling deserves condemnation or dishonor.

Since we are born with a range of possible feelings, we should not honor one feeling over another. Besides joy, laughter and empathy, we must give equal acknowledgment to anger, hostility, shame, humiliation, guilt, remorse, anxiety, fear and sadness. Children need to know that they can function as complete human beings who sometimes feel anger, disgust, contentment or unhappiness. We must recognize, acknowledge and treat *all* feelings with respect.

The expression of feelings helps children maintain control of negative feelings so that they will not act them out destructively against themselves or another person. When we can help children give expression to the painful feelings, the need to hide feelings becomes unnecessary. When they feel understood, children feel closer to us and feel more of the importance of their own selves as individuals. With such self-expression, we clear the way for children to develop into what their true nature intended.

204

— children need their feelings validated.

The power of play

Play is the work of children.[11] Especially during stressful times, parents need to encourage children to spend time solely in playing. Play allows children to relate to many events around them and to express these events in their own simplified way. Their participation in community activities can raise their spirits and occupy them in meaningful ways.

Wartime brings out their imitations of the actions of soldiers, doctors, nurses, parents and other people in events that feel important to them. This spontaneous play, where children think and feel their play into existence, alone or in a group, stimulates their natural path of the development of creativity and getting along with others. Children whose spontaneity has been paralyzed through frightening experiences, and no longer play, often appear passive and withered in spirit. In spite of the many serious demands made of children during wartime, play increases their coping capabilities.

Story telling captivates the minds of children. It is important that caregivers find time to tell the children stories. A story teller visited groups of children during wartime and had children draw objects she had mentioned twice in her stories. The children drew butterflies, houses, rainbows, storms, families and other things that revealed "their concealed inner worlds, their tortured emotions," and made children "forget all the surrounding hardships."[12] Through story telling we can give children opportunities to talk about, write, draw, paint, construct in clay, sand or dirt their memories and feelings so they can express the deeper and more natural emotions about what is happening or has happened in their lives.

The power of dreams

Children's dreams provide a means through which parents and caregivers can help them face the fears produced by forces of violence, tension and stress in their lives. Dreams are a way to help resolve the events in our outer lives and we can use them to heal.[13] Dreams send messages about feelings stored within us about our everyday experiences. Although dreams usually relate to our outer world, they are often clothed in strange or unusual images (likenesses) and follow uncommon story lines as directed by the inner part of us. Children who are experiencing the tension of war often have extremely frightening dream images—monsters or ghosts, acts of violence or other repeating images that continue to awaken them with pounding hearts and screams of terror.

What is happening is that the tremendous force of energy coming from within wants to be felt and recognized. If we do not do so, it will submerge, only to emerge at another time with equal terror.

Using the children's dreams, adults can provide an opportunity for children to connect with the feelings portrayed by these frightful images. When children report these images and feelings to us, we help them by acknowledging their reality; they are real in the reality of the dream world that is depicting our inner life of many hidden feelings.

With the recognition of this reality, a helpful change begins to occur within children. If children are not too frightened the next day, parents can encourage them to draw, paint, mold in clay or sand the dream images of the nightmare, tell the story about them and again visualize or remake them.

With children who are too afraid to approach their terrifying images, acknowledging their terror and their "monsters" may be all that we can do. Later we can encourage them to play out less intense dream images. Even later, with an encouraging adult to help them, they may spontaneously begin work on the threatening dream images. By acknowledging the reality of dreams and bringing the children back to life through this play-type work, we create a safe container for the re-emergence of the dream energy. We approach the fury of the dream in a way that allows the transformation of its powerful energy into life-giving or healing energy for the children's outer life.[14]

The power of routine

Children feel more secure with a stable, or fixed, routine. Although the harassing conditions of war can cause devastation on everyday family life, reestablishing the regularity of everyday events will increase children's feelings of security. Regularity in bed and mealtimes, play, work and study times strengthens children's inner security by providing a sense of order that helps them predict their world. Knowing how tomorrow will be has a settling effect on them.

Sometimes without our realizing it, a routine can place more value on "getting the job done" than on helping children gain security and a sense of belonging by participating in the order of their day. Children can feel that routine chores and obligations are tedious and wearisome when we present these acts as serious duties, scold children when they "mess up," take them for granted and never show any gratitude for their participation. When children view acts as duties lying beyond the voice of appreciation, they may do them in a routine way and perceive them as only meeting the needs of others.

With daily and frequent sincere praise for acts of help and kindness, children thrive on the recognition of participating in important acts. When we center routines around children's fun-loving and enthusiastic nature, they become eager to cooperate because they feel important. When we praise children's efforts sincerely, they want to please us endlessly.

The power of anticipation

Although it is frightening to hear, children are helped by knowing what is happening or may happen to them during times of war.[15] In crisis times, when the normal patterns and understandings of life are disrupted, children and adults feel they are losing something and are often unclear about what it is. They feel that they no longer have the power to keep things under control, and they experience fear and confusion because of the threat to their survival. Children who are old enough to reason need to hear about the dangers they must be aware of, what to do in times of danger and how they may feel when war affects their lives. Parents can help prepare children for the effects of war by explaining about the dangers that may befall them.

207

The childhood experiences of those who have been through persecution can help us understand the dangers of wartime that today's children may experience.[16] When a country is launched into war, parents can prepare the children for what could happen by discussing the possibilities. They may be in a home environment that is somber and frightening, with adults showing tense expressions and speaking in serious tones. The adults may call on the children to be brave and not to weaken the courage of others. It would help the children to know the reasons behind the anxiety of the adults around them.

In times of danger, children may be told to follow exact instructions given them to prevent endangerment of lives, that they may have to depend on others outside the family for their survival and that their lives may depend on their adapting to the circumstances that they may be in. They may be in unsanitary places and may be physically sick from the torment they feel. They may lose control of their bodies and become bed-wetters as worry and distress become lodged within them.

Children may witness terrible brutalities and the suffering of innocent family members or other people. They may see that their community feels terrified of an oppressive army occupying their area. Children may fear being discovered if they are in hiding or being brutalized for no reason. They may feel self-reproach and blame if they survive and others do not.

They may have fears about an unknown future, and anxiety that will make them feel so unstable that an unfriendly look can victimize them. They may have thoughts of wanting to be children again, free to play without fears and wishing to be treated as equals with adults who are kind and comforting to them. They may wish to retain some object that links them to their past. Children may feel that life could never possibly again have any order or predictability. They need to know that their thoughts and feelings are normal for the grave circumstances in which they find themselves. As difficult as it may be, talking to children about the possibility of such events will help them to cope more effectively if any of these tragic experiences should befall them.

Equally important to know is that children in continuous war conditions identify with their group and with hopes of ridding themselves of the enemy. This group identity tends to overcome the development of a personal identity, diminishing the children's personal dreams and visions.[17] When children receive recognition and praise for fighting and continue to hear horror stories about the enemy, not only do they identify themselves with a group at the loss of their own dreams and hopes, but they remain bonded to their wounds, which feed a desire for vengeance. Having a group identity suppresses the development of their true nature, which withers away through faithfulness to an outward force.

The power of adversity

Even children who have suffered severe trauma need firm, loving discipline that provides training and instruction. Some parents and caregivers, however, believe that children need punishment to learn to be civil or polite; such ways are "for their own good," because otherwise children's wills would be too strong if they do not have such strong discipline. Children can then get along with others and become successful adults.[18] To view children in this way is to injure them with doubt, since our actions toward them will suggest our disappointment and displeasure in them as they break valued understandings of what we perceive as "goodness."

Adults do not need to control children's wills. Making children submit to others through fear of humiliation, guilt or punishment leaves them with two choices: to rebel or to disown the righteous anger they feel and submit to another. Since power is unbalanced between adults and children, we can forcibly make them obey by threats, scolding or physical force. Punishment in its oppressive and often subtle forms creates a feeling within children that they are somehow "bad" as a person, and disables their natural ways of developing. They then grow awkwardly through life often feeling dehumanized and misunderstood. Ignoring, scorning or ridiculing children's true feelings blocks their emotional growth. It drives them toward a false destiny because they are unaware of their true selves.

Punished children do not rebound well to life's experiences, even in joyful times. They tend to oppress others when angered. They are unaware that their anger comes primarily from emotions stored-up from being mistreated through previous punishments. This anger is now directed at others. Sometimes, in efforts to win acceptance and power over their circumstances, children can be led to turn on their loved ones and terrorize others in their former communities. They end up conspiring with those who terrorize.

Because of our own vulnerability and because our children's behavior strongly affects us, it is more truthful when we say that we do not like their behavior (arguing, fighting, screaming and so on) and we feel angry, tired or hurt about what has happened or is happening. If we are feeling very tense and vulnerable, we may become extremely angry or annoyed with children and strike out at them.

When this happens, we need to go back to them when we feel in control and reassure them that it was our tension that caused the anger, that it must have appeared that we did not love them and that we will try to approach them more kindly next time.[19] Children learn to solve many of their problems and relate to others by observing how we resolve our frustrations and difficulties and how we relate to other people, including the children themselves.

If we do not see children as lovable and worthy of love in childhood then—whatever their experiences—they will feel rejected. Rejected children often grow up unable to handle the rage that has built up in response to the treatment that demonstrated rejection to them. Some of these children may become adults who pass their rage onto innocent people.[20] Cruel adults were once children born with a capacity to love. But some were disciplined cruelly, without anyone coming to their aid. As children they had no way out, and although they hated what was done to them, they began to believe that aggressive power over others would get them what they want—revenge for their hurtful past.

The power of community

Children also need opportunities for activities that will enhance the feeling that they belong to a community larger than

210

their family. Children need to grow up with their peers (age-mates). When there are opportunities under wise adult leadership, gather children together for work-play activities: cleaning up rubble and ruins from war, helping a particular family in desperate need by cleaning their house, moving things or preparing and planting a cooperative garden. These events provide a channel for children to talk, work, and play with others who previously did not belong to their peer group.

New acquaintances in work-play situations strengthen the developing skills of making friends and enhance a sense of integrity from doing meaningful activities. Other responsible inter-actions are ones where we trust children to carry out an important act: serving a drink to a sick person, visiting the sick, running errands, working at jobs to help the family, reading to elders or young children and taking care of children or others.

Children who are allowed to have responsible interactions with adults and other children help create a meaningful bond between them. The ability to respond compassionately, especially during times of war, amid the chaos that appears unmerciful and cruel, makes life meaningful and stirs a sense of being alive.

Viktor Frankl states that man is not driven to moral behavior but decides how to behave, and he does so because of a commitment to a cause rather than for the sake of having a good conscience.[21] Giving children a cause to which they can commit themselves and therefore behave compassionately is the key to unlocking their empathy and forthcoming good actions. Most important, commitment to any cause must be voluntary to be effective. Providing opportunities for children to act kindly and with understanding pulls on their empathic nature—which otherwise might lie quietly inactive—and urges them into compassionate acts that we can easily recognize and praise sincerely.

The power of need

We can easily identify children in pain. They show symptoms of anxiety, fear, worry and inactivity—or anger, hostility and aggression, although they also nurture fear, anxiety and often

211

despair. A tormented child may display harsh behavior toward his loved ones as a message that he is feeling the constant anxiety of having failed in some unknown way, of having been wronged or of feeling fear that he disguises by his harsh and difficult ways. A child may put herself at the disposal of another who is manipulating her into wrongful acts or who shows off her developing femininity as a means of feeling more powerful. Or the tormented child may be the one who is cast out of a group of companions and ridiculed because of some harmless fault.

These are the children who need an adult who will act as their advocate (supporter and defender). These advocates would help others who will become essential in easing the children's pain and helping them heal. Healing comes about when others understand what the person in pain is feeling and allow this empathy to become acts of kindness.

Children need to know that adults will help them. If we do not help them, their ability to form relationships with others can become damaged. Children can suffer at the hands of many people. Persecution from peers is one example of a very critical and harmful experience for children. It is important that adults (parents, caregivers, teachers and others) come to the aid of children who have become victims at the hands of their peers, by acting as their advocates and guiding them into a structure of a gentle, supportive and transforming experience that will end their suffering.

Injuries cause children to want revenge. When children have been dishonored, they raise their sword of defense through screams, intolerance of others, self-injury and other acts against life's harmony. Had they been treated with respect when injured, they would not continue to defend their honor as a way to heal their hurt. The injured person must make oneself or others pay. Humiliation creates a feeling of shame in the eyes of others, and it can force children into the path of violence. If they become too disabled, children cannot make peace well.

When conditions of conflict abound, tensions mount, unleashing our tendency to blame others, to mock, berate them and even abuse them, in children just as in adults. Despite the despair conflict produces, we can provide a way to transform children's cruel acts of striking-out into acts of kindness toward children in need. (See chapter 16 for ways adults can help children make peace with their peers and in the home.)

As parents and caregivers, we can influence, encourage and instill the idea of compassion in children. It is a blessing that children recognize easily the sufferings of another. With a little encouraging guidance, we can strike the heart of their inborn well of compassion that encourages an uncontrolled desire to help another.

As children continue to be subjected to the violence and cruelty of war, we can rekindle their strength to develop, to survive, to reach out for themselves and for others by drawing on powers that yield encouragement, nourishment and compassion. The powers of patience, love, understanding and kindly guidance become our greatest weapon to weaken the violent thrusts of war on children. Within the deepest recesses of the most discouraged, depressed and angered of children lingers the spirit of joy, compassion and hope waiting to be uncovered.

NOTES

1   J. Garbarino, K. Kostelny and N. Dubrow, *No Place to Be a Child: Growing Up in a War Zone* (Lexington, Massachusetts: Lexington Books, 1991).

2   A. B. Schmookler, *Out of Weakness: Healing the Wounds that Drive us to War* (New York: Bantam Books, 1988).

3   S. Elbedour, R. ten Bensel and D. T. Bastein, *Towards a Symbolic Interaction Theory of Traumatization*, 1993. No publisher given.

4   Schmookler, 1988.

5   S. Elbedour, "The Psychology of Children of War." Unpublished doctoral dissertation, University of Minnesota, 1992.

6   Alice Miller, *Banished Knowledge: Facing Childhood Injuries* (New York: Anchor Books, 1990).

7   Dora M. Kalff, *Sandplay: A Therapeutic Approach to the Psyche* (Boston: Sigo Press, 1980).

8   J. S. Brende, "A 12-step recovery program for victims of traumatic events," *International Handbook of Traumatic Stress Syndromes*, J. P. Wilson and B. Raphael, eds. (New York: Plenum Press, 1993).

9   Kalff.

10 J. Garbarino, F. M. Stott and Faculty of the Erikson Institute, *What Children Can Tell Us: Eliciting, Interpreting and Evaluating Information from Children* (San Francisco: Jossey-Bass, 1989).

11 J. Piaget, *Play, Dreams and Imitation in Childhood* (New York: W. W. Nortons, 1962).

12 Kalff.

13 H. Volavkova, ed., *I Never Saw Another Butterfly: Children's Drawings and Poems from Terezin Concentration Camp, 1942-1944* (New York: Schocken Books, 1993).

14 Ibid.

15 Elbedour, 1992.

16 Goldie Szachter Kalib, *The Last Selection: A Child's Journey through the Holocaust* (Amherst: University of Massachusetts Press, 1991).

17 S. Elbedour and D. T. Bastein, *Identity formation in the shadow of conflict: Projective drawings by children in Gaza, the West Bank, and Israel*, 1993. No publisher given.

18 Alice Miller, *For Your Own Good: Hidden Cruelty in Childrearing and the Roots of Violence* (New York: Farrar, Strauss & Giroux, 1984).

19 Ibid.

20 Ibid.

21 Viktor E. Frankl, *Man's Search for Meaning* (New York: Beacon Press, 1959).

13

A Community of Care:
Ministry to Children in War

Cynthia Blomquist

"The Lord watches over . . . and sustains the fatherless and the widow . . ." (Psalm 146:9a). God's heart is full of mercy and compassion for the widow and the orphan. It was God's intention that his people would care for the orphans and widows in the community. When the Lord first established his plan for his people, he specified the kind of support the widow and orphan should receive (Exodus 22:22, Deuteronomy 14:29).

It is a mandate to be taken seriously: a percentage of the community's produce was to be stored to provide for those who had no allotment of their own. The alien, the fatherless and the widow could eat and be satisfied, "so that the Lord your God may bless you in all the work of your hands" (Deuteronomy 14:29).

God intends for the community of his people to provide care for those stung by grief, loss and trauma. As we face the task of caring for children in war zones, God has granted us both responsibility and resources. We can enter a community with the investment of new understanding and servant hearts. But we serve most faithfully as we participate in the community and discover God's plan of compassion for people. In offering aid we have a responsibility to respect the community, to encourage them to find the resources that God has provided and to walk with them through the process.

Recognizing the impact of bereavement, displacement and trauma on children in a war-torn community, this chapter seeks to present some practical guidelines to approaching a community with relief as development. First, we will explore the concepts of a facilitation approach to community relief and recovery. Second, a practical look at the assumptions of mental health and psychological care unfolds in a "culture-specific" model. Finally, the chapter will address specific concerns critical to caring for a community in crisis.

Relief as development

Relief work in a war zone implies immediate needs. Children need food, shelter, health care and clean water. Yet they also need nurturing and emotional care in a structured environment. We could meet any of these needs with a program that has a "Band-Aid" approach (O'Gorman 1992). With a "Band-Aid" model, resources are simply financed and distributed. Keeping people from starving may require the use of "Band-Aids"; this approach, however, requires little personal involvement and provides little long-term investment in the community. The community learns how to rely on others, and a cycle of dependence can develop. Douglas Millham (1989:251) encourages relief workers to "carry out relief activities in developmental ways which lead to further development." The steps we take into a community can lead to either partnership or reliance.

A facilitation team

An alternate approach to relief emphasizes God's powerful presence in the community. Often, we have heard the idea that "God is already working" in the place we go to minister. This is true of even the most desperate of places—God has created skilled and sensitive people in every culture. A facilitating (or encouraging) partnership between mission relief staff and the community plants seeds of growth that become rooted in the community itself.

The programs do not "spring into being" out of the minds of a few foreign workers. Instead, a facilitation model centers on the people of the community: their concerns, their passions and their abilities.

We could also consider the facilitation team as "animators" in the intervention process; the team brings life and focuses the energy of community members. The animator "help[s] a community discover and use all its potential for creative and constructive team work" (Hope & Timmel 1984:49). The team of facilitators values the assumption that God is already moving among the people. The people know their pain, they want change, and they deserve respect.

The process of facilitation

The first step for a facilitating team is to live among the people and develop relationships. Eating meals together in true fellowship, spending time together and dropping the "business" approach to ministry enables the facilitators to understand the pain of war trauma. Robert Linthicum (1991) calls this move into the community "networking." By listening to the cares of the people and opening their hearts to those concerns, the team members soon learn what the *community* sees as its problems and who the people are who want to see the change.

The team members with sensitivity to psychological and spiritual care for traumatized children will focus on networking with those in the community who are in a caretaking role. You may discover the community caretaker, confessor or adviser through active listening. The community members know who helps others solve conflicts, listens to problems or offers advice. A facilitator might ask a new friend, "Who do you talk to when your heart is heavy?" Remember, part of building these relationships is discovering the culture's language for emotions.

People in a war-torn community may feel suspicious of those persons who enter with many questions and the appearance of an "agenda." The facilitators should discover that they should spend most of their time listening. By keeping their ears open, the team can learn important things: Who cares for the children? What are the caretakers' biggest concerns? How does the community view the children's presence? How would the community describe positive change? If the team approaches the community with an attitude of facilitation, it offers hope to a community that feels powerless.

The unit of action, however, is not the individual or the facilitation team. Through the relationships made during the networking process, the community now knows the facilitators. The next step is for the community itself to take the information gathered through the networking and to form coalitions of community members around what the members believe are the important issues (Linthicum 1991). These people have the passion necessary to motivate them through the pain of change. In this way, the community decides what mental health issues to address, and they bring the energy for developing strategies.

The facilitator's role is to encourage the coalitions to form strategies first around a small but important goal. The community can invest in this step toward change, which also offers the experience of success. A successful first action proves vital to the morale of the community. An example of this first step in caring for traumatized children could simply be organizing a meeting of concerned parents or child care workers in the community. Introducing a place for peer support and encouragement will be a foundational act to providing continued, stable care for the children.

Plans for facilitating mental health care must consider the availability of basic resources necessary for the community's primary survival. Obviously, the community will voice the priority of survival and recovery needs. Initially, the critical need for food and shelter may thwart the development of a counseling network. The community can, however, address mental health issues and physical needs simultaneously. Through the experience of MEDAIR in Liberia, Anne Balfour (1993) suggests that a practical, skill-based program (medical, food or water) that produces visible results in the community works well in combination with a mental health project. Mental health work often produces slow progress, and the tangible success in a skill-based program can boost the esteem of a community struggling to recover from crisis.

218

The next step in Linthicum's "community organizing" is the training of leadership. With mental health issues, training community caregivers faces special concerns due to the need to bring cross-cultural relevance to psychological theory.

Issues in cross-cultural mental health care

As facilitators, we can enter a community equipped with specific skills and ideas. Facilitation, however, requires flexibility and trust in God's *healing*, which is already present in the community. Each culture also has its particular way of approaching issues of emotional pain and problem-solving. The Western model of mental health and counseling is founded on the individual and his or her independent decisions. Western psychology—and some Western theology—also usually ignores the influence of the supernatural. We may miss important resources for caring inherent in that community if we do not seek to understand how that culture defines mental health.

For example, as I described the post-traumatic symptoms of flashbacks or intrusive thoughts to a group of Liberian counselors working with traumatized children, one of them offered his culture's perception of that experience. He explained that some Liberians believe that their enemies can use supernatural forces to make them feel as though they are re-experiencing the painful event. This way, the enemy still had power over the victim's feelings. The Liberians' world view accepted the supernatural more easily than a physical or psychological explanation. It was important that I recognize this spiritual understanding and its powerful influence in the culture. As a Christian, however, I know the power of Christ as the victorious healer. I can encourage caretakers to grasp the healing power of prayer and their culture's effective means of coping with stress.

Uchenna Nwachuku and Allen Ivey (1991) describe an approach to training counselors that brings facilitation into the development of a "culture-specific" counseling model. They suggest that the tendency in cross-cultural work is to bring the Western model in and to attempt to adapt it to the new cultural setting. This attempt to marry Western theory with non-Western culture can inadvertently promote foreign and unwanted values.

The culture-specific process begins as someone (or a group) from that culture considers the key aspects of their world view: values, expectations about the helping relationship and problem-solving. Cultural "informants" then give feedback to clarify these world view questions. Nwachuku and Ivey (1991) use the African-Igbo culture as an example, describing the African-Igbo emphasis on extended family, hierarchy, advice by elders and competition. By using a similar training model, facilitators can discover ways to empower existing mental health values and structures, instead of trying to import new, strange ideas (Ronstrom 1989).

An understanding of the culture's values can be practically incorporated into the counselor's training model. Nwachuku and Ivey used contrasting role plays to distinguish the culturally appropriate and inappropriate methods of therapy. One model therapist acted out a helping relationship that emphasized individual expression and independent decision-making. The culture-specific model demonstrated caring responses that encouraged community involvement and responsibility to the extended family. Counselors with this training learned to lessen their Western-based individualistic approaches and included extended family and community centered values, strengthening the African-Igbo culture.

The foundation of this model for counselor training lies in the expectation that the "experts" have much to learn from those living in the culture. Missionaries who have been living in a community for a long time have important knowledge of the key values of that culture. Informants native to the culture also provide an invaluable resource to clarify questions about the helping relationship that no one may have ever asked.

The care providers should also explore what are the culturally appropriate ways to express emotions. Some communities use active expression like dance, song, story telling or plays. Other groups may feel shame at a public display of pain. With a little creativity, however, you can maintain even this emotional privacy. Community centers have found that telephone counseling can suc-

220

cessfully bypass the shame of a face-to-face relationship in Thailand and Hong Kong (Cheung 1989; Tapanya 1989).

Training in relationship

Once the facilitation team has identified the coalition of caretakers and developed a culture-specific counseling model, it can turn to empowering the people through training. Ted Ward (1975) offers guidelines to encourage more relevant and practical leadership training:

> Reflect: Begin with what people already know. Help people organize what they already know. *Use* it to build on. Even if previous knowledge is small, if it is reflected upon and shared it will serve as a basis for increased self-understanding.
>
> Detect: Provide new information against the background of previous knowledge; thus the contrasts will be visible and the affirmations will be clear.
>
> Project: Help people consider the *active* consequences of what they understand. ("What will you *do* on the basis of your understandings?")

With the foundation of a relationship, training no longer needs to be a hierarchical process. Approaches to teaching communicate a great deal about how the educators value people in the community. Education that allows the students to passively receive information offers little confidence to change (Srinivasan 1983). Actively involving students in the process stretches their God-given abilities, and they will experience the encouragement of the community. People remember best what they discover for themselves. In a training relationship, each participant has the opportunity to be transformed. The trainer is a learner, and the students can be teachers.

There are practical suggestions, however, on how to facilitate this type of nonformal training. The relationship is a crucial focus—both relationships among the facilitators and among the community members. Learning in a group offers the best place to promote a change in attitudes and actions. As the group members

221

interact with each other and act on their surrounding world, they learn together (Srinivasan 1983). Introduction activities should encourage trust between the facilitator and the group, to allow for challenge and risk-taking in the discussions.

The training sessions best serve the community when they offer an incomplete structure open for the participants' involvement. Brainstorming, role-playing, using culturally familiar games and posing problems for discussion—all furnish a place for the community to interact with each other in the learning process (Hope and Timmel 1984).

Concerns for a community in crisis

A vital part of any plan to care for war-traumatized children is the provision of support for those who undertake the care and counseling. Most likely, the adults in the community have also been exposed to excruciating experiences of violence and trauma. You should not ignore their continued need for personal care and ministry.

While working with five Liberian counselors, the stress they experienced while interviewing orphan children about their war experiences constantly challenged me. The women were reminded of their own children, and the men had vivid memories of life-threatening conflicts with soldiers from both sides. It was important to plan a time for these caretakers to talk about their own feelings, both in the group and in a one-on-one relationship. Teaching the community to care for itself requires that individual community members and caretakers learn the skills of recognizing their own pain and accepting care.

The facilitators themselves will also discover that their ability to cope is stretched to its limits. They themselves may develop symptoms of post-traumatic stress related to the stories they hear while participating in the community. Nightmares, hyper-arousal, anxiety and depression were not uncommon experiences for me, even after only a short time in an area of military conflict.

Charles Schulz, the creator of the "Peanuts" comic strip, drew a telling cartoon recently. Snoopy, the family dog, comes to the door of the house in the middle of the night with a frightened expression. Charlie Brown gets out of bed and gives Snoopy a hug and some encouraging words: "Be reassured. The sun will come up; everything will be okay!" Yet, when Charlie Brown goes back to bed, he lies there with his eyes wide open. He asks an important question: "Who reassures the reassurer?"

We can take these concerns very seriously. But be "reassured" that our Lord can provide the resources to heal the broken and traumatized hearts in us and in the community around us. He uses us as skilled channels of his grace and comfort, and as Paul writes: ". . . we can comfort those in any trouble with the comfort we ourselves have received from God" (2 Corinthians 1:4).

Conclusion

Entering a community to provide care for children in war promises both relationships and responsibilities. Each community holds its own set of difficulties and its own resources to face those concerns. A team of facilitators faces the challenge of walking alongside a group of hurting and suffering people. This experience requires an investment of each individual, both in the community and in the facilitation team. Yet, as we invest in this transforming process, God's spirit empowers us to walk through the darkness and to find ways to spread the light.

REFERENCES

Balfour, Anne, ed. "Issues arising from MEDAIR's psychological project in Liberia, Oct. 1991 - Oct. 1992." Unpublished manuscript, 1993.

Cheung, F. M. "The women's center: A community approach to feminism in Hong Kong." *American Journal of Community Psychology*, 17:1989, pp. 99-107.

Hope, A. and S. Timmel. *Training for transformation: A handbook for community workers, Book 2.* Zimbabwe: Mambo Press, 1984.

Linthicum, Robert C. *Empowering the Poor.* Monrovia, California: MARC, 1991.

Millham, Douglas. "Training for relief in development." *Christian Relief and Development*, Edgar J. Elliston, ed. Dallas: Word, 1989.

Nwachuku, Uchenna and Allen Ivey. "Culture-specific counseling: An alternative training model." *Journal of Counseling and Development*, 70:1991, pp. 106-111.

O'Gorman, Frances. *Charity and Change* . Melbourne: World Vision Australia, 1992.

Ronstrom, A. "Children in Central America: Victims of war." *Child Welfare*, 68:1989, pp. 145-153.

Srinivasan, L. *Nonformal Adult Learning*. Boston: World Education, Inc., 1983.

Tapanya, S. "Community psychology in Thailand." *American Journal of Community Psychology*, 17:1989, pp. 109-119.

Ward, Ted. "Increasing relevancy and practicality." Unpublished manuscript, 1975.

Post Counselling Stress Disorder.

14
Providing Care
for the Caregivers

Phyllis Kilbourn

On commercial flights airline personnel admonish passengers that, in an emergency, parents should first put on their own oxygen masks, then give oxygen to their children. We can easily understand that an unconscious parent is of no use to a child in distress. The same holds true for caregivers dealing with children in crisis. Caregivers must take care of themselves to ensure their effectiveness in providing care for traumatized children.

If caregivers are not always mindful of this truth, the traumas stemming from war atrocities will affect children not just directly, but also indirectly through the quality of care the children receive. Dealing with children's war-related crises can be a very stressful experience. The more traumatic the event, the more potential there is for caregivers to become traumatized. As a disaster worker commented after caring for victims of an airline crash, "One cannot walk through the aftermath of a disaster and remain unaffected."

Caregivers also need assurance that they will be provided with the resources and supportive networks they need to become involved in the children's and the community's experiences of loss, pain, and grief. They must be enabled to "first put on their own oxygen masks."

This chapter explores some trauma-producing stress factors caregivers encounter and describes some normal responses to these stress factors. Understanding the stress factors and the caregivers' possible responses can provide helpful insights into their needs. I have also included key elements and principles to assist in planning care for the caregiver.

CONTRIBUTING FACTORS TO TRAUMA-PRODUCING STRESS

Caregivers who experience chronic stress, or have a stress overload, are at risk of becoming emotionally traumatized. Norman Wright describes stress as "any type of action or situation that places conflicting or heavy demands upon a person. These demands upset the body's equilibrium."[1] An overload of stress can erode the caregivers' effectiveness in caring for the children.

Workload

One of the first heavy demands caregivers find themselves handling is an excessively hectic and pressure-filled workload. The demand for their time and energies is enormous, and caregivers often simply cannot begin to meet all of the children's needs. As they discover their limitations, feelings of helplessness, inadequacy and incompetency begin to plague them.

Caretakers have received training for their task and like to feel that they are competent and in control of the situation. In crises, however, they can encounter responsibilities where they only feel minimally competent, or just partially in control of the situation or barely effective. When these feelings take over, a caregiver's confidence can quickly erode, causing an overload of stress. These feelings were evident repeatedly in the Rwandan crisis, which so quickly turned into what many have called the worst human disaster in recent history.

One newscaster vividly depicted the anguish and frustration of a lone doctor who, after surveying the masses of the suffering Rwandans around her, cried out, "I am not God to choose who should live and who should die." Yet, as the only available doctor, choose she must. Hundreds were desperately in need of medical attention, but it was humanly impossible for one doctor to care for everyone suffering from the diseases rampant among the refugees or to treat the innumerable bullet and machete wounds. Should she first attend to the children? The parents or caregivers? The elderly? These were tough, painful choices, because her training had prepared her to save lives at all costs.

Unrealistic expectations

A caregiver's unrealistic expectations can also lead to tension. Especially when faced with catastrophic situations, caregivers can easily feel deep frustration because they can do so little to "fix" the children's pain. The expectation that "I should be able to fix it" leads to feelings of helplessness. Always present are the accusing feelings of "I should be doing more" or "I could have done it better." The tension of faith issues can also surface: "If I pray harder or am more spiritual, I could do more."

When caregivers have unrealistic expectations and cannot live up to them, they can also become severely depressed. Particularly vulnerable are the perfectionists who set very high standards for themselves. Unable to achieve their work standards, they feel their failure deeply and take it personally. Caregivers who tend toward perfectionism also experience difficulties handling the need for flexibility—they are more comfortable following a rigid schedule.

However, rigidly followed schedules rarely, if ever, exist in an emergency care situation. With the rapidly changing dynamics and needs of any given situation, along with limited available resources, caregivers must be willing to practice flexibility. Only in doing so can they discover the most effective methods of handling chaotic situations where basic survival often becomes the primary goal.

The work environment

The environment in which caregivers work can also be a major stress producer. If opposing forces are still waging war near the refugee camp or orphanage where caregivers are caring for chil-

227

dren, the caregivers may fear for their personal safety. Or perhaps they are caring for children who have very limited facilities, resources, food and medical care. Already emotionally involved with the children's plight, it is not easy for them to sit down guilt-free to a meal when some around them are dying of starvation and malnutrition, or to receive priority access to the limited medical supplies. It seems so selfish and unfair. But caregivers must be reminded that if they are sick and exhausted they cannot be of maximum benefit to the children. Once again they must first "put on their own oxygen (lifesaving) masks."

Anger

Injustice is a painful issue to constantly confront, especially when it concerns innocent children who have no control over what is happening to them. Caring for children who are bereft of parents, siblings and friends or who have been physically maimed for life through the actions of people who have no concern for the sufferings they are inflicting can evoke intense rage. A caregiver wants to release rage not just against the injustice and suffering, but also against the perpetrators responsible for the children's victimization.

If left unresolved, this rage continues to boil deep within the caregivers' emotions, making them emotionally crippled. Caregivers struggle with issues of helplessness, depression and the theological implications of forgiveness and suffering. The stress from containing such rage affects not only the "containers" but also those on whom they "dump" it.

Relationships

In even the most ideal work situations, interpersonal relationship problems among colleagues arise that need handling from time to time. Considering the difficulties of working in a stress-laden, emotionally traumatic situation with limited resources at one's disposal, it is not surprising that conflicts occur among caregivers. Perhaps the workers differ in opinions concerning treatment plans, role expectations, use of resources or attitudes toward the children and their situations. Each person has his or her own way of coping, and tensions also can arise over these differences. Unresolved, such conflicts present a serious danger: caregivers may isolate themselves from their co-workers by withdrawing from the conflict. Withdrawal prevents a caregiver from receiving much-needed emotional support from the team.

Roles

Roles are sets of expectations people hold about one another's behavior and work. When caregivers are forced to assume several roles, especially in an emergency, their colleagues expect different behaviors of them. They may have to assume administrative, leadership or teaching roles that are unfamiliar to them or that they were not prepared to assume. If incompatible or inconsistent behaviors occur, stress and conflict can result among colleagues. Just how stressful this situation can be depends on the degree of conflict and the investment the caregiver has in meeting all role demands equally well.[2]

Inability to detach emotionally

Caregivers usually find it difficult emotionally to detach themselves from their work. After a stressful day of dealing with the children's deep emotional and physical wounds, what they have witnessed or experienced continues to swirl in their minds during off-hours and, perhaps subconsciously, even through their sleeping hours. Such vicarious traumatizations leave them physically and emotionally exhausted.

Burnout

Working in a situation that produces overwhelming emotional stress can eventually lead to burnout. Kendall Johnson defines burnout as "a term referring to a lapse in interest and motivation, decline in performance, and lowered professionalism."[3] When we allow stress to reach this level, everyone suffers from the resulting impaired work performance.

COMMON REACTIONS TO TRAUMA-PRODUCING STRESS

The emotions are the outlet for the reactions to traumatic and stressful events. When strong feelings or emotions threaten to overpower the caregivers, however, their natural reaction is to defend themselves from being overwhelmed or incapacitated by their intense feelings. The emotions are there, but they are "frozen" for the sake of self-protection. James Garbarino and his associates warn of this:

> It does not take much introspection to imagine that each of us who will be involved with these children, their families, and their communities will confront head-on a most basic human motivation: the natural and insistent desire to protect ourselves from unpleasant feelings and conflicts that threaten a sense of inner balance and the psychological integrity necessary to continue to function effectively. These feelings may result from deeper, unresolved conflicts (for example, fear of personal safety). Frequently these situations are concerned with violence, abandonment, withdrawal of support, or similar areas that affect people deeply. The feelings may or may not be unconscious, and may not be irrational.[4]

The defenses caregivers raise as survival strategies against their stress and emotional trauma can take many forms. Often they closely resemble the coping strategies children use to mask their intense pain: denying its existence or expressing an unwillingness to share their deepest feelings with others, particularly with people they consider "outsiders."

Often caregivers are too apprehensive to express the deep emotions that churn within them for fear they will "crumble" instead of remain strong. Therefore, using a dominant coping strategy, they become "psychologically numb," burying their emotions and sufferings deep within themselves. Numbness is a form of denial; it is a desensitization to what has happened as a means of dealing with the intense trauma. While numb, a person can keep a calm exterior and employ a "business as usual" approach, appearing strong and emotionally healthy.

230

Numbness may be a helpful adaptive coping mechanism for a time, but eventually these "frozen emotions" must thaw. If they have been allowed to build up, an unchecked and destructive flood can occur.

The hesitancy of caregivers to express their emotions has drastic effects not only on their current and future emotional well-being, but also on the quality of care they can provide. Emotionally, they become unavailable and this may prevent them from assisting and supporting the very children they have come to help.

A willingness to express one's emotions also allows for a deeper identification with the children's suffering and pain. Caught up in the atrocities of war, these children need sympathetic caregivers who can help them come to grips with their trauma and pain. The children need to know that their caregivers understand their experiences and identify with their sufferings.

Caregivers, however, must work on their own emotional needs outside, or apart from, their relationships with the children. While they are with the children, caregivers must contain their feelings; they must not provide opportunities for children to feel that "you can't contain me and my feelings."

PLANNING CARE FOR CAREGIVERS

Devise and implement an ongoing, structured plan to inform and support the caregivers. Almost immediately upon arriving at their posts, caregivers find themselves having to cope with violence, fear and trauma at a disturbing level psychologically. These daily experiences reduce their capacity to meet the children's needs. Work-related tensions and frustrations can leave the caregivers stressed out. Sometimes the urgency of a situation causes them to postpone dealing with their own grief issues.

Caregivers must come to terms with these strong emotions and the difficult conflicts that emerge—or are silenced—in the course of their work. If they do not manage their pain, it will come out in symptoms similar to PTSD (post-traumatic stress syndrome). No matter how hectic the day's schedule or how pressing the need for intervention care, give priority to scheduling adequate time for the caregivers' debriefing sessions and informal group-sharing times. Debriefing helps caregivers identify their thoughts and feelings, allowing healing to occur.

A caregiver's needs vary from situation to situation depending on such factors as how the trauma occurred, the degree of trauma experienced by the children and the caregiver's own background and previous trauma-care experience. For some, this may be their first exposure to suffering and pain on such a massive and inhuman scale; they will need special attention. The following are some key elements and principles to consider when formulating your plan of care for caregivers.

1. When recruiting and selecting caregivers, keep in mind that for some being on a team is a positive experience; it may cripple others. Be alert to the fact that the children's trauma can parallel caregivers' own experiences. A caregiver may bear painful childhood emotional wounds that are not yet fully healed or have not been brought to closure. Effectively caring for children includes a person's willingness to identify with the child's hurt, vulnerability, fear, anger and sense of loss. Unresolved trauma issues may prevent caregivers from helping and supporting the children, although they are sincere in their desire to do so. Andrew Lester stresses the importance of enabling caregivers to resolve these issues both for their own emotional well-being and for competent service to the children.

    > To empathize with the child, to "hang in there" in the face of his or her pain, can only be managed if you have been willing to claim your own personal pain. You must be willing to explore personal experience with grief, loss, guilt, shame, fear, and danger, particularly if experienced as a child. If wounds from the past are left unhealed, it will be difficult for you to allow a child to deal openly with a crisis in your presence. The child's emotional pain will be too threatening to that which lies unresolved in one of your interior closets.

    > On the other hand, if you have been willing to examine your own childhood traumas, reliving them if necessary,

bringing closure and resolution where possible, integrating that experience into your present sense of self-identity, then you will be able to facilitate a child's confrontation with the hurt and pain of crisis without becoming unduly anxious or overwhelmed by your own memories.[5]

2. Plan care for *every* caregiver. Be alert to the fact that a constant denial of pain is common among caregivers. If planners do not seriously consider this fact, they may misinterpret a caregiver's emotional health. This misunderstanding could result in caregivers struggling to cope without a supportive context and system of care.

3. No one should have to carry his or her pain alone—it becomes too heavy a burden to bear. Provide an outlet for caregivers to express their feelings. Just as they encourage children to talk about their pain to facilitate their healing, so you must encourage the caregivers to talk about the painful emotions with which they struggle. You also may find it helpful to use techniques employed with the children for expressing feelings, such as singing, writing, drama or other art forms.

Plan specific, frequent times when caregivers can converse together in an emotionally safe environment where they can feel free to vent their anger, frustrations, fears, inadequacies and other troubling feelings or emotions. Expressing their feelings will also help them gain perspective on their situation and come to an understanding of the causes for their reactions and emotions.

The persons conducting the debriefing sessions might want to first review some particularly traumatic situations the team has recently encountered, sharing some of their own emotional responses to what they observed. Although you want to encourage honest and open sharing, however, be cautious about pushing anyone into opening up prematurely. Some people need extra time and space to reflect and work through issues before they share openly. When you provide a warm, caring and nurturing environment, frozen emotions will begin to thaw and soon come tumbling out naturally.

Time together in a group can also be a forum for peer supervision and support: strategizing, discussion of problems concerning children or work situations, discovering solutions, sharing areas of expertise and prayer support.

4. Elicit professional feedback. A decline in work performance affects professional self-image and creates interpersonal difficulties on the job. Clarify and set priorities regarding role demands and encourage open communication with other team members about mutual responsibilities. To reduce role conflicts and stress, consider reassigning responsibilities.

5. Help caregivers know how to set limits—or boundaries—on their energies, time, competency and resources. Help them to not feel guilty if they must stop before they have completed all their work or if they do not feel qualified to perform a task. Encourage and assist caregivers to set their own reasonable goals and expectations. Empower them to use their skills, knowledge and strength as an investment in the children's lives.

6. Children cannot accept mental health care while they are physically ill or starving. Equip caregivers with a referral list of agencies that can assist with the provision of food, medical care or shelter. Enable them to act as advocates and referral persons when someone approaches them about these necessities. If these resources are not available for the children, then caregivers need help in addressing the crucial question of whether it is appropriate to launch psychological interventions.

7. Set a reasonable work schedule for caregivers. For their off-hours, it is important to provide caregivers with a relaxing environment with social and fun activities that allow them to become temporarily detached from their work. This will provide a change of environment for their minds, relieving them of the heavy burden of work-related stresses.

Children often refuse to play in a traumatic situation. They feel it is not right to play while others are grieving. Caregivers often voice this attitude, feeling guilty for even expressing their sense of humor. Yet many caregivers testify that the only way they could remain sane in deeply traumatic situations was to find ways to express humor and to keep laughing. In times of deep sorrow, to think about relaxing with a comedy program seems almost sacrilegious, yet it can prove to be an effective therapeutic measure for stressed-out caregivers.

8. For additional emotional stability, do everything possible to provide caregivers with a safe and secure working environment. A sense of safety is a basic need for everyone.

9. Especially in a long-term situation, encourage caregivers to become involved with and integrated into the life of the local community. Various community resources may be available to provide additional support and vital networking for the caregivers and to enhance their care of the children: religious leaders, local government bureaus and agencies, civic organizations, recreational facilities, educational agencies and so forth.

10. Help caregivers become aware of and appreciate the ways their care for the children enriches not only the children's lives, but also their own. Some benefits caregivers receive include appreciating life more fully, taking life more seriously, having a greater scope of understanding of others and themselves, forming new friendships, feeling inspired by daily examples of the children's courage, resiliency and hope, being able to experience true compassion and discovering a higher purpose in life. Let caregivers encourage each other by sharing with the group their own discoveries of enrichment. Discuss how these experiences are causing them to mature and develop, and become more holistic in their outlook and attitudes.

Judith Herman points out that by constantly fostering the capacity for integration in themselves and in those with whom they work, engaged caregivers deepen their own integrity. She

235

believes that just as basic trust is the developmental achievement of earliest life, integrity is the developmental achievement of maturity. She defines emotionally healthy integrity as

> the capacity to affirm the value of life in the face of death,
> to be reconciled with the finite limits of one's own life
> and the tragic limitations of the human condition, and to
> accept these realities without despair. Integrity is the
> foundation upon which trust in relationships is originally
> formed, and upon which shattered trust may be restored.
> The interlocking of integrity and trust in caretaking rela-
> tionships completes the cycle of generations and regener-
> ates the sense of human community which trauma
> destroys.[6]

Considering the importance of this kind of integrity for the
caregivers' personal and professional lives, caring for the caregivers
takes on an important added dimension. Those providing care to
the caregivers have the immense task of striving to furnish a
healthy emotional environment that not only enables caregivers to
provide competent care to the children, but also allows those benefits that naturally accrue from healthy service to others to take root.

Success in this provides the caregiver with a developmental
framework in which ongoing professional training and personal
maturity can take place. Such care also provides caregivers with a
broader perspective on life and a deeper sense of purpose. The
challenge is impressive but the results are value-laden for both the
children and their caregivers.

NOTES

1   H. Norman Wright, *Crisis Counseling* (Ventura, California: Regal
    Books, 1993), p. 59.

2   Kendall Johnson, *Trauma in the Lives of Children* (Macmillan, 1989),
    p. 59.

3   Ibid., p. 171.

4   L. B. Wallach, Unpublished notes, Chicago: Erikson Institute, 1991. And James Garbarino, et al., *Children in Danger: Coping with the Consequences of Community Violence* (San Francisco: Jossey-Bass Publishers, 1992), p. 184.

5   Andrew D. Lester, *Pastoral Care with Children in Crisis* (Philadelphia: The Westminster Press, 1985), pp. 80-81.

6   Judith Lewis Herman, *Trauma and Recovery* (Basic Books, 1992), pp. 153-154.

15

Children Helping Children

Clare Hanbury

War, poverty, disaster or conflict often cause children to have learning problems and difficulties in their relationships with others. A secure environment, caring families or understanding adults and young friends help children to develop better.

Understanding children's needs

Besides the basic needs for survival, children need:

- Affection
- Security
- Attention
- Play

Children need help to recognize their own value and their rights. War, disaster and conflict break up and disrupt a normal, healthy pattern of life.

Basic needs: When children are cold, hungry and without shelter they do not develop well and become ill quickly.

Affection: When parents are frightened and trying to survive, they cannot give their children the affection and security they need for proper physical, mental and emotional development.

Security: When violence and catastrophe occur daily, children lose their knowledge of normal, good behavior. Children lose their trust in adults who act violently.

Attention: When war or violence threatens or destroys the people, places and other things that matter to children, and when adults are too worried or unhappy to notice them, children may feel unimportant or useless.

The effects of war, disaster or conflict can leave children:

- Burdened with knowledge of hardship and violence
- Worried and insecure
- Unwilling to trust people, even those who want to help them
- In poor health and with low spirits. This can make children uninterested and slow to learn.
- Angry, restless, overexcited or behaving in surprising ways

Children may appear to be coping well on the surface, but they still have fears and problems that they will need to sort out.

How to help

Twelve-year-old Dan lives in a refugee camp. He has seen many people killed and wounded, including his uncle whom he loved very much. Although in the daytime he is polite, helpful and caring toward his family, during the night he cries, screams out and talks in his sleep as he remembers the frightening things he has seen. His older brother tries to help him by talking to him and reading to him each night before he goes to sleep.

Children need help from adults and other children. Children need a secure environment.

In the family, parents (or other adults caring for the children) must understand the importance of listening to the children, discussing and explaining things to them, being honest and truthful with them, planning things together and giving children a second chance when they make mistakes.

To provide a caring environment, adults will also need help and support from others in the community.

240

Teachers or organizers can encourage discussion with children about things that worry or frighten them. It is important for parents and other adults such as community leaders to understand and discuss children's fears and worries. Teachers or organizers can encourage the children to do so.

Children may find it difficult to talk about their problems. Caregivers must listen carefully to what children are saying and watch what they do; this often explains how children feel. Adults listen to children, watch how they behave, listen to what they do not or cannot say. Children notice when friends are sad or worried, talk and play together and help solve other children's problems.

Activities

There are many activities that are fun and also help children to gain confidence, power to express themselves and to make a contribution and help others. Activities such as meetings, clubs and campaigns can help develop a child's sense of belonging. Sports, making toys and games, drawing or play acting can help restore children's interest in the things around them and build their self-respect.

Working with children who have difficulties is not easy. These children are often uncooperative, destructive or aggressive. Try to find out what is behind these behaviors and give them interesting things to do. Children often respond well if they have responsibility. This helps them earn the respect of others.

Working together as a group

Talking and working things out in small groups can be a good way to develop children's self-confidence and help them express their problems and fears. Many children will not find it easy to work in groups.

When children work together in groups, they will need plenty of encouragement. At first, they may find working together frustrating, but as the activities progress children will become more open with their feelings and opinions. In the end, children should be participating and cooperating well.

Children enjoy making up and keeping rules that help the group work well, such as:

- Raise your hand if you want to speak.
- Only one person speaks at a time.
- Only criticize in a nice way.
- Limit the number of times one person can speak.
- Sometimes, choose a chairperson or someone to take notes.

HELPING CHILDREN FEEL SECURE

Games

The trust circle. A small group stands in a close circle with someone in the center who closes his eyes. He lets himself fall toward the circle of children. Those closest to him catch him and push him gently toward another part of the circle—and so on until the child in the center wants to stop.

The blind walk. Do this in pairs. One child is blindfolded (or keeps her eyes shut). The other child guides her around the room, or outside, explaining the obstacles. Try this with and without talking.

Cat and mouse. The group forms a circle. One child stands in the center of a circle. This is the "mouse." Another child stands outside the circle. This person is the "cat." The cat has to try to catch the mouse. The group tries to stop the cat from catching the mouse.

Relaxation

With their eyes shut, children can:

- Listen to music or sounds outside.
- Squeeze and relax each part of their body in turn.

- Listen to the rhythm of their breathing.
- Listen to a story or a "picture" being painted in their minds by the organizer or by another child such as a beach scene, a mountain scene or some place peaceful and beautiful.

Story telling

Older people can read or tell stories to children. Individually or in groups, children can tell stories; they can act out stories; they can make up new stories or tell traditional stories.

Helping children to listen and express themselves

A role play about listening

Divide into small groups. One person is the speaker and talks about any subject they like for about three minutes. Another person is the listener and must show the speaker that they listened carefully. The third person is an observer and must observe how "well" the listener listened and report on this to the rest of the group. After a feedback session, speakers, listeners and observers can exchange roles.

A listening activity

Select a position in your meeting place where everyone can see a "speaker." Call this the "speaking place." This place might be on a chair in front of a group, on a desk or under a tree. The leader announces a "speaking topic," such as "accidents." Children take turns in telling a story related to the topic. They can begin their story by saying, " When I was very small, I climbed this tree . . ."

Other ideas for topics:

- If I were a rich person, I would . . .
- What makes me feel good
- What makes me angry

The children will have many more ideas. When they get more confident, they can use this time more freely to share experiences and problems.

Group discussions

Children in groups can work together to solve problems. They have to think of peaceful ways to resolve quarrels. Here are two examples:

1. Two families quarrel when the animals from one family have caused damage to the crops growing on the other family's land.

2. In one family, there are many children who make a lot of noise. The neighbors are angry with this family, who do not seem to care about the noise they are making.

Drawing

Children can use drawing to help express their feelings and individuality. They can illustrate stories people tell or their own stories. They can draw on the ground, on paper, on walls, with paints, pencils, chalks, sand and so on. They can draw while listening to music. Caregivers can use drawing as a starting point for story telling, drama or music.

Plays and puppets

Plays are a useful starting point for discussion. You could use the following play about Maria to start discussions, story telling or other drama activities. Children can use the story line or the different characters and make up new plays. Puppets can help children explore sensitive subjects such as missing family or friends, or violent events that children have seen or participated in.

A play

Setting: A home for children separated from their parents.

Scene 1 — In the girls' dormitory

Nine-year-old Maria sits on the floor, looking at a photograph. Five of her friends run out the door to go to a class. Sonia, their housemother, stands by the door.

Sonia: Come on, Maria, hurry up! You will be late for class.

Maria: Sonia, I don't feel well. I want to talk to you. You see this photo . . . do you know—

Sonia: Maria—hurry! I have no time for talking. Go to your class and go quickly!

Scene 2 — On the way to class

Maria is walking alone. Pedro comes running up behind her.

Pedro: Hello, Maria. I'm late too! Come on, let's run together.

Maria: No, I'm not running. I don't feel well. Sonia just told me to hurry up and go.

Scene 3 — At class

The teacher notices that Maria looks miserable.

Teacher: I'm very sorry that you are not feeling well, Maria. Just sit quietly in the back of the room. Take this book, look at the pictures and you can tell me which ones you like the best.

Later, the class is having a discussion about feelings.

Camila: I feel happy today because the beans I planted are grow-
          ing.

Julieta: I am worried because my baby brother is not well.

Tomás: I cried because I saw a big boy shouting at my friend and
          hitting him.

Maria: I am feeling tired and my tummy hurts.

Teacher: Try to think what you can do to solve your problems.

Camila: Why don't you read your brother stories and give him
          lots of boiled water to drink?

Julieta: Keep your friend away from the bullies, Tomás.

Maria: Tell your friend to ignore the bullies.

Tomás: Maria, maybe your tummy hurts because you are hun-
          gry. You can have some of my bread and we can walk
          together around the compound. That might make you
          feel less tired.

Scene 4 — In the evening at the children's home

*Rosa is an older child who came to the children's home at the same time as
Maria. They talk together at supper time.*

Rosa: What have you been doing today?

Maria: Sonia would not talk to me this morning, but my friend
          Tomás gave me some of his bread. He was kind. We
          played together.

Rosa: What are you going to do now?

Maria: I'm not much good at doing anything.

Rosa: That's not true. Why don't we do something together?

Maria: Can I show you my photograph?

Writing

Writing can help children to express their feelings. Children
enjoy writing poems and stories for their friends. The following
poem was written in what was a war-torn part of Uganda. In it, the

247

guns of destruction have been transformed into weapons of knowledge that free people from disease.

> Ah, Mother, Father,
> death and terrible tears
> tears were everywhere in our village
>
> Oh those six great killers
> whooping cough, measles, TB
> tetanus, polio, diphtheria
>
> They are very close friends
> they are powerful fighters
> and their only desire is to kill
>
> Those six great diseases are related.
> Whooping cough is the brother of TB
> Tetanus, the cousin of diphtheria.
> Measles, grandfather of polio
>
> These six relatives move easily.
> They have special vehicles for traveling;
> they have germs as their comfortable cars.
> These cars travel from person to person
>
> When they enter a person's body
> they organize guerilla warfare.
> A person who is not immunized
> will be killed in this war.
>
> But clever mothers take their children for vaccination.
> They become strong; they don't get diseases
>
> Vaccines are the enemies of these great fighters.
> They organize a special resistance army
> and fight the killers
>
> Immunize your children
> and fight the great killers
> whooping cough and TB

diphtheria and tetanus
measles and polio
and be free

Dancing
Older children can teach traditional dances to younger ones. Children can invent and perform dances.

HELPING CHILDREN TO MAKE A DIFFERENCE

The older child as a helper

If a child has problems, other children can help. Often children are better at finding the right way to help. Older children can comfort younger ones, make toys for them, tell or read them stories, teach them songs and dances and help them with school work.

Children as health messengers

Children involved with child-to-child health activities feel that they are doing something useful and important. Children spread health messages and teach others about good health.

The Child-to-Child Trust[1] has activity sheets that cover a wide range of health topics such as: nutrition, safe lifestyles and the prevention and cure of disease. Child-to-child health activities help develop all the skills of group work.

[This chapter was based on Child-to-Child Activity Sheet 8.4. Child-to-Child Activity Sheets are a resource for teachers and health and community workers. They are designed to help children understand how to improve health in other children, their families and their communities. Topics chosen are important for community health and suit the age, interests and experience of children. The text, ideas and acitivities may be freely adapted to suit local conditions.]

NOTES

1   For more information on Child-to-Child activities and a full list of
    publications, contact:

    The Child-to-Child Trust
    The Institute of Education
    20, Bedford Way
    London WC1H 0AL
    United Kingdom

— motivation = care for the children.
             = care for our own children who are
               scared of those who are severely
               traumatized right now.

— Competition may be a North American plague.
  Treated as healthy + necessary, competition may
  well be a social cancer killing our desire to
  help others.

16

Peace Education
and Conflict Resolution

Delores Friesen

As a counselor and teacher, I often meet victims of abuse, igno-
rance and suffering who are so discouraged they want to give up. In
training others to work in the healing ministries of counseling, teaching and evangelism, I try to give at least as much attention to prevention and justice ministries as I do to the healing and caring ministries.

It is appropriate to feed the hungry, heal the wounded and
rescue the perishing, but one also must ask why these persons are
hungry, wounded and dying. A person cannot go on carrying out
rescue operations without trying to find out why people keep
falling into the river of despair and suffering.

If there is abuse, what can someone do to stop the violence?
If there is war, how can the two sides come together in peace? If
there are no options for growth and learning, how can anyone open
such avenues up? This chapter focuses on prevention and healing
by describing some resources for peacemaking and reconciliation
and detailing some basic conflict mediation and resolution skills.

Peace education and conflict resolution: Tools for meeting trauma

Previous chapters have described the kinds of emotions a
traumatized child or person goes through: panic, exhaustion, guilt,

rage, shame, protest, anxiety, denial, intrusive thoughts, numbing, hypervigilance, fear, confusion, impaired functioning and flash-backs. The next stage includes working through the trauma, help-ing the person to discover meaning, mourning and making new plans. In order to survive and grow beyond the crisis, a person needs to recover the ability to work, act and feel. One helpful tool is to give traumatized persons skills in resolving or meeting crisis and conflict, so they can face the future with some practical coping skills and a sense of hope and personal power.

In crisis intervention work, a caregiver rapidly establishes connections and relationships, so that the expression of painful feel-ings and emotions can happen. In discussing the events that have taken place, it is important to assess what has happened and form ideas of what you can do to restore some sense of well-being and safety. You will need both knowledge and skills to help resolve a crisis. Peacemaking and conflict resolution skills are useful both in processing trauma and pain and in working toward the prevention of violence and war. If a person has concrete ways to respond to threats and oppression, this lessens the sense of helplessness and victimization. These skills can bring hope, empower the weak and restore relationships.

If you are working in a religious setting, there are many passages and stories in both the Old and New Testaments that illus-trate and illuminate these concepts. The Beatitudes in Matthew 5, Psalms 34 and 85, Jeremiah 8:11-15, Luke 1:46-55, 68-79 and Matthew 18 are particularly helpful.

Children have most of their problems in one of the follow-ing areas: conflict with others, conflict with self, lack of information about self, lack of skill and lack of information about the environ-ment. As individuals we often have conflict with others. We may also have internal conflict with self, lack of information about self or lack of information about the environment. These areas account for most of the problems human beings encounter. Learning con-flict resolution and peacemaking skills is a very significant way of meeting both personal and interpersonal needs.

Healing through story

Story telling is a very important way of releasing internal feelings and conflicts. In the Liberia conflict, adults and children often recounted what it meant for them to "walk the road." Verbalizing the terrors of seeing persons killed, scattered and lost became part of the healing process for both the speakers and the listeners. Poetry, story writing and drawing may also serve as outlets for feelings and experiences that are unspeakable or difficult to share.

One story telling technique that may help to give support is to have a group of people form a circle. Two to four persons go into the center of the circle to tell their story, and then exchange places with others in the outer circle until all who wish to tell their story have done so. This "fishbowl" method makes the speaker feel listened to and surrounds the speaker with a circle of caring persons.

The other person or persons inside the circle may wish to hold hands or otherwise physically touch the speaker or respond with encouraging gestures or eye contact. This is not a time for discussion, however. Simply let the speakers tell their stories in an environment of support and affirmation. This will encourage the listeners to make peace by grasping the depth of pain and suffering experienced by others. Those who share their stories often experience some release and healing.

If there are other sources of story, life experience and history available in your setting, use them to dramatize and illustrate the principles that follow. For example, in my religious tradition there is a large book called *Martyrs Mirror*, which contains thousands of stories of persons who were martyred for their faith from the time of Jesus through the seventeenth century. When I was a child and young adult, these stories were shared in many settings at home, church and school. They served as an inspiration and example of what it means to follow the way of Jesus in life and death. One of the more famous stories is that of Dirk Willems.

In 1569, Dirk Willems was jailed because of his religious beliefs. He managed to escape, but a prison guard observed him and pursued him across an ice-covered pond. As he reached the opposite side, Willems turned and saw that his pursuer had fallen through the ice. Dirk turned back and saved the man's life. Willems was recaptured, jailed and burned at the stake. Despite his heroic rescue of his enemy, the authorities still killed him. He had the kind of commitment it took to love an enemy and give up his life for doing good. These historical examples help motivate us to exercise faith and learn skills of peace. Nelson Mandela and Mother Teresa are two present-day, living examples whose stories you can tell or dramatize.

You can also create and stage biblical dramas. A biblical drama created in Ghana grew out of a South African sermon on the first Adam and the second Adam. As the preacher told it, the first Adam—the ancestor of all humankind—went to heaven and held a place of honor there. But he had to bear the consequences of his sin. Therefore, from his seat in heaven, he had to watch all the hatred and killing, lying and cruelty that resulted from his sin. He watched Cain kill Abel, Joseph's brothers sell Joseph into slavery, King David with Bathsheba and Uriah and many other events in biblical history, and finally the events surrounding Jesus' crucifixion.

As each event unfolded, Adam hung his head, beat his breast and said, "Oh, my God, my God, what have I begun—the weight of my sin and guilt is too much to bear," or "My guilt, my guilt . . . isn't there anything that can be done?" When finally the second Adam walks into heaven declaring that he has won the victory over sin and death, the sermon and drama close with the powerful words, "And the first Adam had peace."

"Solomon's Wisdom" is another powerful biblical drama created by some participants in the healing and reconciliation workshops in Liberia. They simply portrayed the dilemma of the two mothers who both claimed that one child was theirs and linked that story to that of their country's civil war. It provided a very powerful political and spiritual moment of truth and insight.

Language, drama, music, dance and art are media for the expression of feelings, dreams, vision, hope and despair. It is important to allow the telling of both negative and positive experiences. Healing and reconciliation come only in the acknowledgment of darkness and terror. When in trouble, allow the full, free and total expression of laments. Pouring out a lament is not an expression of a lack of trust. Consider the place of lament in the Psalms, in Job's experience, in literature and music. It is also helpful to engage in illusory thinking, "I would that there were . . ." as a way of moving beyond present despair.

Stories acknowledge the deep human needs for love, safety, shelter and warmth. Listening to and telling stories helps us to belong, to love and to survive. A story telling circle or community is interconnected, balanced and purposeful. It processes pain, lays the foundation for seeking solutions to problems and encourages and strengthens a sense of solidarity and understanding. The Lord God asked the children of Israel to recount his marvelous deeds, lest they forget how they survived the wilderness, the Red Sea and the plagues and oppression of Egypt.

Memorials of stones, places, altars and events can also serve as sacred reminders of the experiences of inhumanity and grief. Remember Job, who wished that his words were engraved in a rock so that no one would forget what he had suffered (Job 19:24). Part of peacemaking within may require some outward symbol or sign of acknowledgment. Naming those who have died, bringing symbols of suffering or healing to a worship table, planting something to symbolize new life or composing a song are some signs that come to mind.

Defining community and conflict

A warm and caring community needs these five qualities:

1. Cooperation
2. Communication
3. Tolerance
4. Positive emotional expression
5. Conflict resolution

Things that work against such a peaceful atmosphere include competition, intolerance, poor communication, inappropriate expression of emotion, lack of conflict resolution skills and mis-use of power.[1] Situations charged with bad feelings, lack of trust, unresolved or suppressed conflicts, irrational or impossibly high expectations, inflexible rules and an authoritarian use of power create an atmosphere of fear and mistrust.

Conflicts tend to fall into three areas: 1) Conflict over resources—two or more parties want something that is scarce; 2) conflict over needs—needs for power, safety, food, self-determination, friendship, self-esteem and achievement; and 3) conflicting values and beliefs. The last area is the most difficult type of conflict to resolve. Challenging a person's values threatens a person's sense of self, and people cling to positions with a tenacity that other types of conflict do not inspire. Goal conflicts are also value conflicts.

Most of us know only three ways to respond to conflict: 1) respond aggressively, that is, physically, verbally or in some other way to defeat our opponent; 2) appeal to a higher authority or someone stronger to battle for us; or 3) ignore the situation.

These are ineffective ways to resolve conflict. Instead, they increase both internal and external stress and tension. Everyone needs to develop peacemaking skills and learn how and when to apply them most effectively.

Conflicts *escalate* (grow bigger and more serious) if:

- There is an increase in exposed emotion, such as anger and frustration
- There is an increase in perceived threat
- More people get involved, choosing sides
- The children were not friends prior to the conflict
- The children have few peacemaking skills at their disposal

Conflicts *de-escalate* or are more easily solved if:

- Attention is focused on the problem, not on the participants
- There is a decrease in exposed emotions and perceived threats

- The children were friends prior to the conflict
- The children know how to make peace, or have someone to help them to do so
- One person cools the conflict, keeping it from spreading and becoming more violent, and channels it along positive rather than negative lines

This is very different from the aggressive and passive ways most of us use to handle conflicts. Physical or emotional hurt, humiliation and suppressed anger accompany passive and aggressive responses. Such responses also tend not to solve problems, are ineffective and leave us at the mercy of a conflict, feeling overwhelmed by it and powerless to respond effectively. "Either the other person wins or I win." This locks persons into a behavior pattern with no apparent way out.

Teaching children to be peacemakers

Preventing conflicts is the work of politics; establishing peace is the work of education. — Maria Montessori

Conflict resolution and peace education means learning a whole range of responses that lie between aggression and inaction. It is looking for constructive alternatives and acting on them. Losing and winning are not the only options.

Instead, a person tries to generate solutions or come to new understandings of the situation: "Let's talk." "Let's look for a solution." "What are the underlying needs and wants?" For example, a fight is a concentration of physical and emotional energy. Anything you can do to divert this energy will help cool the situation. What are the needs of the two persons who are fighting? Does someone feel disrespected? Made fun of? Put down? Are there inadequate resources to go around? The simplest way to deal with a fight is to:

- Break it up
- Cool it off
- Work it out

We can summarize problem-solving techniques as: 1) define the problem, 2) produce solutions, and 3) choose and act. It is not easy to identify problems in terms of needs, but it is an important first step in working toward a solution or an "I win, you win" stance.

William Kriedler suggests considering the following four things when you need to choose a conflict resolution technique:[2]

1. Who is involved? How old, how mature, how angry are they? What are their needs?

2. Is the time right? Do you have enough time to work things out now or should you wait? Do the participants need to cool off first? Is it too soon to talk things out?

3. How appropriate is a particular resolution technique?

4. Should the resolution be public or private? Would the persons involved be embarrassed or would others benefit from seeing the conflict resolved? Could these other beneficiaries help with the resolution?

There are many skills that facilitate the smooth management of conflict. Some of these are cooperation and communication skills, the ability to express feelings constructively and tolerance of diversity. Learning to tolerate and appreciate diversity is another aspect of peacemaking that we should not neglect. Conflicts often arise out of a lack of acceptance or understanding. Learning about other cultures, languages, and religions and noticing the pluses and minuses of having different customs, inheritances and values will help to open the door to fruitful conversation. We need to confront, acknowledge and understand prejudice or it will undermine attempts to resolve conflict and make peace.

A conflict resolution technique simply provides a safe, structured way to air grievances, feelings and differences of opinion so that a conflict can serve a useful purpose. Some useful techniques include:

Cooling off, mediation, smoothing, reflective listening, story telling, time out, written fight forms for children to report problems, role playing, role reversals, the problem puppets and the three "R" strategy: resentment, request, recognition.

There is also the "fight fair" method: state the facts as calmly as possible and refer only to the present situation, not to the past or future. Express how you feel. Talk about your feelings without making negative remarks about the other person. Find out what you can do about the situation. Try to think of a solution that will satisfy all the participants.

Advocacy and action

Too often we give children answers to remember rather than problems to solve. — Roger Lewis

Peacemaking includes internal processing and external action, and witness. Persons whose way of life has been destroyed by violence or trauma often need persons to advocate for them. They also need to learn the skills of advocacy and political action. Four of the steps that bring change are: 1) becoming aware, 2) gathering resources, 3) developing models, and 4) challenging structures.[3]

Paul Tournier says that "the key to the problem of violence is to be found in that of power: that benign violence is that which is put at the service of others, protecting the weak, healing the sick, liberating the exploited, fighting the injustice of the powerful; and that improper violence is violence on one's own behalf, aimed at securing power for oneself, violence which is inspired by the fascination of power."[4] He goes on to suggest that a major difference between power and violence is that power is accessible to reflection, while violence is unleashed passion, a kind of rage that suspends all reason.

Violence has short-term, immediate objectives in mind. Empowerment works out a whole strategy, weighs dangers, sets limits and develops all the stages of progress. Conflict resolution and peacemaking skills are tools to empower and engage persons in settling differences and meeting needs.

259

Teaching students and others to be peacemakers

The following are several lists of issues and topics to discuss in the process of learning to be peacemakers.

A global perspective; global awareness; basic facts and comparisons; global connectedness; global interdependence; trade relations; resources; religion; social, political and economic interrelations between nations; cross-cultural understandings; and an appreciation and respect for diversity, while emphasizing similarities—finding common ground.

Conflict resolution skills, ranging from a personal to a global level: defining conflicts; understanding the causes of conflicts; gathering information; examining facts and feelings; generating and choosing solutions; and using critical thinking skills.

Peacemaking strategies; a study of and participation in strategies resulting in a just and peaceful world, including cultural exchanges and networking; use of nonviolence and pacifism; religions; respect and empathy for human rights; economic, environmental, scientific and other cooperation; force and deterrence; and a historical review of peacemakers.

A conflict resolution model

Although it is not the only way to organize conflict resolution skills, the SIGEP model[5] (Stop - Identify - Generate - Evaluate - Plan) may be one of the easiest to remember.

Stop

When you find yourself being drawn into a conflict, the first step is to stop and decide how you want to handle the conflict. If you decide to negotiate, the first step is to calm down enough to negotiate

Identify the problem

Sometimes the problem is straightforward; at other times it is not. State concerns in terms of "needs" rather than "solutions." A need is the underlying concern. A solution is one way to meet the underlying need. Make sure that both parties agree to what the problem is about. It may be necessary to look at things from the

260

other party's perspective to correctly identify the problem. Stating the problem in terms of needs instead of solutions increases the possible ways to get what someone wants. This also increases the chances of finding something that works well for both parties.

Generate (Gather) ideas

The more ideas you have, the more likely you are to find ones that you can agree on. Try to come up with at least twenty ideas. When you generate ideas, include some "crazy" ideas as well as practical ones. This helps everyone get past the one-sided, typical, too-easy answers. If you cannot move forward, you can return to the problem and review it or look at the "idea starters" below. Remember that this is the time to free your imagination. You can evaluate the ideas after you generate them.

Idea starters: Who else can do it? Where else can we do it? What else can we use to do it or solve the problem? What can we add to make it easier? What can we remove to eliminate the problem? How would an expert solve the problem? What would Jesus do about this? How would God handle the problem?

Evaluate the ideas

Read the list of ideas one by one and check on how everyone feels about each idea. Put a star by each idea for every person who finds the idea acceptable. During this process, people will often object to particular ideas. Jot those objections down also. If you have several ideas that everyone likes, you can go on to making a decision. If no idea has everyone's approval, then consider the ideas with the most supporters and see how you can modify them to make them acceptable to the others. Remind yourselves that you are committed to finding an idea that works for everyone. When you have evaluated all the ideas and at least one idea is acceptable to everyone involved in the conflict, you can then make a decision and implement it.

Develop a plan

Many good ideas falter because there is no plan for implementation and evaluation. Differences arise in people's expectations. There are many issues to resolve. When you make a decision, consider how to implement it. Consider, also, what could go wrong with the decision, and if there is an alternate or "backup" plan that everyone finds acceptable. Plan how you might handle the situation. Unexpected problems rarely cause major difficulties if there is a structure for dealing with them. If things do not work out, go back to the beginning and start again or return to another idea you generated in step three.

Mediation

Sometimes it is necessary to have a third party or outside mediator come in to help with the process. Mediation is simply a process by which the parties to the conflict consult with a neutral third party to settle the areas of disagreement. The mediator does not dictate or decide the solution, but helps both sides listen to each other and work together to find a mutually agreeable solution.

This often reduces the anxiety, anger and communication problems, and it can help to clarify the areas of agreement and non-agreement. A mediator may take several roles: that of educator or expert, translator, message carrier, discussion facilitator, summarizer, rebuilder of relationships, agent of reality, face-saver, lightning rod, idea generator. In other words, a mediator may be able to listen to both sides *when hostility or tension is too high for either party to speak directly to the other*.

See Matthew 18 for some biblical guidelines for when and how to use a mediation process. A mediator keeps a balance between control and participation, makes sure the issues are identified and clarified, points out areas of agreement and disagreement and summarizes.

The process of mediation is very similar to the SIGEP model, but it can often identify blocks or why the process does not work. Mediation usually includes: 1) introduction—who is there, what will happen, ground rules, clarification of the mediator's role, expectations, what happens if the parties cannot agree; 2) gathering information—presenting problems, safety concerns, availability of resources and support; 3) isolating issues and finding hidden agendas—underlying causes, communication blocks, motivations, power differences; 4) development of alternatives - brainstorming, suggestions, recommendations; and 5) decisions and production of agreement.

A mediator needs the following skills and techniques:

◆ Ability to build and maintain trust and confidence

◆ Ability to clarify issues, ask questions, summarize

◆ Ability to break deadlocks or impasses

◆ Ability to help the parties save face

◆ Ability to keep emotions under control

◆ Ability to identify power differences and hidden agendas

◆ Ability to separate needs from motivations and wants

Other roles and methods

Some other roles that may be needed in conflict resolution and peacemaking are that of *observer* (helps to discourage violence, documents what is happening), *sustainer* (helps locate resources and support so the parties will not give up), *legitimizer* (helps establish the credibility of the weaker party's needs, may also verify legal rights), *advocate* (a sustainer and legitimizer who speaks for the weaker party, may represent persons to government or others who hold power), *resources expander* (helps persons access the system and network, so everyone stands to win more) and *activist* (arouses energy that can be channeled toward constructive change).[6]

Another way to think of the conflict resolution process is: introduction, story telling, problem solving, agreement.

In the *introduction* stage you want just the parties involved present (as few people as possible). Establish guidelines for the process.

In the *story telling* stage, persons or sides describe their feelings, talk about when-who-what caused the situation or problem, then try to get to the root cause or "why" questions, before turning to solutions. Listen for facts, feelings, demands, possible solutions and needs to reflect what you are hearing or encourage more detail to clarify the situation. Some examples of what you might say are: "Tell me more about that" "So you felt that was really unfair" "What would you like to have happen next?" "Could you explain that?" "What do you mean by . . .?" "I am not sure I understand that . . ." "Could you elaborate?"

In the *problem-solving* stage, list areas that need resolution and focus on issues of both agreement and disagreement. Ask such questions as: "What will it take to resolve these issues?" "Where does common ground exist?" "Where or from whom can I get what I need to make agreement possible?" This stage may take a lot of patience. It helps to brainstorm solutions, list solution criteria, evaluate the solutions against the criteria established and then develop the best or most acceptable answer. Resolution is based on: satisfying needs, saving face and self-respect. You may need to recognize and express anger, but do so with "I" messages rather than "you" messages. Ask questions in order to learn and to generate possible solutions, rather than to accuse or blame.

In the *agreement* stage, summarize the process and solution clearly and in detail, so everyone understands what it is they have agreed to. "Each of you has agreed to do certain things." "You have agreed to do . . . Is that right?" Establish ownership of the agreement. Sometimes a written or symbolic form is helpful at this point. Follow-up to see if the solution reached is still satisfactory.

What if all attempts fail?

If the parties do not reach an agreement, then it is important to stay in contact with them. Over time, more trust may develop, or there may be new information or developments that will help to soften attitudes. New events tend to work in favor of compromise and resolution. Sometimes parties weary of the frustration and expense of continued discord and fighting. Spiritually and emotionally wounded people may need time to heal and open up to God's grace.

When there is no resolution, agree to meet again. Recognize and help individuals express anger and hurt in safe and appropriate places and ways. Use "I" messages to further define the problem and ask questions to learn more about the needs of each person involved.

When everyone negotiates in good faith, the goal is resolution. A win-win solution preserves the dignity of both parties. It helps to be specific and open to facts. The ability to initiate conversation and maintain a humble spirit that thinks the best of people are two other very valuable peacemaking skills. We can see conflict as a tool that helps us to understand and meet needs. *It can be constructive if it helps to identify evil, and stops violence from happening.* Conflict resolution leads to healing and restoration. It also ensures that needs are met at least in part, or that people are willing to continue the conversational process.

System adaptability depends on leadership, rules and roles, negotiation, organization and values. System cohesion—how to balance autonomy and separateness with mutuality and togetherness—depends on how individuals deal with closeness, support, decision-making, commonality and unity. In order to move from victim to survivor to peacemaker, people must be adaptable and maintain both separateness and connectedness.

Peacemaking and conflict resolution skills are invaluable in developing flexibility in the face of crisis. Individuals have to take responsibility for their own future and emotional well-being, yet remain emotionally engaged with others in the system, even if they are enemies. Resist focusing on changing others, do not get too anxious and keep clear boundaries of safety and self. Jesus, Martin Luther King, Mother Teresa and Nelson Mandela are individuals who have been able to live out these principles in powerful and life-changing ways that have enabled many others to find hope, salvation, healing and *shalom*.

NOTES

1   I am indebted in this section to ideas from William Kreidler's book, *Creative Conflict Resolution* (Glenview, Illinois: Scott, Foresman & Co., 1984).

2   Ibid.

3   C. Dean Freudenberger has elaborated on these ideas in his writings on ways to deal with world hunger.

4   Paul Tournier, *The Violence Within* (San Francisco: Harper & Row, 1978), pp. 113-114.

5   Elizabeth Crary, *Kids Can Cooperate: A Practical Guide to Teach Problem Solving* (Seattle: Parenting Press, 1984), pp. 40-45.

6   Ron Kraybill, *Repairing the Breach: Ministering in Community Conflict* (Scottdale: Herald Press, 1981).

REFERENCES

Aschliman, Kathryn, ed. *Growing Toward Peace*. Scottdale, Pennsylvania: Herald Press, 1993.

Crary, E. *Kids Can Cooperate: A Practical Guide to Teaching Problem-Solving*. Seattle: Parenting Press, Inc., 1984.

Figley, C. *Helping Traumatized Families*. San Francisco: Jossey Bass Publishers, 1989.

James, Beverly. *Treating Traumatized Children: New Insights and Creative Interventions*. Lexington, Massachusetts: Lexington Books, 1989.

Kraybill, R. S. *Repairing the Breach: Ministering in Community Conflict*. Scottdale, Pennsylvania: Herald Press, 1981.

Kreidler, William J. *Creative Conflict Resolution*. Glenview, Illinois: Scott, Foresman & Co., 1984.

McGinnis, J. and K. McGinnis. *Parenting for Peace and Justice*. Maryknoll: Orbis Books, 1981.

McGinnis, K. and B. Oehlberg. *Starting Out Right: Nurturing Young Children as Peacemakers*. The Institute for Peace and Justice and Meyer Stone Books, 1990.

Tournier, P. *The Violence Within*. San Francisco: Harper & Row, 1978.

Van Ornum, William and J. B. Mordock. *Crisis Counseling with Children and Adolescents*. New York: Continuum, 1991.

Part 4

Theological Implications for Intervention Planning

17
Forgiveness in the Healing Process

Dale Henry Schumm

"In your anger do not sin . . ." (Ephesians 4:26a). These are the words of the apostle Paul when he wrote to the believers in the city of Ephesus.

I grew up with the impression that to be angry was to sin; it was not proper for Christians to be angry. The emphasis was on the "do not sin," instead of on the assumption that anger is a part of life.

The second part of the above verse tells us how to be angry and not sin: "Do not let the sun go down while you are still angry." In other words, the writer tells his readers to stay up-to-date with their anger. Do not harbor, hold on to or nurture your anger. He finishes the sentence by saying, "do not give the devil a foothold" (Ephesians 4:27).

What Paul seems to be saying is that it is all right to feel deeply. The depth of that feeling, in this case, is called anger. But, he warns, do not carry it around for long; do something about it. If you do not, it will give the devil a foothold.

When we hold on to anger, it gives the devil an opportunity and quickly turns into hate. In *Getting Bitter or Getting Better*, David Schell starts the introduction with the statement, "Hate poisons,

269

forgiveness heals." Bitterness easily turns into hatred, and hatred, in its ultimate expression, kills.

I witnessed hatred and its devastating effects on individuals, a whole population, and indeed on the entire country as I worked with the people suffering from the trauma of civil war in Liberia, West Africa, in October-November 1991. Liberia was a country with a population of about two and-a-half million before the war, which started in 1989 and continues today. Over 300,000 refugees fled the country and another quarter of a million were displaced within the country. An estimated 150,000 people have been killed, and the UN says up to 200,000 are in danger of starvation and disease in the northern areas controlled by rebel leader Charles Taylor.

After the West African peacekeeping force brought the initial part of the war to a stalemate, the Christian Health Association of Liberia (CHAL) invited me as consultant to help them assess the psychological and spiritual needs of the people. The physical needs were readily evident, but the deeper trauma was what concerned CHAL. Everyone, adults and children, had been deeply traumatized.

Almost every family had experienced death, loss of dignity and loss of possessions. The trauma was so widespread and so profound that the question was not "do we need to do something," but what to do and where to start. During the consultations in Danane, a border town in Côte d'Ivoire, with representatives of CHAL, we decided to focus first on the helping professions, which included teachers, health workers and religious workers.

We developed a five-day workshop to help these professionals begin to get in touch with, and work through, their own trauma to enable them to help the children and others who were coming to them with their emotional and physical needs. All this occurred while Desert Storm was underway. The people of the United States and the news media were so focused on Kuwait, Iraq and Saudi Arabia that other world events did not receive much notice. That is why not much was heard in the West about the Liberian situation.

People in Liberia were shot at close range as they tried to make their way through checkpoints along the roads to reach safer ground. Their homes were looted and burned. Many experienced betrayal by neighbors and friends. They endured tremendous personal devastation, seeing family members being killed in front of their eyes. If anyone dared to show any emotional response to what was happening, he or she would receive the next bullet. The Liberian people were not even allowed to take care of the bodies of their dead loved ones. They were ordered to move on and let the bodies lie where they had been shot. Sometimes family members were mutilated in front of loved ones, including the children. Even then the people did not dare show horror or any other emotion. The trauma was beyond comprehension.

Seth (I have changed all the names in the following stories to protect the identities of the individuals) was an ordained minister, translator and radio speaker. As he fled the capital city of Monrovia, the large group he traveled with was stopped at a checkpoint. A fourteen-year-old fighter pointed an AK-47 at Seth and commanded him to undress completely. What usually happened after a person undressed is that they would receive a fatal shot. As Seth undressed in embarrassment in front of hundreds of his countrymen, a commotion in another direction distracted the soldier, sparing Seth's life. Seth went on, but he could not forget this humiliating experience.

Waldo and his wife owned and operated a pharmaceutical business in the capital city. As they fled the city with their young son, a bullet from an AK-47 hit Waldo's wife in the spine, paralyzing her from the waist down. Waldo picked her up, took his son by the hand and carried his wife on his shoulders for the next several days until they reached a hospital that had been spared looting and destruction.

Yolanda was a well-dressed woman of obvious means in the past. She came to the workshop angry and bitter; she would not do any exercises or engage in any interaction for four days. Her story unfolded bit by bit during the week. Yolanda's three brothers and a sister were in a Lutheran church on July 26, 1990. Government-supported soldiers moved into that church compound and slaughtered 600 people who had taken refuge in the church.

Yolanda had also fled her home, entrusting her house keys to her neighbors. These neighbors had decided that since they were from the "right" tribe, it was safe for them to stay in the area. When Yolanda returned after the fierce fighting had subsided, she discovered that her trusted neighbors had looted and burned her house. So the stories went on day after day and week after week.

These adults are all caretakers of children who also had been severely traumatized by the atrocities of war. It is essential to help parents and caregivers deal with their own grief, trauma, forgiveness and reconciliation issues if they are to be effective in helping the children deal with theirs.

The children also have their own stories to tell: being forced to kill loved ones or to participate in other atrocities, being brutally raped and tortured by soldiers they have come to hate and being treated with injustice, humiliation and lack of respect. Many children are anxious to pick up a gun and seek revenge—not only for their own pain, but for the pain inflicted on family and friends.

How does a person deal with such inhumane treatment? What does a person do with the unforgivable? This is the background and context from which I think about forgiveness in relation to the trauma of war suffered by children and their caregivers. This was the situation that drove me back to the Bible to search for a word of hope and peace in the midst of evil and destruction. It is in this context that I reworked my understanding of forgiveness and the relationship of forgiveness and healing—both mental and spiritual.

Healing and reconciliation

We structured the Liberian healing and reconciliation process around a rhythm of teaching and therapy. The didactic (teaching) and the therapeutic (healing) go hand in hand.

Day One focused on getting in touch with the pain, the wrong, the tragedy, the injury and the woundedness. We encouraged the participants to name their losses and to grieve the losses and tragedy. We focused on helping, healing and a listening that did not reinforce feelings of hatred and revenge. We encouraged the participants to get in touch with the things they were not allowed to be in touch with before, and to grieve their losses.

Day two focused on conflict and mediation. Here we dealt with the causes of conflict and different approaches to conflict resolution, including the traditional tribal approach to conflict. We included an actual mediation experience.

Day three presented an alternative to revenge and hate: forgiveness and repentance. This became the most intense day of the week. It was also the turning point in the healing process.

Day four offered healing and hope. Here we went through several healing rituals that I describe later in this chapter.

Day five projected a new Liberia. In this exercise we used all of the five senses in expectant prayers.

Pain and healing

The Carter Center in Atlanta, U.S.A., monitors wars and at times offers mediation services. According to a January 1991 report from the Center, in 1990 there were 112 wars being fought in our world. Thirty-two of these wars were major wars, which the Center defined as a conflict that caused 1,000 or more casualties. Most of these conflicts were within national boundaries. This is a picture of the world we live in and of the conflict and woundedness within that world.

A narrower view focuses on the individual, not the world. The apostle James in his letter to the dispersed Jewish tribes asks, "What causes wars, and what causes fightings among you? Is it not your passions that are at war in your members? You desire and do not have; so you kill. And you covet and cannot obtain; so you fight and wage war" (James 4:1-2a, RSV).

We know all too well the bruising and pain that many children experience in our world. Many carry wounds, if not because of war, then because of harsh words, beatings, unjust punishment and abuse. Other children come from broken families and carry feelings of betrayal and bitterness. Where is their healing? Would-

273

be healers must first find healing for their own active, contagious infections before they can offer healing to other wounded ones.

As that infection is neutralized and no longer contagious, then healing can take place. The person who has experienced healing can begin to offer healing. The wounded person becomes a healer. This is the concept behind Henri Nouwen's *wounded healer*. Nouwen says that the minister "must look after his own wounds but at the same time be prepared to heal the wounds of others" (1979:84). The healing that is offered is not the removal of pain; rather it is taking it to a level where it can be shared.

"A Christian community is therefore a healing community not because wounds are cured and pains are alleviated, but because wounds and pains become openings or occasions for a new vision" (Nouwen 1979:96). This is the same concept that makes other rehabilitation programs such as Alcoholics Anonymous (AA) so successful. The wounded experience healing and, in return, offer healing to others and so become healers. The twelve steps of AA are merely the structure in which this takes place.

Many therapists during their training as psychological counselors experience a healing treatment for their own needs. Working through their own issues or trauma enables them to help others work through their pain. It is the personal treatment that helps a counselor guard against transferences that hinder instead of aid the healing process.

After a session of family therapy that included our whole family, my son-in-law asked me upon leaving the session, "How can you be doing therapy when you are in therapy yourself?" My response was, "Experiencing therapy better qualifies me to do therapy."

The meaning of forgiveness

Forgiveness is such a common word among Christians that it frequently holds very little meaning for us. Often people will say, "I forgive and forget" but then continue to recount the horrible things the other person did to them years ago. Or someone will say, "I'll forgive, but I'll not forget until he or she is punished in hell."

Forgiveness is not forgetting; forgiveness is neutralizing the effects of the wrong done to us. The apostle Paul in his writings to the churches reminded them repeatedly not to forget their past and where they had come from. In Colossians 3:5, Paul exhorts the Colossians to "put to death . . . whatever belongs to your earthly nature: sexual immorality, impurity, lust, evil desires and greed, which is idolatry." Then Paul reminds them that "you used to walk in these ways . . ." (Colossians 3:7a).

The apostle Peter reminded his readers, "Once you were not a people, but now you are the people of God; once you had not received mercy, but now you have received mercy" (1 Peter 2:10). Do not forget that once you were alienated from God, but now you are reconciled to him. The Bible exhorts us to remember the kind of life we once led so that we do not return to it. As a historian once said, "He who does not know his history is liable to repeat it."

To get to the true meaning of forgiveness, we must go back to the original language of the New Testament. The Greek word translated as "forgiveness" is *aphiemi*, used 146 times in the New Testament but translated forgive only 47 times. The other 99 times translators used other English words that we must examine to get the true meaning, since "forgive" has so little meaning in our current usage.

The translation and usages of *aphiemi* in the New Testament include leave (52 times); forgive (47 times); suffer, let (14); forsake (6); and let alone (6). The remaining 13 renderings include let have, send away, omit, let be, yield up, lay aside, let go, cry, remit, put away (J.B. Smith, Greek-English Concordance:874).

The central idea of *aphiemi* is "to let go." This gives a richness to the meaning of forgiveness that we often miss in our current usage.

God's forgiveness is an *act*. God forgives, and it is finished. But for humans to incorporate forgiveness into our lives and practices often means forgiveness is a *process*. The deeper the hurt, the more profound the injury, the more of a process forgiveness tends to be. Forgiveness is not simple, it is not easy—it is profound.

Criteria for authentic forgiveness

Since we have used the word forgiveness so carelessly and it has lost real meaning for many in our society, we must try to recapture its biblical meaning. I will set forth four criteria for authentic forgiveness that I have adapted from Donald Shirver's treatment on forgiveness in *The Politics of Peace*.

First, name the wrong and acknowledge the pain. Calling judgment against the wrong does not deny its pain and consequences. The offhand phrase "it doesn't matter" is not evidence of authentic forgiveness; the wrong that occurred does matter. It does matter that I hurt. It does matter that I carry the consequences. It does matter that my reputation was destroyed. It does matter that I am a psychological wreck because of sexual abuse. It does matter that a rebel killed my mother and brother. It does matter that my wife is paralyzed for life. The first step in the process of forgiveness is to name the wrong and acknowledge the depth of the pain.

The *second* step is to refuse to seek a penalty from the wrongdoer in the exact proportion of the wrong committed. Before Waldo had processed his wife's injury and the loss of his business and personal goods, he said, "I had such revenge and hatred [in my thoughts] that whenever I would see one of the fighters on the street I would turn around and walk the other way."

Later, Waldo, after going through a healing and reconciliation workshop—where he had a chance to process and to own the depth of his loss and anger—could say, "Rather than wanting revenge, I can walk right past the fighters now." The process of forgiveness is happening.

The *third* criterion is to begin to have some empathy for the humanity of the wrongdoer. Waldo is now saying that the fighters also should have the opportunity to attend one of these healing and reconciliation seminars. Furthermore he also said, "Whereas before I hated him, I now want to talk to the fighter who looted my house and is wearing my coat in the marketplace." For Waldo, hate turned to pity, which in turn became concern and eventually compassion.

On the fifth day of the seminar Seth said, "I had vowed not to talk with anyone from 'so and so' tribe ever again. Now I have been with them for five days and I have been talking with them; we have become friends. They also have been wronged." Seth was beginning to have some feeling of empathy for the wrongdoer. This is a mark of authentic forgiveness happening.

The *fourth* mark of authentic forgiveness occurs when there is the ultimate aim to restore the community relationship of all the parties involved. The ultimate aim is to reestablish the sense of community. Community in this context does not necessarily mean being close or intimate friends, but it is a hope to see the community come back together again.

It is not always possible to accomplish all four steps. There is forgiveness when criteria one and two are present. There is more forgiveness when the third criterion is also present, and still more complete forgiveness when we can meet all four criteria. It is not always possible to achieve number four.

Can there be forgiveness without repentance? Jimmy did not think so when he said, "I'll forgive him when he says that he is sorry." Let me suggest that forgiveness in the healing process is independent of repentance. One tends to encourage the other, however, but neither is dependent on the other and either can come first.

The Greek word for repentance is *metanoia*, which means "to turn," "to change one's view and purpose" and "to feel sorry for or regret."

Criteria for authentic repentance

1. Naming and acknowledging the wrong done by the wrongdoer.

2. A willingness to make restitution. Restitution is not always possible, as in the loss of Yolanda's siblings. There is no way to restore a life that has been taken. The willingness to restore what is possible, however, is an important criterion of repentance.

3. Beginning to have some empathy for the victim's suffering.

277

4. The ultimate aim of repentance is to restore the community relationship of all parties involved. Again, number four may not be possible; neither is number two possible when a life has been taken, but the willingness to make restitution is important.

The goal of repentance and forgiveness

The purposes of repentance and forgiveness are the same:

- To effect change
- To seek freedom
- To heal broken relationships
- To acknowledge the wrong done or the hurt
- To seek justice

Both repentance and forgiveness:

- Attempt to heal old wounds
- Break the cycle of violence and hatred
- Require the same mindset
- Look to a renewed future
- Tend to inspire the other
- Either of them can come first.

The main difference between repentance and forgiveness is whether you are the offender or the offended, the victimizer or the victim. Forgiveness in its judging, empathizing, revenge-refusing and renewing makes a new community possible (Shirver 1991).

Developing rituals

The question we must now ask is how we can make the experience real when it happens. No person can tell another, "You must forgive." We cannot force forgiveness. It is a choice that only the wronged person can make. When forgiveness happens, reinforce it by giving it a definite, concrete form.

Evangelicals often do not have the rituals to make an experience specific or concrete. Catholics have rituals of confession and absolution. How do we seal the experience of forgiveness? I find that it is helpful and important to develop a ritual to make the experience concrete. One such ritual includes the following:

1. Naming the wrong. I often invite people to write on a piece of paper or card all the wrongs they can recall that have wounded them. It often helps children to illustrate their injuries in this exercise. A word of caution: never minimize how horrible a wrong is to a child.

2. The second part of the ritual is "letting go." Here I ask individuals to write (young children may draw) on another card what wrong he or she is ready to let go. Respect the pace of the process in the other person, whether child or adult.

3. Then I invite the participants to bring their cards to a fire and burn them. If having a fire is not possible, I sometimes use a waste can with a garbage bag to dispose of the old hurts. I then ceremoniously take the sealed garbage bag out to the rubbish heap.

4. After the naming of the wrong and the letting go ritual, I offer laying on of hands and a prayer for healing to come in a fuller sense.

5. Finally, we offer anointing with oil for anyone who desires it. Oil, in the biblical context, was used for medicinal (healing) purposes and as a symbol of commitment. Combining both purposes in one ritual has proven meaningful to many, including workshop participants in Liberia.

The prayer I use in the anointing is a very simple one: "I anoint you in the name of God, who blesses, the Son, who heals, and the Holy Spirit, who inspires and empowers."

Rituals are helpful in making the experience concrete and we should not neglect them. Make the rituals culturally relevant and age-specific.

Recently a group of people and I worked through a whole weekend asking what the hurts in the group were, and how they had hurt each other. I invited them to follow step number one of the above ritual, listing their injuries or grievances. This became the agenda for the weekend. At the end of our time together, they were ready to complete the other steps of the ritual.

I conducted the same kind of ritual with another group of thirty to forty people. Everyone in the group had things that they needed to finish and "let go." One young person carried a great deal of anger and hurt from his parents' divorce. In this session he let it go, he finished it. He decided he could not be responsible for his parents' actions and so he let go of his anger and sense of betrayal. In the process, he experienced healing.

The benefits of forgiveness

The benefits of forgiveness are primarily to the person who forgives. The benefits of repentance are first to the person who repents and, second, to the community. The forgiven one may not know or even care whether he or she is granted forgiveness. It is rewarding if and when the wrongdoer cares.

Forgiveness is not indicative of moral or spiritual superiority. It is a means toward good emotional and spiritual health.

To live as a forgiving person requires practice and energy. This is also true of hateful and bitter people who, unfortunately, have practiced hating instead of forgiving. What is the difference? "Forgiveness is constructive and builds strength. Bitterness, on the other hand, is an emotional disease which weakens" (Schell:95).

Forgiveness does not demand trust or respect. We do not need to live with or allow ourselves to be subjected to abusive behavior after forgiveness has taken place. It does not mean trusting someone when a person is not trustworthy. Forgiveness means giving up our right to hate. The right to forgive, to love and exercise compassion is much more productive, assuring, healing, and conducive to growth than hate.

280

Pseudo-forgiveness

Pseudo-forgiveness, or false forgiveness, is defined as "I will forgive but . . . " Any qualifier to forgiveness is false forgiveness. "I'll forgive, but make sure it doesn't happen again" or "I'll forgive, but I pray God will make him suffer as much as I have." In such cases the fury rages on and will affect, or you might say infect, other relationships.

Other forms of pseudo-forgiveness are: "Don't worry about it, I'll get over it" or "I don't let it bother me anymore." Pseudo-forgiveness restricts healing and growth and gives a false appearance of piety. It disguises bitterness. It is an infection that continues to fester. Ironically, it masks hostility, making it look like a virtue. Pseudo-forgiveness is an attempt to short-circuit the process of dealing with the depth of the hurt and anger (Smedes 1984).

Unconditional forgiveness

". . . While we were still sinners, Christ died for us" (Romans 5:8b). Unconditional forgiveness is "I forgive; it's over" or "I forgive, period." The following account illustrates this kind of forgiveness:

> One December day in 1983, Pope John Paul II walked into a dark cell of Rebibia Prison outside of Rome to meet Mehmet Ali Agca, the man who had fired a bullet at his heart. In a quiet moment, alone with his would-be assassin, the Pope forgave him (Lewis B. Smedes in Readers Digest, August 1985).

For most of us, however, forgiveness is not easy. It seems so unnatural. Our sense of fairness tells us that people should pay for the wrong they do. However, vengeance never evens the score. It ties both the injured and the injurer to an endless cycle of violence and retaliation. Forgiving can bring a miraculous kind of healing—sometimes even reconciliation.

Unconditional forgiveness is a personal choice. With this choice we regain control of our inner lives. The other choice is to continue in bitterness, but the responsibility is solely ours (Schell

1990:117). It is a choice between bitterness and freedom and healing.

On December 6, 1991, Terry Anderson gave a news conference upon his release from seven years as a hostage in Lebanon. This was the first news conference with his fellow news reporters. During the news conference one reporter asked him, "Terry, do you feel that the men that took and held you hostage should be pursued and punished?" Terry thought for a moment, looked at his colleagues and said, "I hadn't thought about it." After reflecting a while longer he said, "No, I am a Christian—I must, I want to forgive." In that statement, Terry Anderson acknowledged that forgiveness was a process that he had not yet completed. He had not yet arrived at the point of complete forgiveness.

He seems, however, to have met criterion number one for authentic forgiveness when he said, "They took away seven years of my life." Terry Anderson had also moved beyond criterion number two when he said "no" to punishing them to the extent of his own suffering. By saying that he wants to forgive them, he hinted at both the third and fourth criteria, which aim at restoring the community relationship of all parties involved. He had not allowed bitterness to enter his heart. Instead he said, "I am a Christian and I must forgive." He corrected that when he said, "I want to forgive." Forgiveness, to be authentic, must come from within.

Forgiveness offers no guarantees other than inner peace. "Forgiving is only for the brave—those willing to confront their pain and accept themselves as permanently changed" (Flanigan 1992:39). Forgiveness frees you from the quagmire of hatred and the control of the person who injured you. Forgiveness leads to personal healing and growth.

The Lord's Prayer

Our Father which art in heaven,
Hallowed be thy name,
Thy kingdom come.
Thy will be done in earth,
As it is in heaven.

Give us this day our daily bread.
And forgive us our debts,
As we forgive our debtors;
And lead us not into temptation,
But deliver us from evil:
For thine is the kingdom,
And the power,
And the glory,
For ever. Amen.
(Matthew 6:9b-13, KJV)

REFERENCES

Augsburger, David. *Caring Enough to Forgive*. Scottdale, Pennsylvania: Herald Press and Kitchener, Ontario: Regal Press, 1981.

Flanigan, Beverly. "The Unforgivable War Crimes of the Heart" in *Psychology Today*, September-October 1992, pp. 36-92.

Nouwen, Henri J. M. *The Wounded Healer*. Garden City, New York: Image Books, 1979.

Schell, David W. *Getting Bitter or Getting Better*. St. Meinrad, Indiana: Abbey Press, 1990.

Shirver, Donald W. Jr. *The Politics of Peace*. Brian Frost, ed. London: Darton, Longman and Todd Ltd., 1991.

Smedes, Lewis B. *Forgive & Forget*. New York: Pocket Books, 1984.

Smedes, Lewis B. "Forgiveness: Love's Healing Miracle" in *Readers Digest*, August 1985.

Smith, J. B. *Greek-English Concordance to the New Testament*. Scottdale, Pennsylvania: Herald Press, 1955.

18

How Do We View Suffering?

Edward T. Welch

"The Christian church, and the world at large, consists of people who sit in a pool of their own tears." So believe a growing number of pastors throughout the world as well as those who witness wars, famines and unchecked disease. There are no formal polls or rigorous statistics to prove this assumption, but many Christians would agree with it. More important, God's Word agrees and states that ". . . the whole creation has been groaning as in the pains of childbirth . . ." (Romans 8:22).

Human life entails misery and woe. Broken relationships, agonizing illness, the prospect of one's own death, depression, injustice, quiet yet paralyzing fear, memories of sexual victimization, the death of a child and many other painful problems leave none unscathed. It would be impossible to minimize the breadth and depth of suffering both in the church and in the world.

But this proposition sits at a juncture where Christians are pulled in two directions. Some exalt pain, others deny it. Some prefer to dwell on their pain, others believe that it is wrong to show pain and a sign of weakness to dwell on it. Likewise, some counselors are "pain counselors," others are "sin counselors." Pain counselors are expert at making people feel understood; sin counselors are expert at understanding the call to obedience even when there is pain. Pain counselors run the risk of emphasizing pain and

285

healing to the point where they become the things "of first importance."

Sin counselors run the risk of rendering personal pain of little or no importance. Pain counselors can be slow to lead sufferers in responding to the gospel of Christ in faith and obedience. Sin counselors are in danger of breeding unfeeling stoics whose response of obedience shows a lack of awareness of God's great compassion. Pain counselors might provide a context that enhances blame and a counselee's sense of innocent victimization. Sin counselors may be so concerned about blame-shifting that they have a poorly developed theology of victimization. There are pitfalls to each.

Those who lean toward exalting pain have said or heard, "the Bible doesn't speak meaningfully to my suffering." Nothing has really spoken to the depths of their pain. Yet the Bible is filled with penetrating teaching about suffering.

Pain cries out, and there are times when those cries seem to drown out all other voices, including the compassionate voice of God. Pain, by its very nature, demands attention and relief.

Here is a consequence, however, of letting pain go unchecked by God's Word: our pain problem becomes deeper than our sin problem. We revise our theology to say that pain is the cause of sin. But is this what God says? There are significant problems with granting primary status to suffering. Biblically, we can never further reduce sin to pain. Sin is just sin. Other people do indeed inflict pain on us, but this pain can never lead us into sin or keep us from loving others.

To believe that pain causes our sins and that the alleviation of pain is our deepest need has dramatic implications. First, it reduces sin to self-protection. That is, our greatest sin is protecting ourselves from further pain. This misses the distinctly against-God, law-breaking nature of all sin. Second, when we realize that we are not shielded from suffering, and as we find that "healing" never really loosens the grip of suffering, we believe that God has reneged on his promises and we feel justified in our anger toward him. We also believe God's Word has no meaningful answers to the deepest problems of life. God, however, never promises temporal freedom from suffering. In fact, he speaks to us throughout Scripture to prepare us for suffering.

As difficult as it may sound, the gospel does not take away all present pain. Instead, the gospel goes deeper. It heals our moral problem. The Bible does not provide a technology that removes suffering, but it does teach us how to live in the midst of it.

Those who minimize pain, or call for a stoic acceptance of it, are often more precise in their theological formulations. But they may not offer the full counsel of God to those who suffer. For example, if suffering is a result of being sinned against by another, those who minimize suffering might immediately call the victim to forgive the perpetrator. This theme is critical, so it is no mistake to make forgiveness part of the counseling agenda. Too often, the first and last advice given to a severely victimized person is to forgive the perpetrator.

To compound this problem, some counselors say that forgiveness must be accompanied by forgetting. But counselees typically understand this to mean that they are sinful if they even think about their victimization. They feel guilty if they ever again mention the pain of being sinned against. The result: the victim now becomes the perpetrator.

Those who minimize personal suffering can also attempt to rapidly fix the sufferer. The intent might be praiseworthy; most of us want people in pain to feel better. But the way counselors carry it out can be hurtful. Counselors might barely hear the outline of the suffering before they race in with answers. Counselees often respond by feeling the counselor does not want to hear their pain, and that the pain is in some way wrong.

At other times, the "fix it" intent might not be so laudable. Some people simply do not want to hear about another's suffering. "Just get on with it," is their advice. A brief study of the compassion of Jesus is a profound rebuke to this selfishness. Jesus was characteristically moved with compassion for those who were leaderless, oppressed, destitute or bereaved. The stoic avoids or ignores these clear themes in Scripture.

Ask people who have gone through difficult suffering what most helped them. Many will say, "She was there with me." A friend or counselor was physically present during times of suffering. This friend might not have offered much counsel or advice. Instead, he or she was available so the grieving person did not feel so alone.

Another common pitfall of stoics occurs when a counselor has an internal clock that goes off, announcing that it is time to end the suffering. Perhaps the counselor is compassionate and wants to alleviate the pain. Or maybe the counselor thinks there is a one-month or one-year limit on grief, and then it is time to get on with life. Biblically, however, there are no predetermined stages of grief and suffering. There are sorrows that God will not erase until the last day (Revelation 21:4). Counselors must be patient with everyone, mourn with those who mourn and help people to love God in the midst of suffering.

The practical theological task is to speak with compassion to those in pain, and point them to realities deeper than their pain. In what follows, I will approach this task through two basic questions: Where does suffering come from? How can I help those who suffer?

Where does suffering come from?

Where does suffering come from? When pain comes at me, from what direction is it coming? Is it my fault? Is it Satan's initiative? Or is God the author of it? These questions are different from the inevitable question "Why didn't (or doesn't) God stop it?" Or, "Why me?" But they are critical questions, and the Bible offers practical answers.

1. Others

One answer to "Where did it come from?" is *other people.* Other people kill their neighbors out of old tribal jealousies, they force children to witness brutalities and killings and they brutally rape women. Other people sin against us, and it hurts deeply.

So when a victimized woman asks, "Why?" you might ask a "where" question and answer, "Because of your assailant's

288

wickedness." Perhaps the question she poses is really "Why did God allow this?" The answer continues to be, "It was the perpetrator who did it; it was because of his sin."

This obvious answer does not address all the mysteries that surround the problem of pain, but it is an important answer. Many sufferers rail at God or themselves and ignore the obvious. This answer offers encouragement because it clearly says to victims that the cause of their particular suffering was someone else, not themselves. Although this seems self-evident, victims often say, "I am responsible." God responds by reminding us that we do not cause the sin of other people. They are responsible for their own sin.

This answer can also encourage us because it points us to the heart of love: forgiveness of sins. As Christians, we are not perplexed when someone else has inflicted pain on us. Instead, we have the opportunity to grow in an attitude of forgiveness that may even lead to reconciliation.

There are cautions that surround the suffering inflicted on us by others. God warns us against being self-righteous in our judgments. He tells us that we cannot make other people's sin an excuse for our own disobedience or lack of love. God alone is judge; we must trust his judgments. Therefore, we do not repay evil for evil.

Another caution: "others" are not the only cause of suffering. Occasionally, young children reduce their pain to this cause. If they fall and a parent is close by, they might instinctively say, "Daddy!" as if their father was responsible. Blame-shifting can assign all fault to others.

2. Me

Another obvious answer is *me*. I suffer because I have sinned. I lost my job because I was caught stealing from my employer. I am destitute because I did not care for my crops. I was hurt in a fight that I provoked with harsh words.

The encouragement in this answer is that there is hope for change. Not only does God offer us complete pardon for sin in Christ, but he also gives us power to put off sin. We can change! The Spirit of power gives grace for continual growth in grace.

The cautions about suffering caused by "me" are well known. As others are not the only cause of suffering, neither am I the only cause of my suffering. If there is not an obvious link between a person's sin and suffering, then we must be careful not to assume a relationship. We should remember that some people—especially those whose own families have severely hurt them—embrace this cause rather than avoid it. They are so uncomfortable with the idea that people who are supposed to love them were, instead, very hurtful and sometimes wicked toward them that they prefer to blame themselves. The victim retains the illusion that the perpetrator really loved him or her. The Scriptures counter that we do not cause others to sin; instead, each person is responsible for his or her own sin.

3. Adam

A third cause for suffering is *Adam and the curse*. Although we participate in Adam's sin (Romans 5), it was Adam himself who sinned and brought misery and death to all his descendants. Because of his sin, we experience the curse on all of creation. As a result, we endure accidents that injure, sickness and physical weakness, the loss of loved ones and painful toil.

This may be the most frustrating cause of suffering. It is as if no one is at fault. There is no one to be reconciled with, no one to forgive and no assurance of change. But the curse from Adam's sin keeps us from loving the world too much. It induces us to anticipate something better. When Jesus returns, he will roll the curse away.

4. Satan

Suffering is also from *Satan*. He is ". . . like a roaring lion looking for someone to devour" (1 Peter 5:8). He delights in sending pain to God's people. The book of Job exposes him as an enemy who uses suffering to advance his own agenda. He is a murderer (John 8:44) who inflicts suffering by way of physical pain and loss. The apostle Paul's torments from "a messenger of Satan" (2 Corinthians 12:7) are illustrations of how Satan is just barely out of view. But Satan can inflict pain that goes even deeper than physical torment. Through lies, accusations and promoting division in the body of Christ, Satan strives to lead us into hopelessness and the questioning of God's goodness.

Do you get angry when you see suffering? Satan is the appropriate but elusive target. He is deceptive. We often overlook his hand in suffering. We should warn those who suffer about Satan's purposes so they can be alert to his lies and engage him quickly in battle, by trusting God and following Christ in obedience even as they suffer.

Yet Satan is not the sole cause of suffering. For example, even if Satan is active in all suffering, his presence does not minimize the responsibility that we or others bear. We can never use Satan as a way to share responsibility for the wickedness of sin. No one can say, "The devil made me do it." Judas, not Satan in Judas' body, was the person who betrayed Jesus.

5. God

It is curious that Satan is rarely the target of a sufferer's frustration or even anger. Instead, *God* is. It seems that agnostics and even atheists become theists when going through suffering. They ask, "Why, God, are you doing this to me? What have I done to you?" Is it true that God causes suffering? Naomi believed so. On returning to her homeland, after losing her husband and sons, she said ". . . the Almighty has made my life very bitter" (Ruth 1:20).

Some Bible teachers try to distinguish between what God ordains and what he allows, but the distinction is sometimes a too tidy attempt to justify God. A less technical statement might be this: by the time suffering gets to us it is God's will. "So then, those who suffer according to God's will should commit themselves to their faithful Creator and continue to do good" (1 Peter 4:19). Is it possible to say that some suffering is not God's will? God forbid that we should suggest that something is beyond him. The world is not trapped in the middle of a battle between Satan and God. God is king over all. God is not the author of sin and suffering, but he is over all things, even our suffering. He "works out everything in conformity with the purpose of his will" (Ephesians 1:11b).

291

Figure 18.1: The causes of suffering

5. God's reign over all things

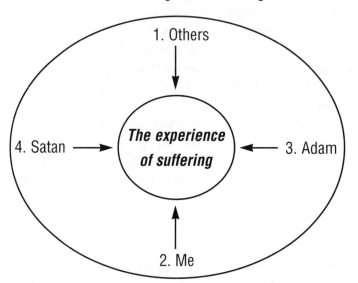

Our faithful God reigns. The world is not in chaos. Neither Satan nor wicked criminals have won, but those who offer counsel must know where the theological boundaries lie. God's sovereignty does not rob creatures of their will. Granted, this is potentially confusing. It is a mystery to maintain that God is ruler over all, while also maintaining that "a man's own folly ruins his life . . ." (Proverbs 19:3a). But God's greatness is such that he has established a world ordained without diminishing human will.

Here is another caution. God is not indifferent to our sufferings. The gospel makes it clear that God is moved with great compassion at the suffering of his people. Jesus Christ entered our suffering (Hebrews 2:14-18).

These five categories (see Figure 18.1 above) answer the question, "Where does suffering come from?" They are important for their mind-clearing effect on sufferers as well as the cautions they provide. These relevant causes can be immensely helpful for those in pain.

But these answers are not always tidy. Suffering rarely falls neatly into any of these categories. Instead, suffering often falls into *all* of them. In any one incident there may be more emphasis on one part of the observable triad of "me," "others," and "Adam," but the issue is one of relative emphasis. For example, in cases of sexual victimization the emphasis is on being sinned against by others. But this does not exclude the fact that the victimization would not have taken place were it not for Adam's sin, and it also does not exclude that we are sinners who will profit from God's discipline in our lives. Apart from Jesus, there is no such thing as an innocent person suffering.

Or consider the case of physical sickness. The most obvious emphasis within the triad of "others," "me," and "Adam" is the curse associated with Adam's sin. We can also relate physical sickness, however, to personal sin, and it can be a result of the sin of other people (e.g., AIDS from a blood transfusion).

Caution people to avoid reducing the cause of suffering to one cause. If we reduce suffering to "others," we become blame-shifters. If we reduce suffering to "me," as Job's counselors did, then guilt and condemnation are ever-present. If it is solely from Adamic sin and the curse we become fatalists. If it is only from Satan we are spiritual warriors who ignore God's purposes and the interpersonal aspects of suffering. The only sure "diagnosis" is that suffering, by the time it gets to us, is God's ordained will for our lives. Yet we cannot reduce the cause of suffering even to God. God is over sin and suffering but he is not their author. The Bible emphasizes that suffering, no matter what the cause, is a time for tears and wrestling, for repentance, for putting our faith in God amid anguish, for following him in obedience.

How do I help those who suffer?

The biblical strategy for helping those in pain is to outweigh it. In other words, at first all the weight seems on the side of suffering. It is as if sufferers cannot see anything outside their own pain. Gradually, as they practice fixing their eyes on Jesus, they encounter "glory-weights" heavier than the weight of their pain.

These glory-weights include the sufferings of Christ, the joy of forgiveness of sins, the contentment of obeying Christ in small ways amid large hardships, the presence of God in our lives and the hope of eternity. To this end, those in pain must be surprised by both the intimate love and the transcendent glory of God; and they must be led to know God so that obeying, trusting and worshiping him become irresistible.

Biblical sufferers can guide us. It is as if these people in Scripture come alongside us, take our hand and lead us to truths that are deeper than our suffering. Consider Job, a companion for many sufferers. In Job 1:21b he says, "The Lord gave and the Lord has taken away; may the name of the Lord be praised." After the most horrifying of losses, this is Job's first response—he worshiped God. The weight of God's glory was more than that of his own suffering. Likewise, Shadrach, Meshach and Abednego had amazing spiritual instincts when, facing a fiery death, they said, "If we are thrown into the blazing furnace, the God we serve is able to save us from it, and he will rescue us from your hand, O king. But even if he does not, we want you to know, O king, that we will not serve your gods or worship the image of gold you have set up" (Daniel 3:17-18). Suffering, or the threat of suffering and death, was a time when they knew they were called to depend on God alone.

The apostle Paul, after recounting his sufferings, says, "Our light and momentary troubles are achieving for us an eternal glory that far outweighs them all." How do you think a person in pain might respond to the apostle Paul's comments? If they did not read the context (2 Corinthians 4), they might say something like this: "Light and momentary? Get real, Paul, you don't know about *my* suffering." But when we recognize the extent of Paul's suffering, he gets our attention. Paul is a credible sufferer to whom we must listen, and he reminds us to look for biblical glory-weights that counterbalance, and thus lighten, our suffering.

The counseling strategy that follows consists of five statements that can guide your support and counsel to those who suffer. They are all prefaced with "God says" as a way to emphasize that God speaks clearly to the sufferer through his word.

294

- ◆ God says, "Put your suffering into speech."
- ◆ In cases of overt victimization, God says, "You have been sinned against."
- ◆ God says, "I am with you and love you."
- ◆ God says, "Know that I am God." *redemption*
- ◆ God says, "There is a purpose in suffering." *can be redemption*

There is a logic to this order, but these five statements are not a step-by-step process. Instead each is overlaid on the one before it. Sufferers do not "finish" one step and move to the next. So while you may emphasize a particular theme, the other themes remain present.

1. God says, "Put your suffering into words." *—before God*

An initial surprise to many people, and a glory-weight in itself, is that God encourages those who suffer to speak honestly to him. Sufferers tend to feel alone and isolated. They often think that God is very far from them. God penetrates this isolation and prods us to put our painful experiences into speech. Not just any speech, of course. Not faithless bitterness. Not pagan laments in a world that is meaningless. God encourages us to direct our speech to himself.

Even though it defies understanding, God desires to hear the depths of our hearts. When we are unable to express ourselves before God, God gives us words to express these silences. God actually "names the silences" in our hearts. The inarticulate groanings become speech:

> . . . My bones are in agony. My soul is in anguish. How long, O Lord, how long? (Psalm 6:2b, 3).

> Why, O Lord, do you stand far off? Why do you hide yourself in times of trouble? (Psalm 10:1).

> How long, O Lord? Will you forget me forever? How long will you hide your face from me? How long must I wrestle with my thoughts and every day have sorrow in my heart? (Psalm 13:1, 2a).

Why are you so far from saving me, so far from the words of my groaning? (Psalm 22:1b).

. . . My soul is full of trouble . . . You have put me in the lowest pit, in the darkest depths (Psalm 88:3, 6).

So counseling begins by being present with sufferers and encouraging them to talk about their suffering, both to you and to God.

But what if counselees are complaining or angry? Should we encourage them to name the silences then? If you read through the Psalms, you will find that God gives much latitude. He gives us words to say things that some would consider almost blasphemous. But there is bad complaining and good complaining. Bad complaining is the cry of one who does not acknowledge who God is. It is the cry of the selfish heart that says, "You must meet my needs." The utmost concern is alleviation of suffering rather than the glory of God. Bad complaining does not believe God's promises; it grumbles and rages *against* God. Good complaining calls out "Why have you forsaken me?" *because* of the knowledge of God. This complaint comes from a heart that knows God and his promises, and is mystified that God seems so far away. They are complaints and appeals *to* God, not *against* God.

Consider a woman who has been sinned against sexually. She may be afraid, be filled with shame, feel unclean and numb. And this is only the beginning. Guilt is almost always present. She may feel responsible for what happened. The story of Job should have changed our minds on this; but many people still think that if something bad happens to them, it must mean that their own behavior brought it on.

This guilt is particularly troublesome because, in a certain sense, it is beyond forgiveness. In other words, these victims have a keen sense that they are responsible and guilty, but they have no idea what to confess. If they find things to confess, the guilt remains. Some women report self-hatred and contempt.

What else might you expect to find in the silences? Pain, a sense of betrayal, helplessness like that of a child, rage toward the perpetrator, but also sometimes love and a desire to protect the perpetrator. Sometimes there is a determination to put hope to death. We perceive hope as an enemy which, if aroused, will only lead to more pain. More hidden are feelings about one's relationship to God: "Why didn't God stop it?" or "Why did he abandon me?"

Expressing your empathy is often the best initial response. Sufferers feel isolated, and that no one really understands their pain. Counselors should actively move into the world of the sufferer, seeking to understand through the eyes of the sufferer. Furthermore, it is critical that counselors express their responses to the sufferer. Are you overwhelmed by the complexity of the suffering? Tell the counselee. Are you grieved by what you hear? Say so. Are you angry at the wickedness of the person who caused the suffering? Express it. Are you moved to tears? Mourn with the person in pain.

Do you do this for an hour? a month? years? How long do you have compassion for the person in pain? How long do you encourage sufferers to name the silences in their souls? The answers are obvious. You have compassion as long as there is pain. You encourage people to speak. The expression of their heart begins a dialog, speaking to God and listening to God.

When people begin to speak, the complexity and emotional power of their experiences may overwhelm you. But if you maintain that the cross of Jesus is central, you will find that you can speak to all the experiences simultaneously. For example, the cross proclaims power to the weak, a lifting up for the humbled, a covering for the naked, love for those who have been hated, redemption for those who are slaves, grace for those who are trying to pay for their sins, forgiveness for sinners and judgment on the enemies of God. God surprises us with the sheer breadth of his work of redemption as well as his love for the oppressed and victimized.

For reflection

a. Read the Psalms through this lens: God encourages the sufferer to speak honestly to him.

b. Put your pain into words, either verbally to a friend or a counselor, or by writing in a journal. Some may prefer to draw a map that captures the complexity of their experience.

c. Go through the Psalms selecting words, phrases, or entire Psalms that express your own heart.

2. In cases of overt victimization, God says, "You have been sinned against."

When it is obvious that other people's sin caused suffering, God speaks to victims. While continuing to encourage them to speak honestly, he helps victims sort out responsibility for the "defilement." Although a victim is a sinner—like all of us—God's initial emphasis is to show that he is for the victim and for justice. Love will ". . . look after orphans and widows in their distress . . ." (James 1:27). If someone who has authority over a woman victimizes her, God holds that authority responsible (Jeremiah 23, Ezekiel 34). God says that he is against the oppressor (Exodus 22: 21-24).

Some counselors are timid to use the biblical category of victimization because it sounds too much like blame-shifting. Oppressed people often do blame-shifting with their responses, justifying sinful self-pity, bitterness or vindictiveness. Victims are also notorious for retaliating: "I am hurting you because you hurt me first." So counselors are rightly concerned that they will leave people helpless, irresponsible and angry. But the categories of perpetrator and victim are biblical. If we avoid them, we ignore God's word to people in pain. The Bible is balanced: "Do not return evil for evil" identifies people as sufferers of evil and challenges blame-shifting.

If suffering is largely a result of the sins of other people, you will probably find that sorting out responsibility is very important. The stage cannot be set for forgiveness if victims do not believe they must forgive. Victims will be paralyzed in their spiritual growth if they have an underlying sense that they are responsible.

For reflection

a. Know what the Bible says about perpetrators of evil. Read Jeremiah 23:1-8, Ezekiel 34:1-16, Luke 17:1, 2.

b. Who do you think was responsible for what happened to you? What does God say about it? Do you believe what God says about it?

3. God says, "I am with you and love you."

The momentum of biblical counsel is outward. It directs our hearts toward the Lord, and it leads us toward loving God and loving others. Now it is time to pull farther away from ourselves and to behold Christ himself. God calls us to see his goodness and love as expressed through his Son.

Seeing God in this way does not come naturally. Satan—the grand deceiver—constantly whispers that God is not good. Satan desires nothing more than that we momentarily appreciate God's manifest blessings during the good times but question his beneficence in the bad. Counselors must be aware that the counselee will often be very reluctant or even angry, and counselors might first have to expose the spiritual warfare that hinders our hearing God.

Consider reading Genesis 3:1-7. Notice how Satan directly contradicts God's word to Adam. The serpent essentially calls God a liar and implies that God is holding back good things from his people. But the gospel of Christ is the definitive statement that God is shocking in his love. This is the dominant battle that many sufferers will face.

In concert with Satan another difficult challenge is the infamous question, "Why me?" "Trust me," says the God of love and power; and to trust him we must know him.

Perhaps you can begin by asking the sufferer if he or she would like to know a fellow sufferer. Have you noticed that suffering seems different in the presence of someone who understands? Have you ever observed that suffering is lighter when you are close to someone whose suffering is greater than your own? This is what happens when we are introduced to the Lamb of God. All our suffering, however tragic, is less monstrous than what happened to the Son of God. Jesus transforms our suffering because of his own suffering.

Here are several passages that might be helpful.

Yet it was the Lord's will to crush him and cause him to suffer . . .
(Isaiah 53:10).

He [Jesus] then began to teach them that the Son of Man must
suffer many things and be rejected by the elders, chief priests
and teachers of the law, and that he must be killed and after
three days rise again (Mark 8:31).

In bringing many sons to glory, it was fitting that God, for
whom and through whom everything exists, should make the
author of their salvation perfect through suffering (Hebrews
2:10).

Deeper or more profound than our suffering are the sufferings of Christ. God does not promise to remove suffering, but as he points us to his own suffering we are reminded that we do not live before a stoic God who is distant from his creatures. Rather, we live before the God-who-suffered.

Next, God surprises sufferers by saying, "You belong to me; I am your God." This is a precious promise to all who have put their faith in Jesus, but it can be especially meaningful to someone in pain. Suffering isolates. Those affected often feel they must be outcasts to have experienced such treatment. They feel shame and rejection. Jesus goes through these walls and assures sufferers that they belong to him (1 John 3, Luke 15). They are part of his family.

As children who belong to him, Jesus listens and understands. He sympathizes (Hebrews 4:15). He shepherds the hurt and lame, and even carries the wounded and weak in his arms (Psalm 23, Jeremiah 23, Ezekiel 34, John 10). He promises to never leave or forsake us (Hebrews 13:5), and he assures us that nothing can separate us from his love (Romans 8:38, 39). God's promise to be *with* us is the ultimate solution to suffering (Revelation 21:3, 4).

Because of his great love, God also covers the shame of those who have been sinned against or defiled by others. The Bible is filled with passages that talk about shame (also defilement, nakedness or being dishonored). Shame is a consequence of our own sin, but there is also a shame that is a consequence of people sinning against us. For example, in Genesis 34 Dinah was shamed

300

or "defiled" by Shechem. In Psalm 79, contact with unclean people and objects shames or defiles the temple. Jesus himself experienced this kind of shame on the cross (Hebrews 12:2). We can legitimately think of the Bible as a story of God covering the shame of his people (e.g., Isaiah 61:10, Zechariah 3:1-5). The premise is that all of us must be covered before God. God, through his initiating grace, transforms the naked one into a beautifully dressed bride (Revelation 21).

Another feature of God's adopting love is that he remembers our suffering and will bring justice. Sufferers feel forgotten, with no one willing to rescue them from oppression. Their complaint seems to go no farther than their own lips (e.g., Psalm 10). If they have been victimized, they often express anger toward both perpetrators and witnesses. It is an anger that says, "I will get justice." The Father, however, does hear. Furthermore, to "hear," in the biblical sense, means to hear and to respond. God's promise is that he will rule justly, and injustice and oppression provoke his anger (Isaiah 1). There will be ultimate justice against God's enemies (Romans 12:19).

The questions "why me" and "why didn't he stop it" may still rage. But as you surprise those who suffer with the suffering and grace of God, many will begin to hear the voice of God over the tumult of their own questions. The weight of suffering may not yet be completely offset, but as a counselor, you can begin to point the way to the ultimate answer to the problem of suffering: "Trust me" is God's most prominent plea. The sufferer begins to see that he or she can trust God.

For reflection

a. Remember your enemy? Satan prowls about and wants to deceive you into thinking that God is not good. Read Genesis 3. What is Satan's strategy? Where do you see it in your own life? How might you combat him?

b. Read the Book of Psalms. This time read them through the lens of Jesus. He is the final psalmist. The words are his words. Especially notice psalms where he speaks

301

about his own suffering. Go back to the psalms that capture your own experience. Now read those psalms as the words of Jesus.

c.   Read Isaiah 1. Notice God's prominent concern for justice and his anger at injustice.

4. God says, "Know that I am God."

To weigh the scales against suffering even further, God comforts us with the fact that the world is not chaotic. He is the sovereign God who reigns. Neither suffering nor Satan is above him.

Here many theologies of suffering fail. They embrace God as a God of compassionate love, but they cannot marry that with a God who is all-powerful. They say that it cannot be both. Modern thinking cherishes the neatness of our minds more than the truths of God's Word. When we encounter a conceptual difficulty, we revise it so it becomes more palatable. We find an example of this in the popular book, *When Bad Things Happen to Good People* by Rabbi Harold Kushner. In his comments about the book of Job he says, "forced to choose between a good God who is not totally powerful or a powerful God who is not totally good, the author of the book of Job chooses to believe in God's goodness."[1]

The biblical response is that God says both: He is love, and he is sovereign over all creation. This does not make God the author of sin or suffering, but it says that he is over both, working all things together for his glory. This apparently posed no obstacle to the people of the Bible. The story of Joseph shows that God's plans were higher than the evil of Joseph's brothers (Genesis 50:20). Naomi says rightly but without a full understanding of God's grace, "The Lord has afflicted me; the Almighty has brought misfortune upon me" (Ruth 1:21b). *lament or fact?*

Job had all his questions answered, or at least rendered insignificant, in a one-sided conversation where God essentially said, "Know that I am God" (Job 38-41). In that conversation, the overwhelming weight of God's glory made Job's suffering seem small. Job saw that there were spiritual realities deeper than his suffering.

Does this end the questions? For many people, it does not. The question often lurks in the shadows: "If God is over all things, why did he allow this evil to happen to me?" Amazingly, God invites this wrestling with him. His response, however, will continue to be, "I am your deliverer, your savior, your friend, your God. Trust me."

For reflection

a. God's thoughts are higher than our own. In our suffering, God does not supply in-depth answers to the "why" questions, but he does comfort us with the fact that he is greater than our suffering. God is in our suffering but is not the author of suffering. Read Job 38-41; take comfort that the world is not chaos.

b. Read the courtroom encounters in Ezekiel 1, Isaiah 6, and Revelation 4. What were the responses of the witnesses? Why?

c. Practice—perhaps for ten minutes a day—the spiritual discipline of quieting the questions in your mind and listening to what God says.

5. God says, "There is a purpose in suffering."

In *How to Handle Trouble*, Jay Adams summarizes a biblical approach to trouble this way: "God is in it, God is up to something, and God is up to something good. Since God is the God of the gospel of grace as well as the King over all creation, it follows that he has kingdom purposes in suffering, and these purposes are good."[2]

The problem for many people is that "good" may not include an immediate end to their suffering. Instead, the good is that God will use suffering to conform us into the image of his Son and, as a result, bring glory to the Father. To paraphrase C. S. Lewis, we settle for too little. We want nothing more than the immediate alleviation of suffering, but God wants to give us much more—things that will last for all eternity.

This is where you might bring the familiar passage, Romans 8:28, to counselees: "And we know that in all things God works for the good of those who love him, who have been called according to his purpose."

As you journey with a counselee toward a greater understanding of God's purposes, it is wise to keep one eye on our adversaries: the world, the flesh and the devil. The world is constantly communicating that this is the only home we have, and we deserve freedom from pain while we are here. The flesh finds pleasure in autonomy from God and resists submitting to his will. And the devil constantly takes our circumstances and suggests that they constitute evidence that God is not really good, that God is holding out on us, that God does not love us. With such adversaries it is clear that we cannot wage the battle without the prayers of God's people.

Suffering exposes hearts

One way God damages these adversaries is by using suffering to expose our hearts. Suffering is a pressure that can squeeze us, revealing either faith or pockets of unbelief and sin that were previously hidden. This does not mean that personal sin always causes suffering. Job's counselors were wrong about this. It is to say that God uses suffering to reveal and to purify those whom he loves. So Job repents of his self-righteousness.

Perhaps you have heard Christians say of suffering, "This is exactly what I needed." Many have learned to be grateful, even joyful, for the spiritual training that these circumstances induce.

To frame it as the book of Job does, suffering places us at a spiritual crossroads. When all the pleasures and comforts of life are removed, will we still worship God? During the good times the answer seems easy: "Of course I will trust God." But suffering exposes the unbelief and self-worship of our hearts. God uses suffering so we know when we are worshiping God for our sake or for his.

The apostle Paul put it this way: "Indeed, in our hearts we felt the sentence of death. But this happened that we might not rely on ourselves but on God, who raises the dead" (2 Corinthians 1:9). Paul was more passionate about conformity to Christ by faith than he was about the immediate alleviation of his own suffering.

Therefore, one purpose of suffering is to produce repentance, faith and obedience. These responses to suffering have eternal longevity. They please God and bring the blessing of peace.

Sin is not the only thing that suffering exposes. Suffering may also expose hearts that are full of faith. Many Christians who have been surprised by suffering find themselves immediately going to God's Word for comfort, and they offer prayers of lament and praise that rival the psalmist's. In such cases we still mourn with people in pain, yet we can also rejoice that the sufferers visibly testify to themselves, to the church and to the world that they are children of God.

Suffering exposes eternity

While suffering can turn the lights on and expose our hearts, it can also lend clarity by exposing even larger kingdom realities. It helps us see eternity. It provokes hope. We can see our present affliction from an eternal perspective. This is where 2 Corinthians 4:17-18 becomes most brilliant.

> For our light and momentary troubles are achieving for us an eternal glory that far outweighs them all. So we fix our eyes not on what is seen, but on what is unseen. For what is seen is temporary, but what is unseen is eternal.

Mother Teresa has said, "From heaven, the most miserable life on earth will look like one bad night in an inconvenient motel."

The encouragement to hope in suffering is a strong theme throughout the Scriptures. If the apostle Paul had a secret, this is it. The hope of eternity was deeper than his pain: "And we rejoice in the hope of the glory of God" (Romans 5:2b). The problem, however, is that we are a generation locked into the present. Yet this is where suffering can do its best work. Suffering reminds us that the world does not keep its promises. It reminds us that there is nothing in this world that sin and the curse have not tainted. Hope can become, by God's grace, more instinctive and settled.

Hope is the grand finale of suffering. Suffering makes what we hope for less shadowy. So it is not surprising that some of the best known Bible passages on suffering end on that note (Romans 5:3-5, 8:18-39; 1 Peter 4:12-14).

How does hope come to a person in pain? You can start by reading biblical passages about hope. Marvel at how the apostles Paul (Romans 5:3) and James (James 1:2) even rejoice in their suffering when they hope. Then notice the expanse between the sufferer's present hope and the hope of Paul and James. Reflect on how we cannot bridge this distance except through prayer, meditating on the consummation and practicing the discipline of hope. Remind counselees that hope will not come in one week but, with persistent encouragement and practice, hope will become more and more of a reality.

When you read the Psalms, it may seem as if hope comes instantly. In many Psalms there appear to be a mere gentle reminder to hope in the Lord and suddenly the psalmist bursts into praise. The Psalms, however, provide condensed summaries of an educational process. Also, they are written by people who were skilled in hope. Indeed, *hope is a skill*. It is not an experience that simply comes over us. It is a discipline that demands stamina and the constant encouragement of the Scripture and God's people.

This is the heart of God's purposes in suffering: exposing our hearts, beholding and trusting the risen Lord, anticipating his return and thus learning obedience. Yet there is one other purpose that can really excite some people. In Job's situation one purpose of suffering was to silence Satan. Satan, our enemy and a prominent cause of suffering and evil, still lives to accuse us and persuade us to disobey the Most High God. The privilege of God's people is to do violence to Satan by trusting and obeying God even in suffering.

The scales are now becoming increasingly lopsided. Suffering still exists and the pain may be great; but the glory-weights are addressing places in our hearts that are deeper than the pain (see Figure 18.2 on page 305).

Figure 18.2: God unbalances the scales of our suffering

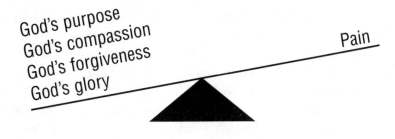

For reflection

    a.   Consider the life of Joseph. How do you see God's loving purpose? Note especially Genesis 50:20.

    b.   Consider the life of Naomi in the book of Ruth. How do you see God's loving purpose?

    c.   What are ways that you can silence Satan?

    d.   Begin to establish a pattern of praying Scripture. That is, if God says it and you do not understand it or believe it, pray that the Lord will make his Word alive to you. Consider starting with passages about hope.

Not stoics but God's suffering servants and responders to his grace

So are we people of pain? People who are healing from pain? People who have been victimized and wounded? Or are we people who need to forget pain and just get on with it? Do we need a tougher brand of Christian who ignores the pain and stays in the battle?

God clearly shows us another way. The Incarnation speaks against the shallowness of the stoics. Jesus' presence on earth shows his solidarity with those who suffer. His ministry was full of compassion and understanding, and it also exposes the shallowness of "the bleeding hearts." Jesus demonstrates that pain, suffering, victimization and death are not the preeminent features of life. He points us to deeper realities, deeper spiritual needs.

We are people-who-have-been-shown-mercy. This does not sound new. It is an identity that even a child can see in the Scriptures. But its commonness belies its ability to revolutionize the sufferer's perspective. For example, people who have suffered at the hands of others sometimes feel that life as a victim is certain. This is who they are, and the most they can do is try to protect themselves from the pain. But God reorients sufferers. He reveals that the grace they received does not compare to the pain they experience. Grace is weighty, suffering is light.

Or consider people who are angry because they feel they do not deserve pain. As recipients of mercy and grace, the astounding cost of the initiative of love that God took toward them suddenly humbles them. They were reactive victims; they become loving responders. The foundation for the life of the Christian is God's grace, not freedom from pain. We were enemies of God who were naked and blind, and he took the initiative toward us: ". . . While we were still sinners, Christ died for us" (Romans 5:8b).

Perhaps "responders" captures our new identity. God is the relentless initiator of liberating grace; we respond to his grace by faith. As responders, we are defined by the one who liberated us, and we become his servants. This does not remove suffering. Suffering will cling to our earthly life. But it does not define or control us. We are responsive, suffering servants.

Here is curious counsel for sufferers: we travel a path that urges us to look outward, toward the triune God. "Let us fix our eyes on Jesus, the author and perfecter of our faith, who for the joy set before him endured the cross, scorning its shame, and sat down at the right hand of the throne of God" (Hebrews 12:2). We begin to ask, "How can I respond to what God has done for me by loving God and loving others?" and "How can I treat others the way Christ has treated me?" The question for sufferers becomes the one for all Christians: "How do I enact the two great commandments, love God and love your neighbor as yourself?"

We are responders who love others

For people who have been victimized, this is when you talk about forgiving the perpetrator. "Do not be overcome by evil, but overcome evil with good" (Romans 12:21). The outward movement of biblical counseling makes this unavoidable. As you have been forgiven, you forgive others. As God has loved you when you did not deserve it, you begin to love your enemies.

What will this look like? There are dozens of possibilities. Sometimes it will take the form of confronting the person, either by letter or in person. Sometimes it will take the form of praying for the perpetrator and not giving up hope for full reconciliation. God's love can inspire many creative initiatives.

We are responders who love God

At the Last Supper, Jesus told the disciples that they would soon experience great grief; but shortly after that pain there would be a joy that no one could ever steal, even during the tremendous persecutions all of them were to face.

> I tell you the truth, you will weep and mourn while the world rejoices. You will grieve, but your grief will turn to joy. A woman giving birth to a child has pain because her time has come; but when her baby is born she forgets the anguish because of her joy that a child is born into the world. So with you: Now is your time of grief, but I will see you again and you will rejoice, and no one will take away your joy (John 16:20-22).

How could this be: constant joy with an overlay of grief and pain? It is a difficult experience to describe, but it is true nonetheless. It is because we worship the risen Lord. Jesus is alive. No matter what happens to us, our great God reigns. Personal hardships and afflictions cannot mute the resurrection. The greatest joy of the Christian is God himself and the fact that nothing can separate us from him.

309

There are, indeed, realities deeper than our pain. The understanding love of Jesus who became a man, forgiveness of sins, knowledge that God has a purpose—these are glory-weights that change our suffering. But the greatest of all glory-weights is God himself. To know him as the true God who deserves our worship and adoration is the greatest glory-weight for any sufferer. It does not end our temporal grief and pain, but it means that we neither exalt our pain nor ignore it. We exalt God amid pain.

"I consider that our present sufferings are not worth comparing with the glory that will be revealed in us" (Romans 8:18).

[Adapted from "Exalting pain? Ignoring pain? What do we do with suffering?" in *The Journal of Biblical Counseling*, Volume XII, Number 3, Spring 1994. Copyright © 1994 by Edward T. Welch. Used by permission.]

NOTES

1. Harold Kushner, *When Bad Things Happen to Good People* (New York: Avon, 1983).

2. Jay Adams, *How to Handle Trouble: God's Way* (Philipsburg, New Jersey: Presbyterian & Reformed, 1982).

— Disappointing chapter.

Part 5

Concluding Reflections

19
Restoring Hope

Phyllis Kilbourn

Chapter one depicted several crucial losses children experience due to the impact of war. Many child researchers believe that the most devastating impact for children traumatized by the brutalities of war and being uprooted from their familiar surroundings is a loss of hope. Without hope children, like adults, give up on life. Paul Cedar says:

> Life without hope is like a beautiful flower cut off from the stem. Like a precious child who has nothing to eat. We cannot live very well or very long without hope. Without it, we shrivel and die.[1]

Having no sense of hope for a future, children maintain a passive outlook on life and feel trapped, with no control over their present or their future. Often their peers, friends and schools are no longer there for them; parents and other significant caregivers also are no longer there for them. Usually the war has dragged on for years with no end in sight; the children can see no way that they will get back to school, back to their familiar villages and family routines. This constant state of insecurity may leave children uncertain about having any kind of future.

Marlys Blomquist earlier touched on the power and importance of providing hope for the children (chapter twelve). She states:

Knowing that healing can arise out of the most chaotic circumstances can be the most powerful inspiration you can give a growing person. If we persevere with courage, we reflect the idea that the most terrible of deeds and circumstances will end, that there are means of healing and a meaningful future to behold. If we suffer but are not being broken by our injuries, our strength increases and can be used with wisdom to help us go beyond our wounds.

George Handzo, describing the faith needs of children in crisis, points out that

> Both children and adults need and want to be in a loving, caring relationship with a benevolent and forgiving God. They both need to know that, whatever their situation, God offers forgiveness and continued presence. They need help in resolving guilt about their part in any tragic events and dealing with any anger they may feel toward a God who did not change things. Most of all they need the hope that comes from knowing that God has not abandoned them.[2]

Before we can offer this hope to the children, however, we ourselves must first have an assurance of hope for their future. As caregivers we must be constantly on guard that the desperateness of the children's situations does not overwhelm us so that we let doubt and uncertainty creep in, especially when hope is one of the most precious treasures we have to offer the children. Children need to sense our expectations of hope: hope that happier times will return, that a sense of stability and order will be restored to their lives and that their future needs can be met.

Where can we derive this sense of hope in the almost total brokenness of their world? This hope must stem from our belief in the truth that children, created in God's image, are of utmost worth to him and, therefore, he is not unconcerned or uninvolved in their sufferings. Instead we must acknowledge that God is in control of their lives, no matter how the situation looks when viewed only through our "natural eyes"—eyes that see the realities of the ugliness, viciousness, unspeakable evils and atrocities of war that surround children. We must believe that God can act redemptively in their lives.

We can reflect on how God can intervene redemptively in the lives of children traumatized by war or other difficult circumstances through the moving story of an everyday childhood crisis experienced by Pastor Wayne Oates' son.[3]

Pastor Oates had made his five-year-old son Billy a balsa wood airplane. The airplane was "powered" by a heavy rubber band. When the rubber band was twisted, it would unwind and turn the propeller, allowing the airplane to glide away. This special toy that his father had given him delighted little Billy. He spent hours in the sunshine playing with it. One day it was raining heavily outside. Billy decided to go to the basement to play. While there he spied his airplane and began to send it zooming across the basement. Then the inevitable happened—there was a crash and the airplane fell in splinters. Billy screamed with anger. His father, hearing his son's cries of distress, raced downstairs to find out what had happened.

Before he reached Billy, he noticed that Billy had stopped crying. Billy not only wiped a tear from his eyes—he smiled. His father wondered what he was thinking. When he asked his son, Billy stooped over, picked up the large rubber band, and replied, "I know what I will do. I will take this rubber band and make me a slingshot out of it!"

As a church family this story represents one of the greatest responsibilities we have toward children in facilitating their recovery and healing from the brokenness they have endured because of their war experiences. We must seriously ask ourselves how we can enable the children—designed and created by their heavenly Father—to find redemptive purposes from their shattered lives; to identify the "rubber band" that remains intact and that they can use for new purposes.

The rubber band was only a small part of the airplane—yet it was a vital part. It powered the airplane and remained intact during the tragedy of brokenness. So we must discover those parts of the children's lives that have remained intact during their time of brokenness—intact even if crushed or bent out of shape—and guide the children in learning how *God* can act redemptively in their individual situation. This is a task that Oates describes as "setting about perceiving a new design, a new pattern, a new use of the old pieces."

The following news clips vividly illustrate the importance of discovering hope through God's redemptive action for the children's future.

> These children must grow up to take charge of the country, to [rear] their own children. And I wonder how they can do that unless in some way they can come to terms with the terrible things that have been done. People here [in Mozambique] talk of a lost generation, but we cannot afford to lose a generation.[4]

> Two generations of children of this war [in the Philippines] have grown up carrying their unresolved fears and traumas as seeds which sprout into an often troubled and violent adulthood. A third generation is already on its way.[5]

As countries cannot "afford to lose a generation," so the church cannot afford to stand by and experience "a lost generation" either. To prevent this, we must help the children learn that there is good news for them by sharing the liberating word that God hates what is happening to them, and that his love extends to each and every one. They need to know in the deepest part of their beings that Jesus Christ weeps for them and has finished the work that forgives anything and everything they have done or have been forced to do. Through God's love and forgiveness there is healing—and hope.

We must also understand that the children's healing will not come quickly or easily, but will be part of a prolonged process. It is a process during which we must continually ask ourselves how we can help the children use their experiences to create new structures. Children will never be the same after enduring prolonged,

Pupils of Gaza's Greek Orthodox Christian primary school crowd in front of a spray-painted Palestinian flag, resistance fighter and information in Arabic script in the school's courtyard.

difficult and tragic war experiences. They will never recover by only referring to their old frames of reference.

The responsibility on the church and families to provide new, meaningful structures in the lives of the children is a challenge and responsibility that we must face for a long time. We must help children regain a sense of control and provide them with a hope for their future. This will include returning some of their "safe places" to them. It will also mean enabling them, with God's help, to reconstruct their fragmented lives.

Our ultimate goal in providing rehabilitating interventions must be to restore the children to full health: emotionally, spiritually, mentally and physically. Achieving this goal will also restore a brighter hope for their future.

REFERENCES

1   Paul Cedar, "Where is Hope?" in *Pursuit* (Volume 1: Number 4, 1993).

2   Andrew D. Lester, ed. *When Children Suffer: A Sourcebook for Ministry with Children in Crisis* (Philadelphia: The Westminster Press, 1987), p. 175.

3   Wayne E. Oates, *Your Particular Grief* (Philadelphia: The Westminster Press, 1981), pp. 113-114.

4   Angela Neustatter, quoted from "The Independent" of London in *World Press Review* (November 1992), p. 27.

5   News Release: Philippine International Forum; Cebu City, 1992.

MARC

Bringing you key resources on the world mission of the church

MARC books and other publications support the work of MARC (Mission Advanced Research and Communications Center), which is to inspire fresh vision and empower Christian mission among those who extend the whole gospel to the whole world.

New MARC titles include:

Transforming Health: Christian Approaches to Healing and Wholeness, Eric Ram, editor

Explores how God is bringing about health, healing and wholeness throughout the world today. Dr. Ram encouraged more than twenty of his health care colleagues around the world to share their newest insights on practices of health and healing.   **350 pages $21.95**

Survival of the Fittest: Keeping Yourself Healthy in Travel and Service Overseas, Dr. Christine Aroney-Sine

No one wants their ministry hindered by illnesses that can be prevented. This informative guide helps you prepare for trips and take preventative measures against common illnesses. Once abroad, it will help you maintain your physical, emotional and spiritual well-being.   **112 pages $9.95**

Focus! The Power of People Group Thinking, John D. Robb

A practical manual for planning effective strategies to reach the unreached. This revised and expanded edition contains new information on prayer and networking as keys to mission progress. Will help your ministry develop strategies that are relevant to the people you are trying to reach.
                                                           180 pages $10.95

God So Loves the City: Seeking a Theology for Urban Mission, Charles Van Engen and Jude Tiersma, editors

An international team of experienced urban practitioners explore the most urgent issues facing those who minister in today's cities. Each team member shares a story that illustrates the challenges to urban ministry in the face of injustice, marginalization and urban structures. From a retelling of these stories through the lens of Scripture, we see the first steps toward a theology of mission for the city.   **315 pages $21.95**

Japan's Post War Protestant Churches, Hugh Trevor

A detailed analysis of the growth of Christianity in modern Japan. Drawing from Japan's most exhaustive databases and statistical sources, the author compiles a comprehensive list of Japan's Protestant churches and sects with detailed charts and in-depth statistical data on individual denominations.

139 pages $17.95

Mission Studies Resources for the Future, Stephen L. Peterson

Highlights the results of an 18-month investigation of the international base of research resources for the study of mission and world Christianity. Identifies ways to share resources with the international community of scholars engaged in mission studies and looks at the role of technology in information gathering and sharing.   **43 pages (8 ½" x 11") $6.95**

Other MARC titles include:

The Changing Shape of World Mission, Bryant L. Myers

52 pages of easy-to-read color graphs, charts and maps to help you and your church understand the changing shape of the Christian church, the unfinished task of world evangelization, the available resources for mission and the major challenges to mission in the 1990s. Provides a bird's-eye view of the state of the world from the context of Christian mission and evangelism. Also available in color slides and overheads—makes a great presentation package!   **Book   52 pages $ 5.95**
Overheads $99.95
Slides $99.95

The Mission Handbook 1993-95: A Guide to USA/Canada Christian Ministries Overseas, John A. Siewert and John A. Kenyon, editors

The standard guide to North American mission agencies, with 525 pages of vital information on over 833 agencies including: countries of service, types of ministry, key contacts and phone numbers, analysis of mission finance and distribution of personnel. Also available in software format. With the computer version of *The Mission Handbook 1993-95*, you can: combine and view descriptive and statistical data according to criteria you select; print agency lists, phone and fax numbers; use the select, sort, retrieve, view and other functions to guide you through the database.

Book $ 39.95
Software $ 99.95
Book and software $119.00

Bridging the Gap: Evangelism, Development and *Shalom*, Bruce Bradshaw

From a holistic approach to Christian ministry, the author seeks to bridge the gap that occurs between evangelism and development when we perceive the two as separate enterprises of Christian mission. Examines the biblical concepts of creation, redemption and *shalom* and searches for a fuller understanding of God's redemptive plan for all creation. **183 pages $11.95**

Empowering the Poor, Robert C. Linthicum

The award-winning author of *City of God, City of Satan* presents a bold strategy for community organizing in the city, including how to build coalitions, network in the city and develop leaders in the neighborhood and church. The author shows how we can empower rather than serve the poor.
118 pages $8.95

Patching God's Garment: Environment and Mission in the 21st Century, W. Dayton Roberts

Roberts provides a scientifically accurate foundation for Christian environmentalism while showing us what we need to understand about our ecosystem. Also shows how the environmental crisis affects the church's evangelistic mission. **174 pages $13.95**

Companion to the Poor: Christ in the Urban Slums, Viv Grigg

The author's compelling story of Christian presence, witness and change in the Manila squatter settlement of Tatalon and his challenge to establish a church there. Also available in Spanish language version.
205 pages $ 8.95
Spanish version **$13.00**

Cry of the Urban Poor, Viv Grigg

In his sequel to *Companion to the Poor*, Grigg examines the principles of church planting among the poor and addresses the question, "Do we need to live with the poor to establish the kingdom among them?"
295 pages $10.95

Order toll free in the USA: 1-800-777-7752

Visa and Master Card accepted

Ask for the MARC newsletter and complete publications list

MARC a division of World Vision International
121 E. Huntington Dr.
Monrovia, CA 91016-3400